TOP 10 AMSTERDAM

FIONA DUNCAN & LEONIE GLASS

EYEWITNESS TRAVEL

Left **Hollandse Manage** Right **Magere Brug**

LONDON, NEW YORK,
MELBOURNE, MUNICH AND DELHI
www.dk.com

Produced by DP Services, 31 Ceylon Road, London W14 0PY
Reproduced by Colourscan,Singapore
Printed and bound in China by Leo Paper Products Ltd

First published in Great Britain in 2003 by Dorling Kindersley Limited 80 Strand, London WC2R 0RL A Penguin Company

Reprinted with revisions 2005, 2007, 2009

Copyright 2003, 2009 © Dorling Kindersley Limited, London

All rights reserved. No part of this publication may be reproduced, stored in a retrieval system, or transmitted in any form or by any means, electronic, mechanical, photocopying, recording or otherwise, without the prior written permission of the copyright owner.

A CIP catalogue record is available from the British Library.
ISBN 978 1 40533 348 1

Within each Top 10 list in this book, no hierarchy of quality or popularity is implied. All 10 are, in the editor's opinion, of roughly equal merit.

We're trying to be cleaner and greener:

- we recycle waste and switch things off
- we use paper from responsibly managed forests whenever possible
- we ask our printers to actively reduce water and energy consumption
- we check out our suppliers' working conditions – they never use child labour

Find out more about our values and best practices at www.dk.com

Contents

Amsterdam's Top 10

The information in this DK Eyewitness Top 10 Travel Guideis checked regularly.
Every effort has been made to ensure that this book is as up-to-date as possible at the time of going to press. Some details, however, such as telephone numbers, opening hours, prices, gallery hanging arrangements and travel information are liable to change. The publishers cannot accept responsibility for any consequences arising from the use of this book, nor for any material on third party websites, and cannot guarantee that any website address in this book will be a suitable source of travel information. We value the views and suggestions of our readers very highly. Please write to: Publisher, DK Eyewitness Travel Guides, Dorling Kindersley, 80 Strand, London, Great Britain WC2R 0RL.

Cover: Front – **Corbis:** Wolfgang Kaehler main; **DK Images:** Kim Sayer bl. Spine – **DK Images:** b. Back – **DK Images:** tc, tr; Tony Souter tl.

Left **Eerste Klas Café, Centraal Station** Right **Prinsengracht**

Left **Café de Jaren** Right **Montelbaanstoren, Oude Schans**

AMSTERDAM'S TOP 10

TOP 10 Amsterdam Highlights

Amsterdam has an appeal that is absolutely unique. It's a vibrant place, a treasure-trove of extraordinary artistic riches, and the living embodiment of 900 years of history, during which it rose to become the centre of a huge global empire. After a period of decline, it matured into today's relaxed and tolerant modern metropolis. Elegant and serene, Amsterdam also has its seamy side, and this too is part of its character, as much as its famous network of canals. Whatever you are looking for, this small city packs a big punch.

1 Canals and Waterways

Amsterdam's canals – in particular, the elegant ring of three 17th-century canals known as the Grachtengordel – are its defining feature *(see pp8–11)*.

2 Rijksmuseum

The country's largest national museum houses an unrivalled collection of 17th-century Dutch art, and much besides. Vermeer's *Milkmaid (left)* and Rembrandt's *Night Watch* are among the star sights *(see p12–15)*.

3 Van Gogh Museum

The Van Gogh Museum houses simply the most comprehensive collection of the artist's work to be seen anywhere in the world – including some of his most famous paintings. The collection also includes works by other 19th-century artists *(see pp16–19)*.

4 Museum Ons' Lieve Heer op Solder

Things are not always what they seem, and that is certainly true of this gem of a 17th-century house in the Red Light District: tucked away on its upper floors is a rare example of a perfectly preserved hidden Catholic church. The rest of the museum is fascinating, too – the interior has changed little since the Golden Age *(see pp20–21)*.

5 Begijnhof

A haven of peace, the Begijnhof was built as a refuge for the Beguines, a lay Catholic sisterhood. Amsterdam's oldest house is here *(see pp22–3)*.

6 Amsterdams Historisch Museum

Housed in the old city orphanage, this vibrant collection traces the history of Amsterdam from the 12th century *(see pp24–7)*.

7 Oude Kerk

This great Gothic basilica preserves a number of its treasures, despite being stripped of its paintings and statuary during the Iconoclasm *(see pp28–9)*.

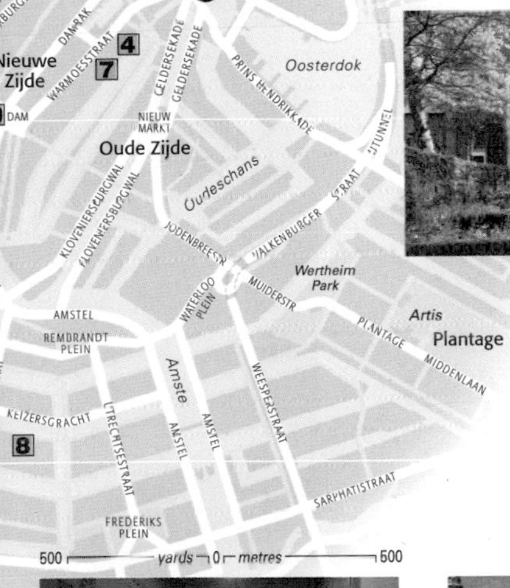

8 Museum Van Loon

Visitors to the Van Loon family residence on the Keizersgracht, lovingly restored in the style of the mid-18th century, have a rare opportunity to see behind the façade of a grand canal house – and to wander freely about it *(see pp30–31)*.

9 Anne Frank Huis

The hiding place of Anne Frank and her family, before they were discovered, arrested and sent to their deaths, is today a deeply moving museum *(see pp32–3)*.

10 Dam Square

This is where it all started: Amsterdam's main square is on the site of the dam on the Amstel around which the city grew. Now it hosts markets, events and all shades of city life *(see pp34–5)*.

TOP 10 Canals and Waterways

With their delightful views, pretty bridges (1,281 in all), idiosyncratic gabled houses and relaxed waterside cafés, Amsterdam's 75 km (47 miles) of canals are great fun to explore: full of interest and perfect for a leisurely stroll. They are a constant reminder that the Netherlands is the world's flattest country, half of which has been reclaimed from the sea with the aid of dykes, canals and, more recently, huge tidal barriers. Before you start exploring Amsterdam's canals on foot, however, you should take a boat tour (see pp10 and 136) *for a fascinating overview.*

Café Van Puffelen

Three perfect canalside cafés are Papeneiland, at Prinsengracht 2, Van Puffelen, where you can sit on a barge in summer *(see p102)*, and De Sluyswacht *(see p80)*.

If you are in the centre of Amsterdam, with no time to explore the city's canals, at least take a stroll to the Huis op de Drie Grachten, (House on Three Canals), step-gabled on all three of its canal-facing sides, at Oudezijds Voorburgwal 249.

Top 10 Canals and Waterways

1. Herengracht
2. Keizersgracht
3. Prinsengracht
4. Entrepotdok
5. Reguliersgracht
6. Amstel River
7. Brouwersgracht
8. Bloemgracht
9. Leidsegracht
10. Singel

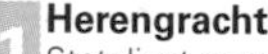

1 Herengracht

Stateliest canal of the Grachtengordel *(see p11)*, the Herengracht is famous for its Golden Bend – a grand but rather lifeless stretch of mansions built for the richest merchants. A more beautiful stretch lies between Huidenstraat and Leidsestraat, best viewed from the east side.

2 Keizersgracht

The central canal of the Grachtengordel has fine stretches between Brouwersgracht and Raadhuisstraat, and again between Runstraat and Leidestraat.

3 Prinsengracht

The outermost canal of the Grachtengordel, designed for warehouses and artisans' housing, has a breezy, laid-back air. It is peppered with cafés, art galleries and houseboats. Cycle its 3 km (2 mile) length, or explore short stretches on foot.

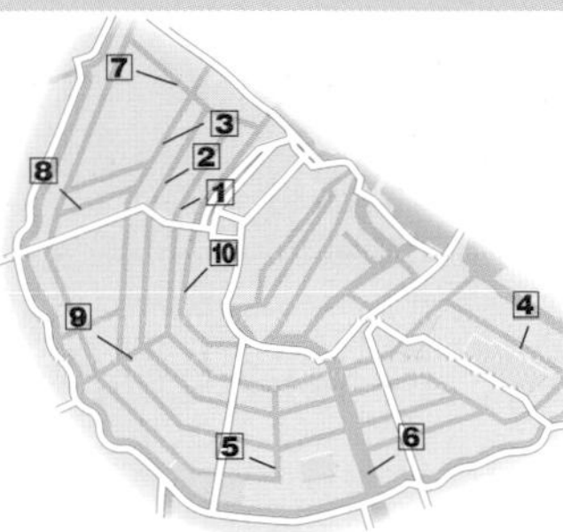

4 Entrepotdok

An imposing stretch of former dockland has been restored to provide offices and apartments, with outdoor cafés overlooking colourful houseboats.

5 Reguliersgracht

Much loved for its pretty houses and hump-backed bridges, Reguliersgracht was cut in 1664. Look out for Nos 57, 59 and 63.

6 Amstel River

Until the construction of the Grachtengordel pushed it out of focus, the river Amstel was the city's *raison d'être*. It is still used by barges to transport goods to the city's port.

7 Brouwersgracht

The happy-go-lucky feel of the "brewers" canal' makes a pleasant contrast to the sophisticated elegance of the Grachtengordel.

8 Bloemgracht

A charming canal crossed by cast-iron bridges, Bloemgracht is known locally as "the Herengracht of the Jordaan", because of its elaborately gabled houses.

9 Leidsegracht

This lovely – and exclusive – canal was cut in 1664, when it was the main barge route from Amsterdam to Leiden.

10 Singel

Once a fortified moat, the Singel is now home to Bloemenmarkt, the domed Ronde Lutherse Kerk and the soaring Neo-Gothic Krijtberg church.

How Amsterdam's Houses are Built

Each house is built on wooden piles sunk into the marshy, porous subsoil. It wasn't until the 17th century, when the piles could be sunk deep enough to reach the hard layer of sand that lies at 13 m (42 ft), that any real stability was achieved. Some reach even further, to a second layer of sand at 18 m (58 ft). If piles come into contact with air, they rot, so today, concrete is used instead of wood.

Left **Canal tour boat on the Oude Schans** Right **De Poezenboot**

Top 10 Unexpected Sights on a Canal Tour

1 The Safest Vaults

The vaults of the Dutch National Bank are sunk some 15 m (48 ft) below ground level. In the event of an alarm, they have been designed to allow the waters of the Singelgracht to flood into them.

2 The Prison Bridge

The Torensluis – the widest bridge in Amsterdam – spans the Singel on the site of a 17th-century sluice gate. A lock-up jail was built into its foundations.

3 The Cat Boat

Hundreds of feline waifs and strays are given refuge in *De Poezenboot* (The Cat Boat), moored on the Singel *(above)*.

4 The Drunken Tsar

In 1716, Peter the Great got drunk at his friend Christoffel Brants' house at Keizersgracht 317, and kept the mayor waiting at a civic reception. That night, he stayed at the house of the Russian ambassador, Herengracht 527, where Napoleon also stayed in 1811.

Peter the Great

5 The Narrowest House

Is Singel 7 the smallest house in Amsterdam? No, it's simply the back door of a wedge-shaped house, whatever your tour guide tells you.

6 The Oldest Café

Which is really the oldest café in Amsterdam? It's Café Chris, in Bloemstraat, dating from 1624. A curiosity: the loo is flushed from the bar.

7 The Most Crooked Café

Teetering Café de Sluyswacht, built in 1695, makes an alarming sight as you glide by along the Oude Schans *(see p80)*.

8 The Wrapped-up House

Look carefully at Victoria Hotel, near the station, and you will see two tiny 17th-century houses embedded in the monumental 19th-century façade. A little old lady, so the story goes, refused to sell up, so the hotel had to wrap itself around them.

9 The Floating Pagoda

The vast Sea Palace, Amsterdam's famous floating Chinese restaurant, makes an unusual sight in Oosterdok. With its twinkling lights and many windows, it makes a romantic dinner spot.

10 The Tower of Tears

This medieval defensive tower has the saddest of names: Schreierstoren (Tower of Tears), where weeping women waved farewell to their seafaring men.

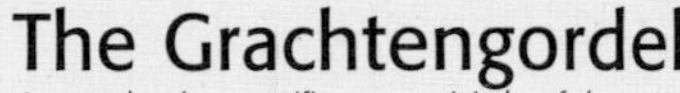

Top 10 Bridges

1. Magere Brug (Amstel)
2. Blauwbrug (Amstel)
3. Hogesluis (Amstel)
4. Nieuwe Amstelbrug (Amstel)
5. Berlagebrug (Amstel)
6. Torensluis (Singel)
7. St Antoniessluis (Zwanenburgwal)
8. Seven hump-back bridges (Reguliersgracht)
9. White wooden drawbridges (Western Islands)
10. Sleutelbrug (Oudezijds Voorburgwal)

The Grachtengordel

Amsterdam's magnificent semicircle of three canals – Prinsengracht, Keizersgracht and Herengracht – is the city's defining characteristic. Lined by elegant gabled houses, and connected by intimate cross-streets, it was devised in the early 17th century to cope with the rapid rise in population, and was built in two stages during the century. This costly Plan of Three Canals was purely aesthetic, taking no account of existing waterways. The land along the banks was sold in single plots; the wealthy bought two together so that they could build larger houses.

Amsterdam had its unlikely beginnings some 400 years before, when a fishing settlement grew up on the marshy banks of the river Amstel. (It was dammed in 1222 – hence the name, a contraction of Amstelledamme.) As the town began to expand, canals were cut to drain more land and provide transport channels, and outer canals were fortified. A glance at a map clearly shows the limits of the medieval town, bounded by the curved Singel, with the Grachtengordel fanning out beyond.

Magere Brug

Built in 1672 and so narrow that it was named the Skinny Bridge, this much-loved double-leaf wooden drawbridge was rebuilt in 1969.

Plan of Amsterdam (1648) showing the Grachtengordel

For details of canal tours **See p136**

TOP 10 Rijksmuseum

The magnificent national museum of the Netherlands possesses nearly seven million works of art, only a fraction of which is on display. It was established by King Louis Napoleon in 1808 in the Royal Palace on the Dam, moving later to the Trippenhuis on Kloveniersburgwal. In 1865, the architect P J H Cuypers designed a new home near the Vondelpark; the Rijksmuseum opened in 1885. The main building is being renovated (until 2010) and only the Philips Wing is open.

Façade of the Rijksmuseum

There is no café in the Philips Wing but Café Cobra on Museumplein is a good place to stop or head for Indonesian Sama Sebo, on P. C. Hoofstraat, or Café Americain ***(see p101).***

Be prepared: this is a difficult museum to get to grips with in a single visit. In 2003 the main building closed for major restoration, during which the Philips Wing has remained open where the museum's finest works can be seen. Work should be completed in 2010.

• Stadhouderskade 42/Hobbemastraat 19 (Philips Wing entrance: Jan Luijkenstr. 1) • Map D5 • 020 674 7000 • www.rijksmuseum.nl • Open 9am–6pm (to 8:30pm Fri); closed Jan 1 • Admission €10 (under 19s free); garden free

Key

Basement

Ground floor

First floor

1 St Elizabeth's Day Flood

Look carefully at this pastoral scene, highlight of the museum's Dutch History collection, and you will see that a tragedy is unfolding. Painted by an unknown artist in 1500, it recalls a disastrous flood of 1421, when some 20 villages were swept away by floodwater.

2 The Night Watch

The museum's most prized possession is *The Military Company of Captain Frans Banning Cocq* – otherwise known as *The Night Watch* (1642), given pride of place at the head of the Gallery of Honour *(see p15).*

3 The Jewish Bride

In creating one of the most tender double portraits ever painted (1667), Rembrandt depicted – in an unusually free style – an unknown couple in the guise of biblical characters Isaac and Rebecca.

4 The Milkmaid

The sense of realism in this magical painting by Vermeer (c.1658) is conveyed by his mastery of light, colour and perspective. Seen slightly from below against a bare wall, the simple, sturdy girl seems almost tangible – quiet and still, but for the milk flowing from her jug *(left).*

Bear in mind that from late 2003, the museum will undergo a major and lengthy restoration **See panel above**

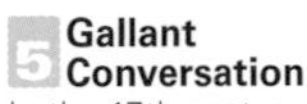

Top 10 Works

1. St Elizabeth's Day Flood
2. The Night Watch
3. The Jewish Bride
4. The Milkmaid
5. Gallant Conversation
6. The Windmill at Wijk
7. Winter Landscape with Skaters
8. Delftware
9. Dolls House of Petronella Oortman
10. Portrait of Woman in Turkish Costume

5 Gallant Conversation

In the 17th century, paintings of everyday scenes, called genre paintings, became very popular. In this one, by Gerard Ter Borch (1655), a scruffy dog, a candle and a bed convey sexual meaning, and the man appears to hold up a coin.

6 The Windmill at Wijk

In this impressive painting (1670) by Jacob van Ruisdael, a calm scene becomes a dramatic picture, full of excitement.

7 Winter Landscape with Skaters

Dutch landscape artist Hendrick Avercamp specialized in winter scenes packed with delightful detail, such as this one painted in 1608. The longer you gaze at it, the more you notice.

9 Dolls House of Petronella Oortman

An exquisitely detailed 17th-century miniature Dutch house, belonging not to a child but an adult.

10 Portrait of Woman in Turkish Costume

Swiss-born Jean-Etienne Liotard was a portrait artist who used pastels with great skill. After a spell living in Istanbul, he dressed as a Turk, and he liked to array his sitters in Turkish costume as well as in this subtle and delicate painting of 1745.

8 Delftware

The Rijksmuseum has a superb collection of Delftware, including an astonishing pyramid vase (c. 1700) more than 1 m (3.2 ft) high, with spouts for displaying highly-prized tulips *(right)*.

Gallery Guide

There are three entrances, two at the front, either side of the central driveway which runs under the building, and one in the Philips Wing on Hobbemastraat. At peak visiting times, it's quicker to use this entrance, housing Asiatic Art, European Paintings, Costume and Textiles and temporary exhibitions, then make your way through to the main building. The museum's highlight collections – Dutch Paintings and Dutch 17th-century Sculpture and Decorative Arts – are on the first floor.

For more on Dutch Artists **See pp46–7**

Left, Centre ***Works by Edvard Munch and Gerard Ter Borch*** Right ***Seated Guanyin***

TOP 10 Rijksmuseum Features

1 The Building
The architect P J H Cuypers attracted strong criticism from the Protestant community, who took exception to the building's Neo-Gothic roofs and ornately decorated façade. King William III refused to set foot inside.

2 The Garden
A little-known, immaculate haven, it is studded with statues and architectural curiosities.

3 Dutch History
The museum's collection includes a chronological display of artifacts tracing the history of the Netherlands. Highlights include *St Elizabeth's Day Flood* *(see p12)* and *The Battle of Waterloo* by Jan Willem Pieneman.

4 Dutch Paintings
Walk through the Gallery of Honour to survey *The Night Watch*, then begin the tour proper with paintings of the Middle Ages (Room 201). The museum's core is its astonishing array of 17th-century Dutch art, in which every important Dutch artist is represented by a selection of his greatest works. Move on to the 18th- and 19th-century collections, including a Van Gogh self-portrait.

Museum Floorplan

5 European Paintings
Veronese and Goya are among the Italian and Spanish masters represented here. A collection of pastels is displayed separately.

6 Sculpture and Decorative Arts
Highlights include Delftware, dolls houses *(see p13)*, glassware and furniture, as well as the remarkable Chinese Room from Leeuwarden.

7 Costumes and Textiles
Magnificent costumes and textiles, mostly 18th- and 19th-century, are displayed in temporary, themed exhibitions.

8 Asiatic Art
Here, the fruits of Dutch association with the Orient are on display – including beautiful works of art from India, Indonesia, China and Japan.

9 Print Room
The museum owns almost a million works on paper – a small selection is shown in temporary exhibitions in the Print Room on the ground floor.

10 ARIA
The ARIA computer system offers information on 1,250 items from the collection, and helps you to design your own route around the museum.

Rembrandt and *The Night Watch*

Popular belief holds Rembrandt's greatest painting, The Night Watch *(1642), responsible for his change in fortune from rich man to pauper. In fact, it was more a case of poor financial management than of public dissatisfaction with the artist, although it's very likely that the militiamen who commissioned the portrait would have been dismayed at the result.* The Night Watch *differs radically from other contemporary portraits of companies of civic guards, in which they are depicted seated, serious and soberly dressed* (see p26)*. Rembrandt, by contrast, shows a tumultuous scene – the captain issuing orders to his lieutenant, the men taking up arms ready to march. This huge painting was originally even larger, but it was drastically cut down in 1715, when it was moved to the town hall, and the other pieces were lost. In 1975 it was slashed, but repaired.*

Self-Portrait as St Paul

Rembrandt's series of self-portraits, painted throughout his life, provide an extraordinary insight into his character.

The Military Company of Captain Frans Banning Cocq* – better known as *The Night Watch

Top 10 Events in Rembrandt's Life

1. Born in Leiden (1606)
2. Studies with Pieter Lastman (1624)
3. Receives first important commission and marries Saskia van Uylenburgh (1634)
4. Reputation grows; buys large house in Amsterdam (1639) – now the Museum het Rembrandthuis
5. Titus, his only child to survive into adulthood, is born (1641)
6. Saskia dies; *The Night Watch* completed (1642)
7. Hendrickje Stoffels moves in (1649)
8. Applies for bankruptcy (1656)
9. Titus and Hendrickje acquire the rights to his work
10. Death of Titus (1668); in October of the following year, Rembrandt dies

TOP 10 Van Gogh Museum

The most comprehensive collection in the world of Van Gogh's work was amassed by his art dealer brother Theo, and is housed in this museum. It includes more than 200 of his paintings, over 500 drawings and hundreds of letters, as well as his Japanese prints and works by contemporaries – though not all are on permanent display. Gerrit Rietveld's airy building, opened in 1973, sets off the paintings to perfection. The display follows Van Gogh's development from the murky peasant scenes of the early 1880s to the anguished final works. An ellipse-shaped extension designed by Kisho Kurokawa was added in 1999.

Van Gogh Museum façade

The museum has a useful self-service café, situated on the ground floor.

To avoid the crowds, arrive at opening time or buy tickets at the museum's website *(see below)*. Stick to the chronological order of the display.

- *Paulus Potterstraat 7*
- *Map C6*
- *020 570 5200*
- *www.vangoghmuseum.com*
- *Open 10am–6pm daily, 10am–10pm Fri*
- *Admission: adults €12.50; children 13–17 €2.50 (under 13s free)*
- *Audio tours €2.50–4; group tours by appointment*

1 Sunflowers

This vibrant painting (1889) was intended to be one of a series of still lifes to fill the "Yellow House" at Arles. Van Gogh chose sunflowers because he was expecting Paul Gauguin, and knew his friend liked them. The predominant yellows and oranges contrast with strokes of brilliant mauve and red.

2 The Potato Eaters

The culmination of his years in Nuenen, this was Van Gogh's first major composition (1885). He wanted to portray the peasants realistically, not glamorize them, but the painting was not the critical success he had hoped for.

3 The Bridge in the Rain

This work, painted in 1887, illustrates Van Gogh's interest in Japanese art, in particular Utagawa Hiroshige. However, Van Gogh used far brighter colours and greater contrasts.

Top 10 Paintings

1. Sunflowers
2. The Potato Eaters
3. The Bridge in the Rain
4. A Pair of Shoes
5. Self-Portrait as an Artist
6. Fishing Boats on the Beach at Les Saintes-Maries-de-la-Mer
7. Vincent's Bedroom in Arles
8. The Reaper
9. Almond Blossom
10. Wheatfield with Crows

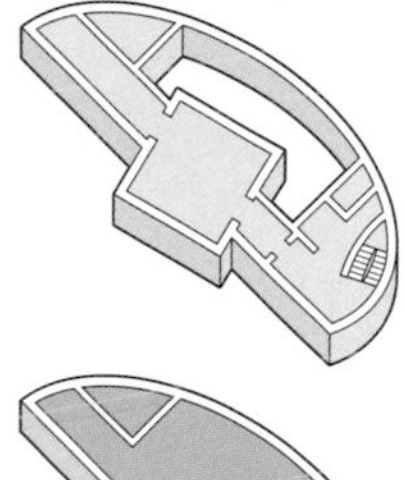

Key

- Basement
- Ground floor
- First floor
- Second floor
- Third floor

4 A Pair of Shoes

Van Gogh gives character to a pair of worn boots in one of the first paintings after his move to Paris (1886). The dark palette harks back to his Nuenen work.

5 Self-Portrait as an Artist

The last and most accomplished in a series of self-portraits painted in 1887, shortly before he left Paris, reveals Van Gogh's distinctive interpretation of Pointillism. He chose himself as subject since he could seldom afford models.

6 Fishing Boats on the Beach at Les Saintes-Maries-de-la-Mer

A trip to the sea in 1888 produced these colourful, stylized boats. Look close and you will see grains of sand, blown on to the canvas and fixed there forever as the paint dried.

7 Vincent's Bedroom in Arles

The mastery of this painting (1888) lies in the simplicity of the subject and the subtly alternating blocks of colour. Van Gogh was so happy with the result that he made two copies *(see p19)*.

8 The Reaper

While undergoing treatment in Saint-Rémy, Van Gogh found solace painting people who worked the land. He painted three versions of The Reaper (1889).

9 Almond Blossom

Van Gogh made this picture of white almond blossom against a blue sky for his new nephew, born in January 1890 and named after him.

10 Wheatfield with Crows

One of the panoramic landscapes that Van Gogh painted in 1890, during the last days of his life, this famous picture with its dead-end track and menacing, crow-filled sky, perhaps reveals his tortured state of mind.

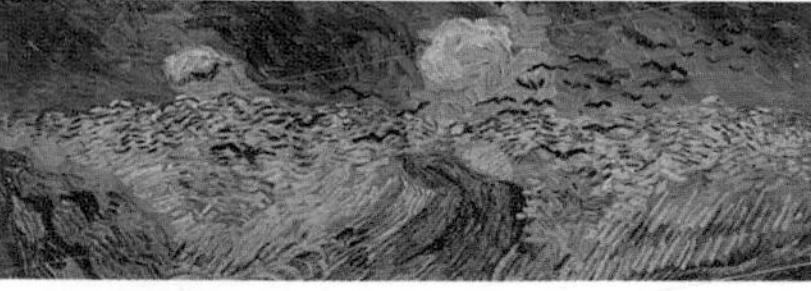

Museum Guide

Van Gogh's paintings are displayed by date and place of execution on the first floor of the main building. Works by contemporaries are split between ground and third floor. Exhibitions of drawings and graphic art are staged on the second floor, which also has a study area, where drawings and documents too fragile to be displayed can be viewed. The new wing has three floors, devoted to temporary exhibitions.

For more Amsterdam museums **See pp40–41**

Left **Exhausted Maenads** Centre **Amsterdam cityscape by Monet** Right **Gauguin self-portrait**

TOP 10 Van Gogh Museum: Other Artists

1 View of Prins Hendrikkade and the Kromme Waal in Amsterdam

Monet painted this cityscape in winter 1874 from a boat on the IJ river.

2 Young Peasant Girl with a Hoe

Jules Breton was an idol of Van Gogh. In rural scenes like this one (1882), he places an idealized figure in a realistic setting.

Museum Floorplan

3 Exhausted Maenads after the Dance

In this Lawrence Alma-Tadema painting of 1874, three devotees (maenads) of the wine god Bacchus have fallen asleep.

4 Portrait of Guus Preitinger, the Artist's Wife

The vivid use of colour in Kees van Dongen's portrait of his wife (1911) is characteristic of Fauvism.

5 Young Woman at a Table, "Poudre de Riz"

This early painting by Toulouse-Lautrec (1887), who became a friend of Van Gogh, is probably of his mistress, Suzanne Valadon.

6 Portrait of Bernard's Grandmother

Van Gogh swapped one of his self-portraits for this painting (1887) by Emile Bernard.

7 Saint Geneviève as a Child in Prayer

An oil study (1876) by Puvis de Chavannes for the huge murals he painted on the theme of St Geneviève's childhood at the Panthéon in Paris.

8 Self-Portrait with a Portrait of Bernard, "Les Misérables"

In his powerful self-portrait (1888), Gauguin identified himself with the hero of *Les Misérables*, Jean Valjean.

9 "Grand Paysan"

Jules Dalou shared Van Gogh's preoccupation with peasants, whom he saw as heroic labourers. He devised this life-size sculpture in 1889.

10 Two Women Embracing

Van Gogh's influence on the Dutch artist Jan Sluijters is obvious in the brushwork and colour of this painting of 1906.

Portrait of Bernard's Grandmother

The Life of Vincent van Gogh

Born on 30 March 1853 in Zundert, Vincent van Gogh was the eldest son of a pastor and his wife. Aged 16, he joined his uncle's business Goupil & Co., art dealers. Seven years later, displaying increasingly erratic behaviour, he was dismissed. After a couple of false starts as teacher and evangelist, in 1880 he decided to be a painter. From 1883 to 1885, he lived with his parents in Nuenen, but in 1886 he went to Paris to study in Fernand Cormon's studio. He lived with his brother Theo, met renowned artists and changed his style. In 1888, he moved to Arles where he dreamed of establishing an artists' colony with Paul Gauguin. Soon after Gauguin arrived, the friends had a fierce argument, and during a psychotic attack, Van Gogh cut off a piece of his own left ear lobe. He enrolled as a voluntary patient in a clinic in Saint-Rémy in 1889. The following year he left for the rural village Auvers sur-Oise, where his state of mind deteriorated and he shot himself in the chest on 27 July 1890. He died, with Theo at his bedside, two days later.

Vincent Van Gogh

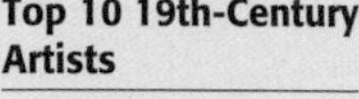

Top 10 19th-Century Artists

1. Vincent van Gogh (1853–1890)
2. Claude Monet (1840–1926)
3. Pierre Auguste Renoir (1841–1919)
4. Paul Cézanne (1839–1906)
5. Auguste Rodin (1840–1917)
6. Edouard Manet (1832–83)
7. Edgar Degas (1834–1917)
8. J M W Turner (1775–1851)
9. Eugène Delacroix (1798–1863)
10. Jean-Baptiste Camille Corot (1796–1875)

Vincent's Bedroom in Arles

TOP 10 Museum Ons' Lieve Heer op Solder

Contrasting sharply with its surroundings in the shabbiest corner of the Red Light District, this lovely 17th-century house has a surprise in store. Concealed in its upper floors is a hidden church, Ons' Lieve Heer op Solder *(Our Lord in the Attic), a rare, perfectly preserved example of the many clandestine churches that were built after the Alteration* (see facing page). *Local Catholics worshipped here from 1663 to 1887, when nearby St Nicolaaskerk was built. Its little-changed interiors transport you back in time to the Dutch Golden Age.*

Amstelkring façade with spout gable

For refreshment, head to Himalaya around the corner *(see p81)* or walk to the Nieuwmarkt, where In de Waag is an excellent café-restaurant.

Take one of the free plans and follow the suggested tour of the museum. If you are confused at first, don't worry – all the rooms are clearly marked and you won't miss anything.

- *Oudezijds Voorburgwal 40*
- *Map P2*
- *020 624 6604*
- *www.opsolder.nl*
- *Open 10am–5pm Mon–Sat, 1–5pm Sun, public hols. Closed 1 Jan, 30 Apr*
- *Admission: €7; concessions: €5; under 19: €1*

Top 10 Features

1. The Building
2. The Front Parlour
3. The Sael
4. The Priest's Room
5. The Hidden Church
6. The Folding Pulpit
7. The Maria Chapel and Peat Room
8. The Confessional
9. The Rear Houses
10. The Kitchen

1 The Building

The spout-gabled canal house was built in 1661 for Jan Hartman, a Catholic merchant. He combined its attic with the attics of two smaller houses behind to create the hidden church, which was extended in c.1735.

2 The Front Parlour

This *(above)* was the merchant's shop, with the wood-floored office behind and a separate entrance for customers. The family and their guests entered though the porch into the dimly-lit marble corridor.

3 The Sael

Adhering to strict rules of proportion and symmetry, the family's formal parlour *(sael)* is a superb example of the Dutch Classical style fashionable in the 17th century *(below)*. It contrasts with the simpler Canal Room, which would not have been used to receive guests.

For more on Amsterdam's churches **See pp42–3**

4 The Chaplain's Room

Formerly the servants' quarters, the Chaplain's Room is in a corner on a bend in the stairs. It's a tiny, enclosed bedroom with a box bed, simply furnished as it would have been for the priest of the hidden church, who lived in the house.

Key

- Ground floor
- First floor
- Second floor
- Third floor
- Fourth floor
- Fifth floor

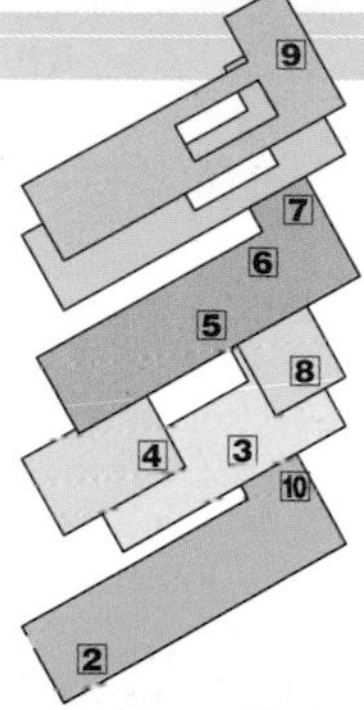

5 The Hidden Church

At the top of the stairs, the hidden church *(schuilkerk)* proves a charming and highly unusual sight *(left)*. In c.1735 it was remodelled in Baroque style, with the addition of two tiers of galleries, suspended from the roof by cast-iron rods, to provide extra seating.

6 The Folding Pulpit

With space-saving in mind, the ingenious pulpit was designed to fold away under the left column of the altar when not in use. The altar painting is *The Baptism of Christ* by Jacob de Wit (1695–1754).

7 The Maria Chapel and Peat Room

The congregation kept warm with footwarmers fuelled by peat stored in this room above the Maria chapel, which now houses the church's silver.

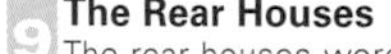

8 The Confessional

In 1739, this living room in the middle of the three houses became the church's confessional. One of the two wooden confessional boxes still remains *(right)*.

9 The Rear Houses

The rear houses were gradually taken over by the church, but there are still signs of their original use as family rooms.

10 The Kitchen

Once part of the sacristan's secret living quarters, the charming 17th-century kitchen *(left)* has Delft wall tiles, an open hearth, stone sink and black-and-white floor.

The Alteration

The revolt of the (Calvinist) Northern Netherlands against the (Catholic) Spanish Habsburgs began in 1568, but Amsterdam did not decide where its loyalties lay until 1578, when the city joined William of Orange in a peaceful revolution known as the Alteration. Calvinists seized power and Amsterdam became the Protestant capital of an infant Dutch republic. Catholics were no longer allowed to worship in public, but Dutch tolerance ensured that they were able to continue in private.

For more on the Dutch Golden Age See p27

TOP 10 Begijnhof

Away from the bustle of the city, this bewitching sanctuary of elegant houses around a tranquil green was founded in 1346 for the members of a lay Catholic sisterhood, the Beguines, the last of whom died in 1971. Although none of the original buildings survive – nor the early design in which the courtyard was surrounded by water – there is a fascinating example of a 15th-century wooden house, a lovely church of the same period, and an appealing hidden chapel. Visitors are asked to respect the privacy of the current residents.

The elegant houses of the Begijnhof

Trendy Café Esprit and traditional Café Hoppe are just round the corner in Spui (at Nos 10 and 18 respectively).

Services are held in Dutch (daily) and French (Sundays) in the Roman Catholic Begijnhof Chapel. Services in English are held in the Protestant Engelse Kerk (Sundays).

In summer, go to a lunchtime concert at the Engelse Kerk.

Pick up an information booklet from Het Houten Huis.

- *Spui (entrance on Gedempte Begijnensloot)*
- *Map M4*
- *020 623 3565*
- *(chapel) www.begijnhofamsterdam.nl*
- *Open 9am–5pm daily; Begijnhof Chapel open 1–6:30pm Mon, 9:30am–6:30pm Tue–Fri, 9am–6pm Sat & Sun*
- *Free*

Top 10 Features

1. Engelse Kerk
2. Begijnhof Chapel
3. Het Houten Huis
4. Courtyard with Wall Plaques
5. Mother Superior's House
6. 17th- and 18th-Century Houses
7. Statue of a Beguine
8. The Beguine in the Gutter
9. Wall Plaque on No. 19
10. Spui Entrance

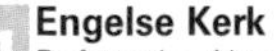

1 Engelse Kerk

Before the Alteration *(see p21)*, the Beguines worshipped in this pretty 15th-century church *(below)*. Confiscated in 1578, it was let in 1607 to a group of English and Scottish Presbyterians, who renamed it.

2 Begijnhof Chapel

The city's first clandestine chapel was created in 1665, when the Beguines converted two ordinary houses into a little church *(see pp20–21)*. The Miracle of Amsterdam *(see p38)* is commemorated here.

3 Het Houten Huis

No. 34, Het Houten Huis, is the oldest house in Amsterdam *(below)*, and one of only two wood-fronted houses in the city. It predates the 1521 ban on the construction of wooden houses, introduced to reduce the risk of fire.

4 Courtyard with Wall Plaques

Set into the wall of the courtyard behind Het Houten Huis is a remarkable collection of wall plaques salvaged from demolished houses. In keeping with the religious nature of the Beguines, each one tells a Biblical story.

5 Mother Superior's House

The grandest house, No. 26, belonged to the Mother Superior *(above)*. In the 20th century, the last of the Beguines lived together here.

Plan of the Begijnhof

6 17th- and 18th-Century Houses

After several devastating fires, most of the existing houses were built in the 17th and 18th centuries. They are typically tall and narrow, with large sash windows and spout or neck gables. They were the property of the sisterhood, so if a Beguine left or died, outsiders could not claim her house. Today they provide homes for 100 or so single women.

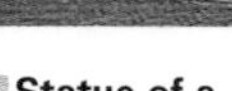

7 Statue of a Beguine

The statue shows a Beguine dressed in her traditional *falie* (headdress) and long garment of undyed cloth.

8 The Beguine in the Gutter

To make amends for her family's conversion to Protestantism, Cornelia Arents requested in her will not to be buried in the church, but in the gutter outside. Her coffin was left inside the church on 2 May 1654, but the following day it had miraculously moved outside, where she was eventually buried. A plaque marks the spot.

9 Wall Plaque on No. 19

This handsome plaque *(above)* illustrates the return from Egypt to Israel of Jesus, Mary and Joseph after the death of Herod.

10 Spui Entrance

Members of the public use the arched entrance from Gedempte Begijnensloot, but be sure to peep discreetly into the pretty vaulted and tiled passageway leading to Spui.

The Welfare System

Charity lies at the heart of Amsterdam's long tradition of caring for the poor and needy, which goes back to the Middle Ages and continues to the present day. In the 14th century, primary responsibility for social welfare passed from the church to the city authorities. They distributed food to the poor, and set up institutions to care for orphans, the sick and the insane. In the 17th century, a number of wealthy merchants funded almshouses – *hofjes* – providing subsidized mass housing. Some of these *hofjes* are still used for their original purpose today.

For more on hofjes **See p92**

TOP 10 Amsterdams Historisch Museum

The Historical Museum houses the city's most fascinating collection of artifacts, archaeological finds, clothes, jewellery, maps, paintings and sculptures. Originally a convent, in 1580 it became the city orphanage. Handsome extensions were added by Hendrick and Pieter de Keyser before Jacob van Campen's magnificent rebuilding of 1634. The orphans moved out in 1960, and in 1975 the museum moved in. Its stunningly presented exhibits and interactive displays chart Amsterdam's growth and metamorphosis over the centuries.

Kalverstraat entrance, 1581

The David & Goliath café is inside Joost Bilhamer's Kalverstraat entrance.

Start your sightseeing here; it will help you understand the city when you begin to explore.

The electronic map in Room 1 traces Amsterdam's development from AD 1000 to 2000.

Don't miss the delightful façade stones set into the wall of the museum in St Luciënsteeg.

- *Kalverstraat 92; Sint Luciensteeg 27; Nieuwezijds Voorburgwal 357*
- *Map M4*
- *020 523 1822*
- *www.ahm.nl*
- *Open 10am–5pm Mon–Fri, 11am–5pm Sat, Sun and hols. Closed 1 Jan, 30 Apr, 25 Dec*
- *Admission: adults €7; children 6–18 €3.50 (under 6s free); concessions €5.25*

Top 10 Works

1. Bird's-eye View of Amsterdam
2. The Return from the Second Voyage to the East Indies
3. Terrestrial and Celestial Globes
4. 19th-century Jewellery Collection
5. Dam Square
6. Turbo Shell
7. Orphan Girls going to Church
8. Dr F M Wibaut (bronze head)
9. The Anatomy Lesson of Dr Jan Deijman
10. Model of the Oosterdok

1 Bird's-eye View of Amsterdam

Cornelis Anthonisz's 1538 map of Amsterdam (the oldest extant) includes the Dam, Oude Kerk and Nieuwe Kerk.

2 The Return from the Second Voyage to the East Indies

Hendrik Corneliszoon Vroom's painting (1599) celebrates the first successful expedition to the Far East to buy spices.

3 Terrestrial and Celestial Globes

A pair of costly globes lent prestige to any self-respecting 17th-century intellectual. Joan Willemsz Blaeu must have made this unique pair after 1644 because they show the Australian coast, just discovered by Abel Tasman *(see p39)*.

4 19th-century Jewellery

Sophia Lopez Suasso-de Bruijn was a passionate collector of jewellery; even on her deathbed, she spent 5,400 guilders on watches and snuff-boxes. Most of the stunning pieces on display are Italian.

5 Dam Square

George Hendrik Breitner based his cityscapes on photographs; despite its Impressionist style, this famous painting (1895–98) still has a photographic quality.

6 Turbo Shell

This exquisite mother-of-pearl *turbo marmoratus* is covered in tiny engraved animals. It dates from around 1650 and was probably brought from the Orient by the Dutch East India Company (VOC).

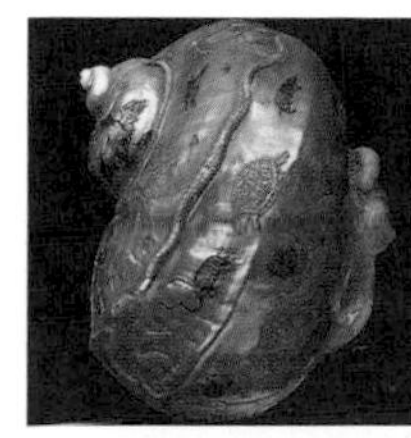

Key

Ground floor

First floor

Second floor

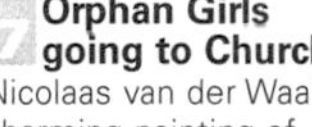

7 Orphan Girls going to Church

Nicolaas van der Waaij's charming painting of around 1895 hangs in the anteroom to the Regents' Chamber.

8 Dr F M Wibaut

This powerful bronze head was made in 1934 by Tjipke Visser, favourite sculptor of the Social Democratic Workers' Party (SDAP). The subject was Floor Wibaut, SDAP Councillor for housing in the 1920s, who dedicated himself to building new apartments for the working class.

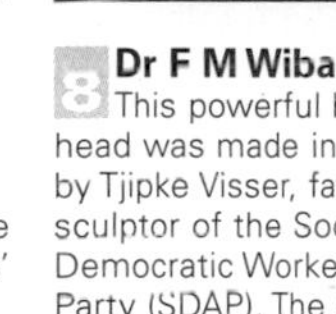

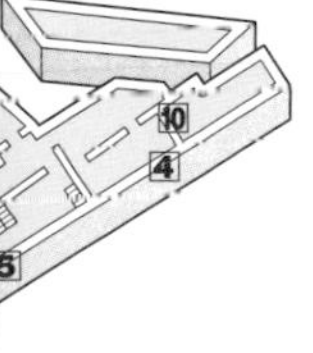

9 The Anatomy Lesson of Dr Jan Deijman

In Rembrandt's original, eight surgeons watched Dr Deijman dissect a corpse. Fire destroyed most of the painting in 1723, but the frontal perspective of the remaining group is still quite remarkable.

10 Model of the Oosterdok

This wonderful model of the Oosterdok Lock dates from 1831, the year work started on the lock itself. It was part of a larger project to counteract a build-up of silt, which barred large ships from the harbour.

Museum Guide

The permanent exhibition is arranged on three floors; the "Young City: 1350–1550" is on the ground floor; the "Mighty City: 1550–1815" is split between ground and first floors; the "Modern City: 1815–2000" is split between first and second. A temporary exhibition room and the Civic Guards Gallery are inside the Kalverstraat entrance to the left. The door into the Regents' Chamber is opposite the ticket desk. There is wheelchair access at the St Luciënsteeg entrance.

For more Amsterdam museums **See pp40–41**

Left **Dam Square with the New Town Hall under Construction** Right **Civic Guard**

Top 10 Historisch Museum Rooms

1 Civic Guards' Gallery
These 16th- and 17th-century group portraits of the Civic Guard are arguably the highlight of the museum (entrance free).

2 Regents' Chamber
The orphanage governors met in this 17th-century room, sympathetically restored in Old Holland style.

Museum Floorplan

3 Room 2: Walking through the City
Aptly named, this room includes a superb collection of 14th- and 15th-century leather shoes, well preserved after centuries in mud.

4 Room 4: Turbulent Times
Displays from the late 16th century include the Civic Guard's Italian-made armour, and silver that escaped melting down for "crisis coins" in 1578.

5 Room 6: The Dam
The bustling heart of the city was a popular subject in 17th-century paintings like Lingelbach's *Dam Square with the New Town Hall under Construction*.

6 Room 9: Social Care, Stern Discipline
In 1613, the city appointed six Almoners with responsibility for the poor and needy. The paintings in this room show them at work.

7 Room 12: The 18th Century
The 18th century saw the decline of Amsterdam and, ultimately, the Republic's defeat by the French. Highlights include *The Arrival of Napoleon at Dam Square* by van Bree.

8 Room 15: 19th-century Cabinet
There was a 19th-century trend for rich industrialists to collect art: old masters as well as contemporary works. These important collections helped establish the public ownership of art.

9 Room 22: Amsterdam 1940–1945
A room devoted to memorabilia of the German occupation.

10 Room 24: Café 't Mandje
A meticulous reconstruction of leather-clad motorbiker Bet van Beeren's famous café on Zeedijk – the first where homosexuals could be open.

Café 't Mandje

The Golden Age

The economic boom of the 17th century laid the foundations for the flowering of the arts in Amsterdam. Plans were laid to surround the city with a triple ring of canals lined with fine houses, a project which required the work of many architects. The most powerful city in the Dutch Republic recognized the importance of the arts, and rewarded its artists well – and with the supremacy of the Protestants came the freedom to paint secular subjects. To show their wealth and status, rich patrons commissioned portraits of themselves and their families. The artists' best clients, however, were the municipal bodies such as the guilds, who commissioned group portraits, as well as decorative pieces of silver and glass. Painters began to focus their energies on a single area of painting – whether historical, portraiture, interiors, genre, still lives, urban scenes, landscapes or seascapes – and this specialization greatly enhanced the quality of their workmanship.

Silver Marriage Cup
The hinged bowl above the woman's head forms one cup, her full skirt a second. Once the wedding was in full swing, bride and groom would down both together.

Top 10 Highlights of the Golden Age

1. *The Night Watch* by Rembrandt (1642, Rijksmuseum) *(see p15)*
2. The Grachtengordel, designed by Hendrick Staets (begun in 1613) *(see p11)*
3. Museum Amstelkring (1663) *(see pp20–21)*
4. Westerkerk by Hendrick de Keyser (1631) *(see p91)*
5. Huis met de Hoofden, sometimes attributed to Pieter de Keyser (1622) *(see p91)*
6. Claes Claeszhofje (1616)
7. Silver Marriage Cup by Gerrit Valck (1634) *(right)*
8. Café Hoppe (c.1670) *(see p50)*
9. Delftware (second half 17th century)
10. Burgerzaal (Paleis op de Dam) Koninklijk Paleis *(see pp34 & 39)*

Dutch Battle Ships **by Ludolf Backhuysen**

For more Amsterdam museums **See pp40–41**

Oude Kerk

The city's oldest monument and first parish church stands on the site of an early 13th-century wooden chapel that was destroyed by fire. Rebuilt as a small stone hall church in the 14th century, over the years it expanded into a mighty Gothic basilica, now in the heart of the Red Light District (see p77)*. The interior is stark, stripped of its Catholic treasures during the Iconoclasm of 1566, but it boasts some exquisite stained glass, rare ceiling paintings and a world-famous organ. It is dedicated to St Nicholas, patron saint of the city.*

Exterior of the Oude Kerk

For food and people-watching, head for Nieuwmarkt; In de Waag (Nieuwmarkt 4) is recommended.

Go to the Dutch Reformed Church service at 11am on Sundays, one of the Spring or Summer concerts, or the World Press Photo exhibition (late April to early June).

Don't miss the votive ships hanging from the choir ceiling.

- *Oudekerksplein South Entrance*
- *Map P2*
- *020 625 8284*
- *www.oudekerk.nl*
- *Open 11am–5pm Mon–Sat, 1–5pm Sun. Closed 1 Jan, 25 Dec, 30 Apr*
- *Admission €5; concessions €4 (separate charge for exhibitions)*
- *Guided tours by appointment; Tower Apr–Sep: noon–4pm Sat–Sun; Oct–Mar: by appointment (phone 020 689 2565)*

Top 10 Features

1. Great Organ
2. Maria Kapel
3. Ceiling
4. Saskia's Grave
5. Red Door into the Old Sacristy
6. Decorated Pillars
7. Misericords
8. Spire
9. Stained Glass of the Burgemeesters
10. Little Organ

1 Great Organ

With its eight pairs of bellows, magnificent oak-encased pipework, marbled wood statues and gilded carving, the great organ is a glorious sight *(right)*. Built by Christian Vater in 1724 and renovated by Johann Caspar Müller 14 years later, it is known as the Vater-Müller organ.

2 Maria Kapel

The most stunning stained glass is in the three windows of the Lady Chapel. All date from the 16th century; two show scenes from the Virgin's life, above the customary picture of the family who donated the window.

3 Ceiling

The massive wooden vaulted ceiling is claimed to be the largest in Western Europe, but it was only during restoration work in 1955 that the beautiful 15th-century paintings were revealed.

4 Saskia's Grave

Among the great and the good buried here is Saskia van Uylenburgh, Rembrandt's first wife, who died in 1642. Her grave is number 29K in the Weitkopers Kapel.

Share your travel recommendations on traveldk.com

5 Red Door into the Old Sacristy

Rembrandt passed through this door to announce his marriage. "Marry in haste, repent at leisure" is inscribed above it.

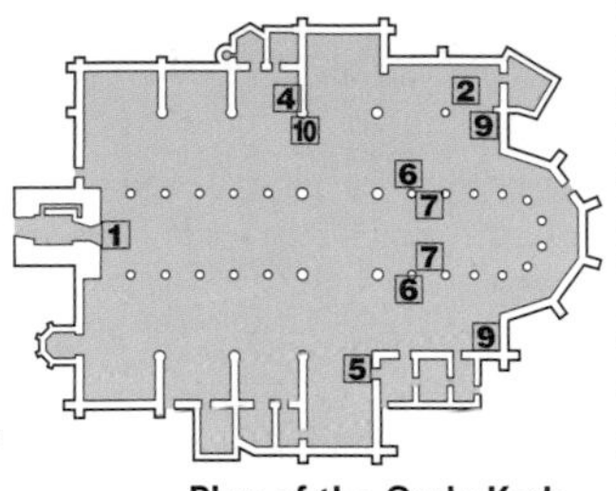

Plan of the Oude Kerk

6 Decorated Pillars

Relics of the period before 1578, these pillars once supported niches for statues of the Apostles destroyed in the Iconoclasm, and were painted to look like brocade, since the real thing was too expensive, and unsuited to the humid atmosphere.

7 Misericords

The 15th-century misericords helped choristers take the weight off their feet *(left)*. They are decorated with charming carvings illustrating traditional Dutch proverbs.

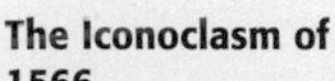

8 Spire

From the graceful late-Gothic spire, built by Joost Bilhamer in 1565, there are splendid views over the Oude Zijde. The tower contains a 47-bell carillon, a 17th-century addition which rings out every Saturday afternoon.

9 Stained Glass of the Burgemeesters

The colourful stained glass windows flanking the chancel depict the arms of the city burgomasters from 1578 to 1807 *(left)*. One was designed by De Angeli in 1758; the other by Pieter Jansz in 1654.

10 Little Organ

Attractively painted shutters form the original casing (1658) – however, the pipework was replaced in 1965. Tuned as it would have been before 1700, early music can now be part of the repertoire.

The Iconoclasm of 1566

In the 1566 Iconoclasm, or *Beeldenstorm* – precursor to the Alteration of 1578 *(see p21)* when the city became Protestant – the Calvinists looted Catholic churches and destroyed their treasures, among them the Oude Kerk's pictures, altars and statues. Only the ceiling paintings and stained glass were spared, as they were out of reach. The Calvinists also disapproved of the beggars and pedlars who gathered in the church, and threw them out, ending its role as a city meeting place.

For more Amsterdam churches **See pp42–3**

TOP 10 Museum Van Loon

Step back into the 18th century at this delightful canal house on Keizersgracht, which has been the property of the prestigious Van Loon family (co-founders of the Dutch East India Company, later bankers and royal courtiers) since 1884. In the 1970s, the family opened it to the public, having painstakingly restored it to its appearance in the 1750s, when it was owned by Dr Abraham van Hagen and his heiress wife Catharina Trip. It is beautifully furnished with Van Loon family possessions throughout.

Façade of the Museum Van Loon

There is no café; head for nearby Nieuwe Spiegelstraat or Utrechtsestraat for a good choice.

Serene and elegant, the Museum Van Loon makes a perfect visit for adults, but is not so well suited to young children.

- *Keizersgracht 672*
- *Map E5*
- *020 624 5255*
- *www.museumvanloon.nl*
- *Open 11am–5pm Wed–Mon*
- *Admission €6; concessions €4*
- *Guided tours on request*

Top 10 Features

1. The Building
2. The Staircase
3. The Family Portraits
4. The Wedding Portrait
5. The Garden
6. The Dining Service
7. The Gold Coin Collection
8. The Painted Room
9. The Romantic Double Portrait
10. The Kitchen

1 The Building

In 1672, Jeremias van Raey built two large houses on Keizersgracht. One he occupied himself, the other – No. 672, now the Museum Van Loon – he rented to Rembrandt's most famous pupil, Ferdinand Bol.

2 The Staircase

The balustrade was installed by Dr Van Hagen, who had his and his wife's names incorporated into the ornate brass work. When the canals ceased to freeze over regularly, the 18th-century sledge in the hall found a new use as a plant stand.

3 The Family Portraits

Portraits of the Van Loon family are displayed throughout the house.

4 The Wedding Portrait

Jan Molenaer's first major commission in Amsterdam portrays the whole family. It's a second marriage: the bride holds her stepson's hand in an act of acceptance, while the fallen chair symbolizes the groom's deceased brother.

5 The Garden

Laid out in the 1970s according to a plan of the property of 1700, the peaceful garden ends in the false Neo-Classical façade of the coach house *(below)*. Look carefully and you will see that the upstairs windows are in fact painted, pretty curtains and all.

Key

- Ground floor
- First floor
- Second floor

6 The Dining Service

Rare 18th-century Dutch porcelain and 19th-century Limoges ware grace the dining room.

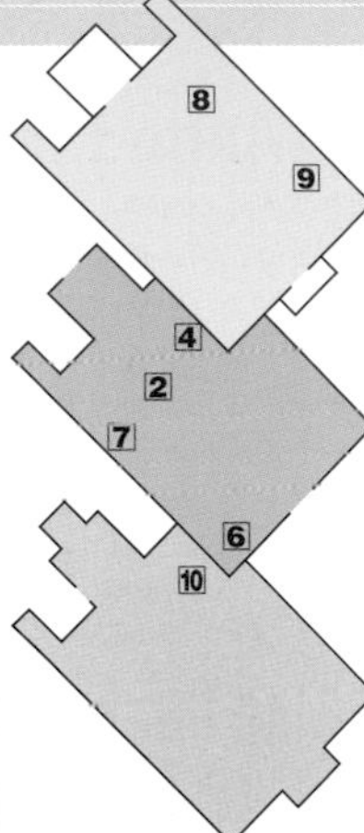

7 The Gold Coin Collection

Over the centuries, five Van Loon couples have celebrated their golden wedding; each had gold coins specially minted.

8 The Painted Room

Painted wallpapers such as these, featuring ruins, Classical buildings and human figures, were very popular in the 1700s.

9 The Romantic Double Portrait

Painted by J F A Tischbein in 1791, this intimate, relaxed portrait of these Van Loon ancestors is typical of the Age of Enlightenment, conveying love and happiness as well as duty.

The Kitchen 10

Cosy and inviting, the basement kitchen has been recently restored to look as it did in a photograph of 1900.

Museum Guide

Visitors are welcomed as guests in a private house and encouraged to wander around freely. They are allowed to walk on the carpets and nothing is roped off. Temporary exhibitions of modern art and sculpture are often on display in both the house and garden.

Top 10 Anne Frank Huis

This deeply moving museum tells a tragic story. When in 1942 the Germans began to round up Jews in Amsterdam, the Frank and Van Pels families went into hiding. For 25 months, they hid in a secret annexe in Otto Frank's business premises on Prinsengracht, now the Anne Frank Huis. In August 1944, they were betrayed and deported. Only Otto survived. The diary of his daughter, Anne, who died in Bergen-Belsen concentration camp in March 1945 at the age of 15, has made her one of the most inspiring figures of the 20th century.

Façade of No. 263 Prinsengracht

There is a pleasant, airy café, with a great view of the Westerkerk.

Book on-line to avoid the long queues.

Take care around the house as the stairs are steep and narrow.

The visit is a moving experience, so plan something contemplative afterwards: climb the Westerkerk spire, or walk to the Western Islands.

- *Prinsengracht 263 (entrance at 267)*
- *Map L2*
- *020 556 7105*
- *www.annefrank.org*
- *Open mid-Sep–mid-Mar: 9am–7pm daily; Jul–Aug: 10am–10pm daily; mid-Mar–mid-Sep: 9am–9pm Sun–Fri, 9am–10pm Sat. Closed Yom Kippur*
- *Admission adults €7.50; children 10–17 €3.50; children under 10 free*
- *No disabled access*

Top 10 Features

1. The Warehouse
2. The Offices
3. The Moveable Bookcase
4. The Secret Annexe
5. Anne's Room
6. The Chestnut Tree
7. The Front Attic
8. The Diary Room
9. Multimedia Resources
10. The Exhibition Room

1 The Warehouse

Otto Frank ran a business making pectin for jam, and spice and herb mixtures. The annexe in which the families hid was over his warehouse, so they had to keep quiet for fear that the warehouse workers would hear them.

2 The Offices

Visitors continue upstairs to the offices of Otto Frank and the staff who helped to hide him and his family, along with Otto's business partner, Hermann Van Pels, and his wife and son. In Anne's diary, the Van Pels became the Van Daans.

3 The Moveable Bookcase

To camouflage the entrance to the annexe, one of the helpers made a swinging bookcase. As Anne wrote, "no one could ever suspect that there could be so many rooms hidden behind..."

4 The Secret Annexe

The claustrophobic rooms in which the eight lived have been left unfurnished, as they were when the Germans cleared their possessions after their arrest. On one wall, pencil marks record the growth of Anne and her sister Margot.

5 Anne's Room

After a while, Margot moved in with her parents, and Anne had to share her room with a new member of the group, a dentist called Fritz Pfeffer – in Anne's estimation, "a very nice man". Anne's film-star pin-ups are still up on the wall.

Key to floorplan

- Ground floor
- First floor
- Second floor
- Third floor
- Attic

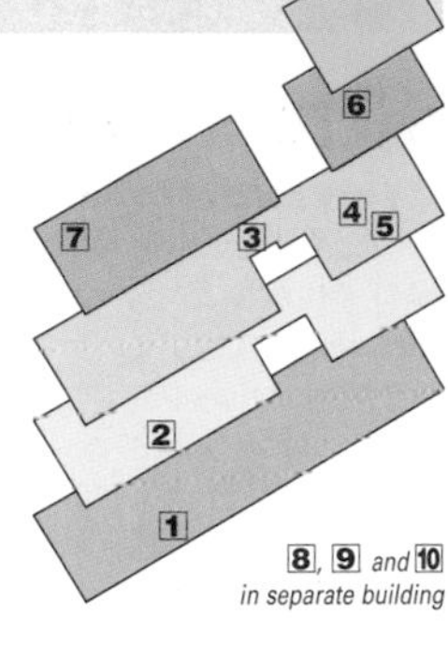

6 The Chestnut Tree

This tree, visible from the exhibition room, was a favourite of Anne's. It has been pruned and anchored and is estimated to last for another 10–15 years.

7 The Front Attic

In a moving display, the fate of each member of the group unfolds. Anne and Margot died a month before Bergen-Belsen was liberated.

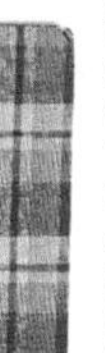

8 The Diary Room

As well as the now famous red-checked diary, which she kept every day, Anne wrote short stories and ideas for novels. As time went on, she began to edit her original diary with a book called *The Secret Annexe* in mind.

9 Multimedia

In the musuem's multimedia space, visitors can go on a "virtual" journey through the Secret Annexe to find out more on the people in hiding and on World War II.

10 The Exhibition Room

The Anne Frank Huis promotes racial tolerance through education. After the tour, visitors can participate in a video presentation on related issues.

Anne Frank's Diary

On the day the family were taken away, Miep Gies found Anne's diary. With the words "here is your daughter Anne's legacy to you", she handed it to Otto Frank on his return from Auschwitz. He prepared a transcript, and the diary was published to great acclaim in the Netherlands in 1947, and in Britain and the United States in 1952. It has since been published in more than 65 languages. Over 900,000 people visit the museum each year.

For more Jewish sights in Amsterdam **See pp48–9**

TOP 10 Dam Square

The very heart of Amsterdam, Dam Square – or "the Dam", as the locals call it – marks the site of the original 13th-century dam on the Amstel river (see p11). *An architectural parade spanning six centuries includes the glorious Nieuwe Kerk and the Koninklijke Paleis. By the 17th century, with the town hall here and the Exchange nearby, the Dam had become the focus of Amsterdam's political and commercial life. The passage of years may have eroded some of its grandeur – but certainly none of its colour or its vitality.*

A horse and trap near the Nationaal Monument

There are cafés in Madame Tussaud's, De Bijenkorf and the Nieuwe Kerk – the latter with a terrace overlooking the Dam.

Go to one of the concerts or exhibitions held at the Nieuwe Kerk.

- *Map M3, N3*
- *Koninklijk Paleis: closed for renovation until 2009 (check website: www.koninklijkhuis.nl). 020 620 4060. Admission: adults €4.50; children 6–16 €3.60; under 6s free*
- *Nieuwe Kerk: during exhibitions: 10am–6pm daily (to 10pm Thu). 020 638 6909. www.nieuwekerk.nl Admission charge*
- *Madame Tussaud's Scenerama: Peek & Cloppenburg Building. 020 522 1010. www.madametussauds.nl Open 10am–5:30pm daily. Admission: adults €19.95; children 5–16 €14.95; under 5s free*

Top 10 Sights

1. Koninklijk Paleis
2. Nieuwe Kerk
3. Nationaal Monument
4. Madame Tussaud's Scenerama
5. Damrak
6. De Bijenkorf
7. Rokin
8. Kalverstraat
9. Grand Hotel Krasnapolsky
10. Street Performances and Events

1 Koninklijk Paleis

Built as the town hall, Jacob van Campen's unsmiling Classical edifice symbolizes the civic power of 17th-century Amsterdam *(above)*. It is still used for state occasions *(see p39)*.

2 Nieuwe Kerk

Now a venue for exhibitions, the Nieuwe Kerk has hosted royal events since 1814. Its treasures include a Jacob van Campen organ and an elaborately carved pulpit by Albert Vinckenbrinck *(see p42)*.

3 Nationaal Monument

This 22 m (70 ft) obelisk commemorates the Dutch killed in World War II *(above & centre)*. Embedded in the wall behind are urns containing soil from the Dutch provinces and colonies.

Sign up for DK's email newsletter on traveldk.com

4 Madame Tussaud's Scenerama

Displays at this outpost of the London waxworks range from the fascinating to the bizarre. Special effects, including animatronics, bring to life scenes from Holland's past.

5 Damrak

Damrak was once the medieval city's busiest canal, with ships sailing up to be unloaded at the Dam. In 1672 the canal was filled in, and Damrak developed into the hectic shopping street it is today.

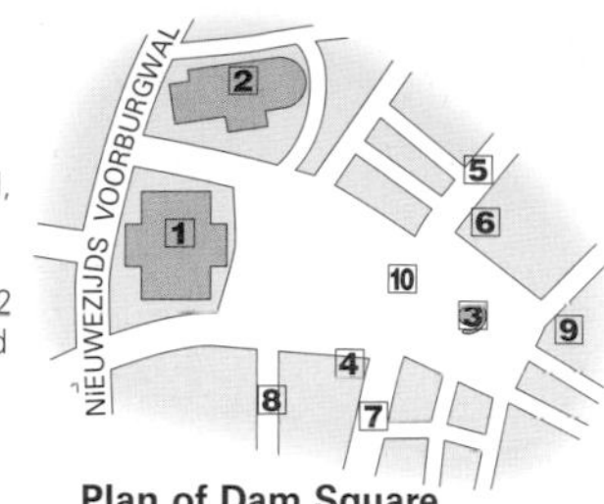

Plan of Dam Square

6 De Bijenkorf

Amsterdam's best-known department store has a vast perfumery, designer fashion boutiques and much more.

7 Rokin

The Rokin had its heyday in the 19th century, when its broad sweep was a promenade for the well-to-do.

8 Kalverstraat

Music shops jostle for space with tacky clothes stores at the Dam end of this pedestrian shopping street.

9 Grand Hotel Krasnapolsky

Adolf Wilhelm Krasnapolsky, an emigré Polish tailor with ambition, rented the down-at-heel Nieuwe Poolsche Koffiehuis in the 1870s, swiftly transforming it into a fashionable hotel *(below)*.

10 Street Performances and Events

Busking, mime, funfairs, book fairs, exhibitions, concerts – such things have gone on in the Dam since J Cabalt introduced his puppet show in 1900.

Inside the Koninklijk Paleis

The ponderous exterior belies the magnificent interior – especially the dramatic Burgerzaal (Citizen's Chamber). See fine sculptures by Artus Quellien and Rombout Verhulst, ceilings and friezes by Rembrandt's pupils, and Empire furniture of Louis Napoleon. The *Vierschaar* (Tribunal) is a macabre room, still intact, where judges meted out tough – and often terminal – justice.

For more Amsterdam churches **See pp42–3**

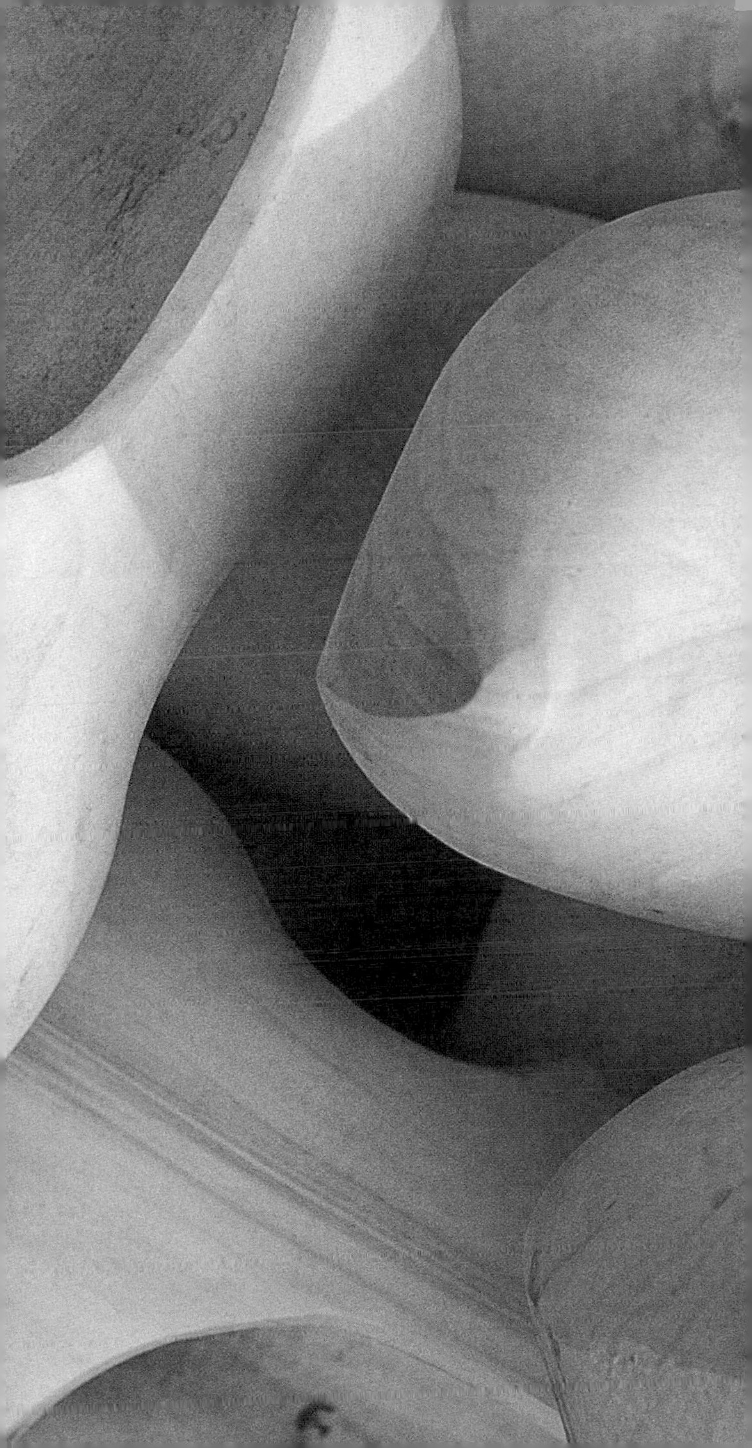

Left **The Arrival of Napoleon at Dam Square** Right **German wartime propaganda poster**

TOP 10 Moments in Amsterdam's History

1 c.1125: First Settlers

Fishermen settled at the mouth of the Amstel river, building huts on man-made mounds called *terps* for flood protection. With the growth of the new settlement came feudal conflict between the self-made Counts of Holland and Lords van Amstel.

2 1275: Freedom from Tolls

In the earliest document to refer to Amsterdam, Count Floris V of Holland granted its citizens exemption from tolls when transporting their goods by river across his territory at The Hague.

3 1345: Miracle of Amsterdam

At a house in Kalverstraat, a priest gave a dying man the last sacraments. He was unable to keep down the communion wafer, so it was thrown on the fire. Next morning, the wafer was found intact among the embers. News of the miracle spread, and Amsterdam soon became a place of pilgrimage.

Miracle of Amsterdam

4 1566 and 1578: Iconoclasm and Alteration

As Protestantism swept northern Europe, Dutch Calvinists rebelled against their intolerant Spanish Catholic ruler, Philip II. In the *Beeldenstorm* or Iconoclasm, the Calvinists stormed the Catholic churches and destroyed their religious artifacts. The city finally became Protestant, in a peaceful revolution known as the *Alteratie* or Alteration *(see p21)*.

5 1609: Plans for the Grachtengordel

The dawn of the Golden Age, when the arts flourished in Amsterdam *(see p27)*, saw ambitious plans for a triple canal ring around the city *(see p11)*. Herengracht, Keizersgracht and Prinsengracht were built in two stages, starting in 1613 and 1663.

6 1634–37: Tulipmania

The Dutch passion for tulips dates from the late 16th century, when the first bulbs were imported from Asia. In 1634, the tulip was quoted on the Stock Exchange, and speculation began. Fortunes were made overnight as the craze led to spectacular price increases; the inevitable crash caused scores of bankruptcies.

7 1806: Kingdom of the Netherlands Established

After the formation of the Batavian Republic in 1795, rule was shared between the invading French and the Dutch Patriots. In 1806, Napoleon Bonaparte took over the Republic, created the Kingdom of the Netherlands and installed his brother, Louis Napoleon, as head of state.

8 1940–45: German Occupation

Despite Dutch neutrality, Germany invaded Holland in May 1940. With the deportation of Jews to concentration camps from 1942 onwards, the Dutch Resistance became active and underground newspapers thrived. Canadian troops liberated Amsterdam on 5 May 1945.

9 Mid-1960s: Provo Demonstrations

The radical Provo movement took off in the 1960s, fuelled by antagonism to the city's transport and housing policies. Street demonstrations turned into full-scale rioting on 10 March 1966, the day of Princess Beatrix's wedding to German aristocrat Claus von Amsberg. The Provos won seats on the city council, but their popularity was short-lived.

10 2002:Wedding of the Crown Prince

On 2 February 2002, Crown Prince Willem-Alexander married Máxima Zorreguieta in the Nieuwe Kerk, followed by a reception in the Koninklijke Paleis. After a difficult start, due to her father's involvement with the Videla regime in Argentina, Máxima won the hearts of the Dutch public.

Wedding of the Crown Prince

Top 10 Historic Characters

1 William of Orange
"William the Silent" (1533–84) led the Protestant rebellion against Philip II. He was assassinated.

2 Willem Barentsz
This explorer (1550–97) failed to discover the north-east passage but left behind invaluable maps.

3 Frederik Hendrik
An effective politician, William of Orange's youngest son (1584–1647) became *Stadhouder* in 1625.

4 Pieter Stuyvesant
Stuyvesant (1592–1672) was Governor of the colony of Nieuw Amsterdam, later to be New York, from 1646–64.

5 Abel Tasman
In search of trade routes to South America, Tasman (1603–c.1659) discovered Tasmania and New Zealand.

6 Michiel de Ruyter
This revered Dutch admiral (1607–76) set fire to the English fleet in the Medway in 1667.

7 Jan de Witt
A leading politician in the Anglo-Dutch Wars (1625–72), he was killed by a mob.

8 William III
William (1650–1702) was *Stadhouder* from 1672 until his promotion to King of England in 1688.

9 Louis Napoleon
Brother of Napoleon I, Louis (1778–1846) was King of the Netherlands between 1806 and 1810.

10 Johan Thorbecke
Liberal Prime Minister Johan Rudolf Thorbecke (1798–1872) was architect of the 1848 Constitution.

Left **Rijksmuseum** Right **Nederlands Scheepvaart Museum**

Top 10 Museums

1 Rijksmuseum

The world's greatest collection of 17th-century Dutch art is housed in this grand municipal art museum – and there's so much more to see besides *(see pp12–15)*.

2 Van Gogh Museum

The permanent home for hundreds of works by this troubled artist also displays work by his contemporaries *(see pp16–19)*.

3 Amsterdams Historisch Museum

First a convent, then the city orphanage, now a wonderful museum charting the history of Amsterdam and, in particular, its meteoric rise during the Golden Age *(see pp24–7)*.

Amsterdams Historisch Museum

4 Museum Ons' Lieve Heer op Solder

The 17th-century domestic interiors would be fascinating in themselves, but the astonishing thing about this historic canal house is the secret Catholic church hidden on its upper floors *(see pp20–1)*.

Stedelijk Museum

5 Stedelijk Museum

At time of writing, the national museum of modern art, in its specially designed building by A W Weissman, is closed for major renovation work. The museum is due to reopen in 2009 with a new wing, designed by Benthem Crouwel Architects. The new wing has increased the exhibition space considerably and also contains a café-restaurant with a terrace overlooking Museumplein *(see p115)*.

6 Anne Frank Huis

This world-famous yet movingly simple museum is dedicated to the young diarist who hid here from the Nazis with her family *(see pp32–3)*.

7 Museum Van Loon

Another canal-house-turned-museum, the Van Loon recreates high-society life in the 18th century *(see pp30–31)*.

8 Museum Willet-Holthuysen

Like the Museum Van Loon, the Willet-Holthuysen affords a rare glimpse inside a grand canal house – and into the lives of the wealthy merchants who lived there. Built in 1685, the interior is decorated in 18th-century style. A mild sense of melancholy pervades the building *(see p107)*.

Museum Het Rembrandthuis

9 Nederlands Scheepvaart Museum

Holding the largest collection of boats in the world, and crammed with fascinating objects, the Nederlands Scheepvaart became a museum in 1973, when the Dutch Navy vacated the building. Solid and four-square, Daniel Stalpaert's imposing classical-style arsenal was built for the Admiralty in 1656 during the Golden Age of Dutch maritime history. Among the museum's treasures are weapons, paintings and meticulously accurate models *(see p123)*. The museum will be closed for renovation from late 2007 until 2010.

10 Museum Het Rembrandthuis

Completely restored to look as it did in Rembrandt's day, this handsome red-shuttered house was the artist's home during his years of prosperity (1639–58). Entering the rooms is a little like stepping into a painting: they are typical Dutch interiors with black-and-white tiled floors, traditional box beds, and paintings by Rembrandt's contemporaries. Perhaps the two most fascinating sights here are the recreation of his studio, and the room – in a new wing – devoted to his magical etchings, many of which show his compassion for the common people: quacksalver, pancake woman, beggars, street musicians. A video about the recent restoration work is shown in the basement *(see p77)*.

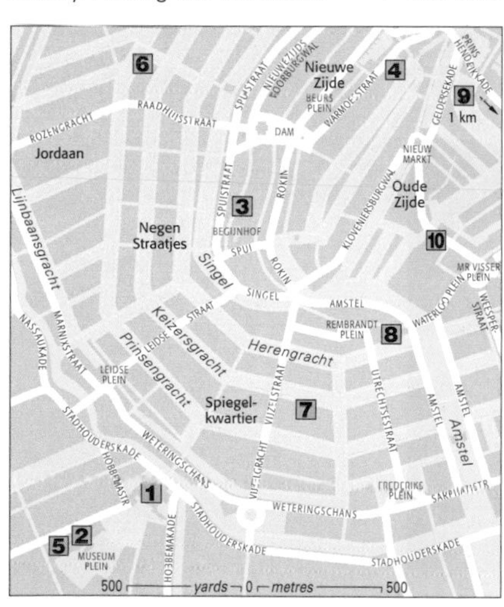

Left **Noorderkerk** Right **De Krijtberg**

TOP 10 Churches

1 Oude Kerk
The oldest and greatest of Amsterdam's churches *(see pp28–9)*.

2 Nieuwe Kerk
The second parish church in Amsterdam was built after the congregation outgrew the Oude Kerk. Burnt down several times, its oldest part is the choir, dating from around 1400 *(see pp34, 83)*.

3 Westerkerk
After the Alteration of 1578 *(see p21)*, the first Dutch Protestant churches to be built were the Zuiderkerk, the Noorderkerk and the Westerkerk – all designed by Hendrick de Keyser. The Westerkerk has the city's tallest tower, topped by the gaily painted imperial crown of Maximilian of Austria *(see p91)*.

Väter-Müller organ, Oude Kerk

4 Zuiderkerk
The splendid spire, with its columns, clocks, pinnacles and onion dome, was much admired by Sir Christopher Wren, and is still a prominent city landmark, even though the Zuiderkerk ceased to function as a church in 1929. Today it is an information centre for urban development *(see p81)*.

Zuiderkerk

5 Noorderkerk
Hendrick de Keyser's last church, begun a year before he died in 1621 (its completion was supervised by his son Pieter), is quite different in style. Built for the poor of the Jordaan, it is an austere brick building with only the shortest of spires. Designed on a Greek Cross plan, it has a central pulpit and four hipped roofs. *Noordermarkt 44–48 • Map D2 • Open 11am–1pm Mon, Thu, Sat (also open for regular afternoon concerts and 11am–3pm Wed, noon–5:30pm Sun Apr–Oct) • Free*

6 Engelse Kerk
In the middle of the Begijnhof, the pretty English Reform Church got its name from the English (and Scottish) Presbyterians who worshipped there after it was requisitioned in 1578. There has been a church on this site since the end of the 14th century *(see pp22)*.

7 De Krijtberg

Like many Catholic churches in Amsterdam, De Krijtberg (meaning Chalk Mountain) is known by its nickname rather than its official name, Franciscus Xaveriuskerk (after St Francis Xavier, a founding Jesuit monk); designed in 1884 by Alfred Tepe, it replaced a clandestine Jesuit chapel *(see p21)*. It's an impressive building, with an elegant, twin-steepled Neo-Gothic façade and an ornate interior that stands in marked contrast to the austerity of the city's Protestant churches. *Singel 448 • Map M5 • Open 1:30–5pm Tue–Thu, Sun and 30 mins before services: 12:30pm & 5:45pm Mon–Fri; 12:30pm & 5:15pm Sat; 9:30am, 11am, 12:30pm & 5:15pm Sun • Free*

8 Mozes en Ääronkerk

Here, the nickname comes from two gablestones depicting Moses and Äaron on the house fronts that hid a clandestine church within. It was replaced in 1841 by the present Neo-Classical building, its towers inspired by St Sulpice in Paris. *Waterlooplein 205 • Map Q5*

9 St Nicolaaskerk

Dedicated to the patron saint of seafarers, the church was commissioned by the congregation of *Ons' Lieve Heer op Solder (see pp20–21)*. A C Bleys, the architect, came up with a Neo-Renaissance building. *Prins Hendrikkade 76 • Map Q1 • Open noon–3pm Mon & Sat; 11am–4pm Tue–Fri; mass 12:30pm Mon–Sat; 10:30am, 1pm (Spanish) Sun (10:30am Fri Spanish also) • Free*

St Nicolaas Kerk

10 Waalse Kerk

This church – founded in 1409 – is all that is left of the convent of St Paul. Its name means Walloon Church, a reference to the Low Countries (now Belgium), from where Huguenots fled the Catholic terror. In 1586 they were given use of the Waalse Kerk so that they could continue their worship in French. It has a historic organ dating from 1680, renovated in 1734 by master organ builder Christian Müller. The church is a popular concert venue. *Oudezijds Achterburgwal 159 • Map P4*

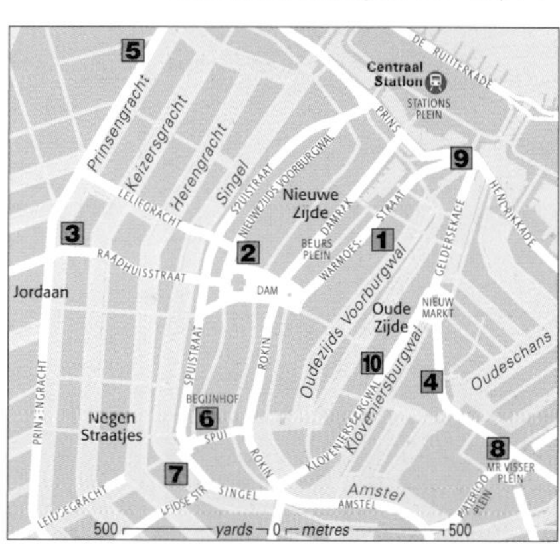

Left **Paleis van Justitie** Right **Greenpeace Building**

Historic Buildings

1 Schreierstoren

The Schreierstoren (Tower of Tears) is one of Amsterdam's oldest buildings *(see p10)* – a surviving fragment of the medieval city wall. *Prins Hendrikkade 94–5 • Map Q2*

2 In't Aepjen

One of two remaining wood-fronted houses in Amsterdam *(see p22)*, In't Aepjen was built in 1550 as a sailors' hostel, and is now a bar. The name means "In the monkeys": when sailors couldn't pay, they would barter – sometimes with pet monkeys *(see p80)*.

De Gooyer Windmill

3 Oostindisch Huis

Seen from the courtyard, the impressive red-brick façade, with its ornate entrance and stone-dressed windows, was the height of corporate fashion. Headquarters of the once mighty Dutch East India Company (VOC), it was built in 1605, probably by Hendrick de Keyser, and is now part of Amsterdam University. The 17th-century meeting room of the VOC lords has been restored. *Oude Hoogstraat 24 (entrance Kloveniersburgwal 48) • Map P4 • Open noon–5pm Tue, 9am–5pm Wed (meeting room)*

Schreierstoren

4 De Gooyer Windmill

If you are lucky, you might see the vast, streamlined sails of this 18th-century corn mill creak into motion. Built in 1725, the whole octagonal structure was painstakingly moved to its present site in 1814. *Funenkade 5 • Map H4*

5 Pintohuis

Named after the Portuguese merchant Isaac de Pinto, who paid an exorbitant 30,000 guilders for it in 1651, the building boasts an Italianate façade and ceiling paintings by Jacob de Wit. A branch of the public library is housed here. *Sint Antoniesbreestraat 69 • Map Q4*

6 Trippenhuis

Justus Vingboons' grandiose façade with false middle windows (1662) concealed the two separate homes of the powerful Trip brothers – arms dealers, hence the pair of chimneys resembling cannons. *Kloveniersburgwal 29 • Map P4*

Scheepvaarthuis

7 Westindisch Huis
The city of New York was conceived in the Dutch West India Company building, and Pieter Stuyvesant's statue still surveys the courtyard *(see p39)*. Built in 1615, its classical proportions belie its origins as a meat market. *Haarlemmerstraat 75 • Map D2*

8 Paleis van Justitie
This sober, monumental building in Empire style is a conversion of the Almoners' Orphanage by city architect Jan de Greef. *Prinsengracht 434–6 • Map K6*

9 Eerste Hollandsche Verzekeringsbank
Gerrit van Arkel's eyecatching 1905 building is a fine example of *Nieuwe Kunst*, the Dutch version of Art Nouveau. Built for an insurance company, it now houses lawyers' offices and PR companies. *Keizersgracht 174–6 • Map L2*

10 Scheepvaarthuis
Designed as shipping company offices by van der Mey, de Klerk and Kramer, this fanciful building (1916) is smothered in nautical whimsy – mariners, monsters, and mermaids. It is now a luxury hotel. *Prins Hendrikkade 108 • Map Q2*

Top 10 Architectural Features

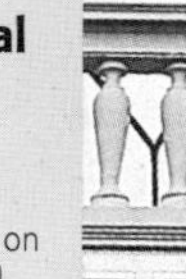

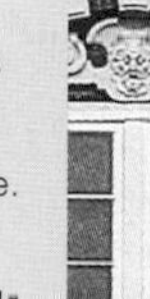

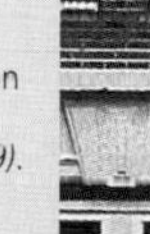
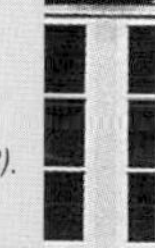
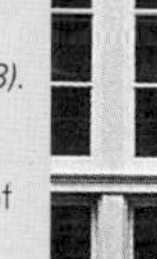

1 Triangular Gable
This simple triangular-shaped gable can be seen on Het Houten Huis *(see p22)*.

2 Bell Gable
Fashionable in the late 17th and 18th centuries, bell-shaped gables can be flamboyant (Prinsengracht 126) or unadorned (Leliegracht 57).

3 Neck Gable
Made popular by Philips Vingboons, this gable has a raised centrepiece; Oude Turfmarkt 145 is an example.

4 Spout Gable
This plain triangular gable topped by a spout was used for warehouses, like those at Entrepotdok *(see p123)*.

5 Step Gable
Common from 1600 to 1665, this gable has steps on both sides: Huis op de drie Grachten has three *(see p79)*.

6 Wall Plaque
Before numbering was introduced, houses were identified by plaques *(see p23)*.

7 Claw Piece
Sculptures – frequently of dolphins – were made to fill the right angles of gables, as in Oudezijds Voorburgwal 119.

8 Mask
This type of Renaissance decoration depicts a human or animal face, and can be seen at Oudezijds Voorburgwal 57.

9 Cornices
From 1690, gables fell out of vogue and decorative top mouldings came in: examples line the Herengracht.

10 Pediment Carvings
Carvings often decorate the triangular or rounded form above doorways: see the Felix Meritis Building *(see p57)*.

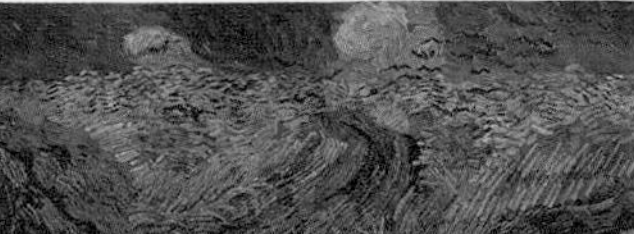

Left ***Allegory of Painting*** **by Vermeer** Right ***Wheatfield with Crows*** **by Van Gogh**

TOP 10 Dutch Artists

1 Jan van Scorel
After prolonged stays in Germany, Venice and Rome, where he studied the works of Giorgione, Michelangelo and Raphael, Jan Van Scorel (1495–1562) returned to Utrecht in 1524. He introduced the techniques of the Renaissance to the Northern Netherlands; his portraits fuse Italian solidity of form with Netherlandish delicacy.

2 Rembrandt van Rijn
The greatest artist of the Dutch Golden Age *(see p15)*.

3 Frans Hals
Much loved for his technique of capturing character and fleeting expression in his sitters, Frans Hals (1580–1666) brought a new realism to portraiture in the 17th century. His fine group portraits of civic guards are displayed in the Frans Hals Museum in Haarlem *(see p72)*.

4 Johannes Vermeer
Relatively little is known about the life of this sublime Delft artist (1632–75), who inherited his father's art-dealing business and painted purely for pleasure. He gained some recognition in Holland during his lifetime, but his importance was not established until the late 19th century, and rests on less than 40 known works – mainly domestic interiors with figures – that are extraordinary in their handling of space, light and colour. He was married with 11 children. On his death, his wife was declared bankrupt, and his baker kept two of his paintings against unpaid bills.

Self Portrait at a Young Age **by Rembrandt**

5 Jan Steen
A prolific painter of the genre (everyday) scenes so popular in the Dutch 17th century, Jan Steen (1625–79) was an innkeeper as well as an artist. His often bawdy tavern and household narratives were packed with hidden messages (red stockings for prostitution, oysters for sexual liaison, broken eggshells for mortality), creating allegories with a moral purpose.

6 Jacob van Ruisdael
Born in Haarlem, Jacob van Ruisdael (1629–1682), though not highly regarded in his own day, has come to be seen as one of the finest landscape and seascape painters of the Dutch school. His works are filled with restless skies and naturalistic details. Even calm scenes such as *The Windmill at Wijk* have a sense of dramatic grandeur.

For more on Dutch paintings **See pp12–19**

7 Pieter Claesz

As well as portraits, genre paintings and landscapes, still lives had an important place in Dutch 17th-century art. Peter Claesz (1597–1661) reached a peak of technical skill in his harmonious if academic compositions, which are replete with symbolic detail.

8 Vincent van Gogh

A troubled genius who left a vast body of work, despite his tragically short life *(see p19)*.

9 Piet Mondriaan

Although he lived in London, Paris and New York (and few of his works are on show in Amsterdam), Mondriaan was born and grew up in Holland (1872–1944). A leading member of the De Stijl movement, he created an abstract style using the simplest elements: straight lines and blocks of primary colour, arranged on the canvas to create harmony and balance.

10 Karel Appel

Karel Appel (1921–2006) was one of the founders of the Cobra movement, started in 1948, which combined expressionist, abstract and surrealist influences *(see p128)*. His colourful works display a savage, forceful directness combined with an almost childlike optimism. "I paint like a barbarian in a barbarous age", he said.

***Children with* Dog by Karel Appel**

Top 10 Dutch Literary Figures

1 Desiderius Erasmus

Scholar and humanist (1466–1536). Friend of Thomas More, no friend of Luther.

2 Hugo Grotius

Statesman and philosopher (1583–1645). Author of *De Jure Belli et Pacis*, the foundation stone of international law.

3 Gerbrant Bredero

Satirical poet and playwright (1585–1618), best known for *De Spaanse Brabander*.

4 Joost van den Vondel

Important playwright and poet (1586–1679) famed for his ornate style. Author of *Gijsbrecht van Amstel*.

5 Jan Six

Poet, playwright (1618–1700) and friend of Rembrandt, who painted his portrait.

6 Baruch Spinoza

Philosopher (1632–77) expelled by Amsterdam's Jewish community for his secular beliefs.

7 Multatuli

Pen name of Eduard Douwes Dekker (1820–87), whose work in colonial Java inspired his best-known novel *Max Havelaar*.

8 Anne Frank

Teenage victim (1929–44) of the Holocaust. Her eloquent diary has sold in its millions.

9 Gerard Reve

Novelist (1923–2006) influenced by his Catholicism and his homosexuality.

10 Cees Nooteboom

Prolific man of letters (b.1933) whose fiction is at best observant and poignant, at worst experimental and elusive.

Sign up for DK's email newsletter on traveldk.com

Left **Joods Historisch Museum** Right **Jodenbuurt**

Top 10 Jewish Sights

1 Anne Frank Huis

The plight of Jews like the Franks, forced into hiding by the Nazis, was brought to light by Anne's poignant diary; the house where they hid for 25 months is now a museum *(see pp32–3)*.

2 Joods Historisch Museum

This remarkable museum represents all aspects of Judaism and the history and culture of the Jews who settled in the Netherlands. On show are some marvellous paintings by Jewish artists, fascinating displays about the diamond industry, and exhibits that bring home the true horror of the Holocaust *(see p78)*.

3 Portugees-Israëlitische Synagoge

Inspired by the Temple of Solomon in Jerusalem, Elias Bouman's bulky red-brick synagogue is still the core of the small Sephardic community for whom it was built in 1675. The massive wooden barrel-vaulted ceiling is lit by more than 1,000 candles *(see p78)*.

4 Jodenbuurt

When the Jews arrived in Amsterdam in the late 16th century, they moved into a lacklustre area to the east of Oude Zijde, around present-day Waterlooplein. Although several synagogues, diamond factories and street markets have survived, the heart of the Jodenbuurt was decimated by post-war redevelopment and the building of the Metro. *Map Q5*

De Dokwerker

5 De Dokwerker

Mari Andriessen's evocative bronze statue (1952) is a memorial to the dockers' and transport workers' strike of February 1941 over the arrest of 450 Jews for the killing of a Nazi sympathizer. The event is commemorated every 25 February. *Jonas Daniel Meijerplein • Map Q5*

6 Hollandsche Schouwburg

Jewish families were rounded up at this operetta theatre before being transported to the death camps. A moving memorial and a small exhibition of memorabilia keep their memory alive *(see p125)*.

Hollandsche Schouwburg

Interior of the Tuschinski Theater

7 Tuschinski Theater
This extraordinary 1921 theatre was the creation of its obsessive owner, Abraham Tuschinski, a Jewish emigré who died at Auschwitz. The sumptuous interior crosses Art Deco with the Orient *(see p108)*.

8 Ravensbrück Memorial
Dedicated to the women of Ravensbrück, one of the most disturbing of the city's Holocaust memorials (1975) incorporates a sinister soundtrack and eerily flashing lights. *Museumplein • Map C6*

9 Verzetsmuseum Amsterdam
The Resistance Museum's brilliant displays give a vivid sense of life in an occupied country, as well as an insight into the ingenious activities of the Dutch Resistance. Exhibits include photographs, heart-rending letters thrown from deportation trains, film clips and room sets *(see p124)*.

10 Nooit Meer
In stark contrast to its peaceful surroundings, Jan Wolkers' Auschwitz memorial *Never More* features a slab of shattered glass. The fragments reflect a distorted view of the heavens, mirroring the damage done to humanity by the Holocaust. *Wertheim Park • Map R5*

Top 10 Jewish Historical Events

1 1592 onwards
Sephardic Jews from Portugal and Spain, fleeing the Inquisition, settle in Amsterdam, attracted by the city's religious tolerance.

2 1630s
Ashkenazi Jews start to arrive from eastern Europe (mainly Poland and Germany).

3 1796
Jews are given equal civil rights during Napoleon's Batavian Republic.

4 1860
Drawn to Amsterdam by its new industries and housing, Jews emigrate from Antwerp.

5 1932–7
These years see the rise of the Dutch Nazi Party under Anton Mussert; they also see waves of Jewish immigration from Hitler's Germany.

6 1941
In February, nine months into the German Occupation, the dockworkers strike in protest at the arrest and round-up of 450 Jews.

7 1942
The deportation of the Jews to Nazi death camps begins. Many Jews, including Anne Frank's family, go into hiding. Of the 80,000 living in pre-war Amsterdam, only 5,000 will survive the war.

8 1945
Amsterdam is liberated by Canadian troops on 5 May.

9 1947
Anne Frank's diary is published *(see pp32–3)*.

10 1975
Violent protests break out against the destruction of the Jodenbuurt – the old Jewish Quarter – in the Nieuwmarkt.

Left **Het Blauwe Theehuis** Right **De Taart van M'n Tante**

Top 10 Cafés

1 De Jaren

Wood, air, glass and light seem the building elements of this spacious, multi-levelled grand café. Have a leisurely leaf through international newspapers at the reading table, pile up your plate at the salad bar, or sun yourself beside the canal on one of the best terraces in town *(see p86)*.

Café de Jaren

2 De Kroon

Waiters in long white aprons glide beneath crystal chandeliers at the grandest of grand cafés, in the heart of Amsterdam's night-life district. The glassed-in balcony is a great late breakfast spot and things hot up at night on Thursdays, Fridays and Saturdays with a live DJ. *Rembrandtplein 17 • Map N6 • 020 625 2011*

3 Backstage

The half-Mohawk owner of this brightly-coloured café appeared in the 1958 movie *South Pacific*, along with his late twin brother. Drop by for a delicious sandwich, a choice of cakes and a quiet chat. *Utrechtsedwarsstraat 67 • Map E5 • 020 622 3638*

4 De Bakkerswinkel

Refined cream teas, delicate sandwiches, scrumptious cakes and mouthwatering quiches all baked on the premises. This huge, high-ceilinged lunchroom is suitably housed in an old tea warehouse. *Warmoesstraat 69 • Map P2 • 020 489 8000*

5 Het Blauwe Theehuis

"The Blue Teahouse" in the middle of the Vondelpark is a 1930s architectural treasure, a trendy night spot and a great terrace café all in one. Snack on well-filled sandwiches under the trees, dance the night away to DJs upstairs, or just stop by for a coffee on your walk through the park *(see p119)*.

6 Land van Walem

Sip a champagne cock tail on the canal-side terrace, or show off your latest designer wear to the fashionable crowd inside one of Amsterdam's most popular cafés. Piles of magazines and intriguing artworks help while away the time *(see p102)*.

7 De Taart van M'n Tante

My Aunt's Cake is the campest tearoom in town and is run by couture cake creators

Recommend your favourite café on traveldk.com

who supply Amsterdam's elite, including the mayor and the Dutch royal family. *Ferdinand Bolstraat 10 • Map D6 • 020 776 4600*

8 Pacific Parc

Inhabiting a vast industrial building on the grounds of a former gas works, this characterful café has wi-fi access, an open fire in winter and canalside terrace in summer. DJs feature most nights. *Polonceaukade 23 • 020 488 7778 • €€€*

9 1e Klas

A station café? If that gives you the horrors, think again. A minute or two in this stunningly decorated, classy 19th-century former first-class waiting room, and you're transported back in time. Station bustle becomes part of the atmosphere – though when you're back on the platform, it comes as a shock to find there are no steam trains. *Platform 2b, Amsterdam Centraal Station, Stationsplein • Map P1 • 020 625 0131*

10 Tis Fris

A few steps from the Waterlooplein Flea Market *(see p63)*, this light and spacious split-level café serves healthy quiches, salads and soups as well as alcohol. A perfect mid-shop pitstop. *St Antoniesbreestraat 142 • Map Q4 • 020 622 0472 • €*

1e Klas, Centraal Station

Top 10 Types of Café

1 Bruin Café
Snug, smoky and old-fashioned, these brown cafés are places for beer and gossip.

2 Grand Café
Always grand in size, sometimes these cafés are grand in style too.

3 Eetcafé
Eetcafé means, unsurprisingly, Eat Café, and eat is exactly what you do in one. Good cooking at a little below restaurant prices.

4 Hip Hangouts
Some cafés flash their designer credentials – and attract a suitably hip and trendy crowd.

5 Music Cafés
Live music or top DJs make a good start to an evening of clubbing *(see pp54–5)*.

6 Games Cafés
Devotees of billiards, chess, darts or board games will find entire cafés given over to single pursuits.

7 Coffee & Cake
Sometimes there's no alcohol at all, just tea, coffee and more calories than you'd care to mention.

8 Nachtcafés
When all else is closed, these night cafés open their doors through the wee hours, though tread carefully – some may be a little seedy.

9 Gay Cafés
From the stylish to the sweaty, Amsterdam's famous gay cafés cater to all tastes.

10 "Coffeeshops"
Here, intoxicants take a different form, and smoking rather than drinking is the predominant activity.

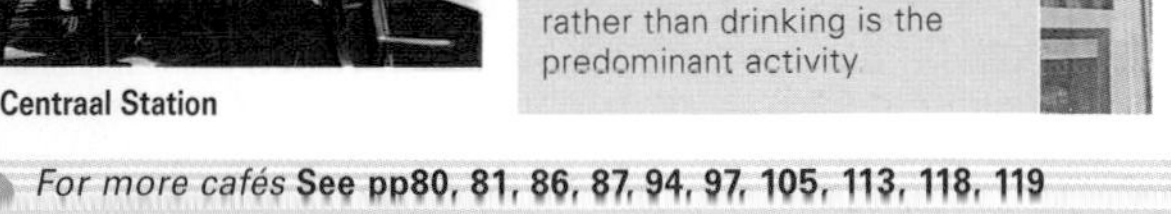

For more cafés See pp80, 81, 86, 87, 94, 97, 105, 113, 118, 119

Left **Freddy's Bar** Right **Getto**

TOP 10 Bars

1 ARC

Champagne and cocktails are the order of the day at this stunning bar which crowns Amsterdam's popular Reguliersdwarsstraat. There are three bar areas, a garden courtyard and a restaurant serving oysters and kangaroo steaks. Happy Hour runs from 5–7pm: try an Absolute Arc or a fresh mint julep, just two of the cocktail specialities at this trendy spot. *Reguliersdwarsstraat 44 • Map M6 • 020 689 7070*

2 Brouwerij 't IJ

Adjacent to a landmark 1814 windmill and within a former bathhouse, this micro-brewery produces excellent local beer. There is a daily tour of the brewery held by the barman every afternoon. Special seasonal beers are produced and bottles can be taken away after closing. *Funenkade 7 • Map H4 • 020 622 8325 • Open 3–8pm daily*

3 The Getaway

Run by artists, this upbeat DJ bar near Dam Square draws a hip yet unpretentious crowd – with a vibe to match. A perfect prelude to hitting the clubs. *Nieuwezijds Voorburgwal 250 • Map M3 • 020 627 1427*

4 Suite

Sip on cocktails in the retro 70s "living room" area, or devour exquisite Mediterranean-infused French cuisine in the white-linen dining space. This sprawling premises also has a basement club and a chilled Arabic lounge. *Sint Nicolaasstraat 43 • Map N2 • 020 779 8314*

5 TWSTD

Declaring itself "Holland's smallest club", this DJ bar may be tiny but it packs a punch. Its eclectic daily programme sees both established and novice mixers hit the decks, while its annual contest presents over 160 DJs going head to head over 80 rounds. The bar boasts an ever-growing list of internationally celebrated DJs who have played here and is located just a short walk from the bustling Leidseplein. *Weteringschans 157 • Map D5 • 020 320 7030*

XtraCold

For more bars **See pp80, 86, 87, 94, 97, 102, 110, 118**

Wijnand Fockink

6 Wijnand Fockink

Proeflokalen, the "tasting houses" of local distilleries, were once places to knock back a quick *jenever* (Dutch gin) before re-emerging into the winter's air. Crooked and cosy, with wooden barrels lining the walls, this one dates back nearly 400 years. Drop in for a quick one *(see p80)*.

7 XtraCold

Amsterdam's infamous ice bar always makes for a novel experience – three life-size sculptures of Dutch sporting heroes greet you upon entry. Warm up afterwards with sublime cocktails and tapas in the second bar – a modern, scarlet red lounge bar. *Amstel 194–6 • Map P6 • 020 320 5700*

8 Getto

A haven of light and charm, a beacon of good taste and friendliness on the edge of Red Light district sleaze. Great cocktails, big smiles and a mixed, attitude-free clientele are all part of the magic formula. DJs, bingo evenings and other activities liven up the week – and there's a good restaurant too *(see p86)*.

9 Freddy's Bar

Named after the late Freddy Heineken (he of beer fame), who was a frequent guest, this quiet city-centre classic, complete with piano music, leather upholstery, soft lighting and discreetly friendly barman, is ideal for a classy pre-dinner drink. Dress up, act suave, and bring someone you want to impress. *Hotel De l'Europe, Nieuwe Doelenstraat • Map N5 • 020 531 1777*

10 De Koe

Downstairs, people are tucking in to good, basic food; upstairs, they're shoulder to shoulder around the bar. Order a beer and you're instantly part of a no-nonsense neighbourhood bar atmosphere, with just a touch of merry mayhem, and everyone aiming headlong at a good night out. *Marnixstraat 381 • Map K6 • 020 625 4482*

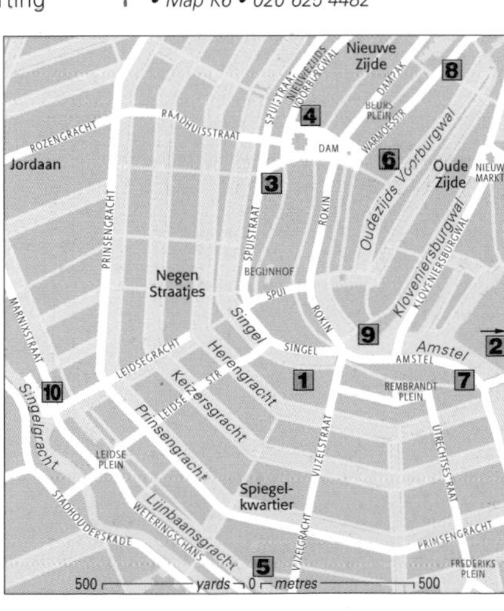

Left **Winston International** Right **Paradiso**

TOP 10 Clubs

1 Arena Hotel

Dating from 1890, this cool three-star hotel on the east side of town was originally a Roman Catholic orphanage, and later an asylum. On Fridays and Saturdays the madness continues, when some of Amsterdam's top DJs spin at Tonight, the hotel's adjacent two-floor "church-club". A bit of a trek if you're staying centrally, but worth the effort. *'s Gravesandestraat 51 • Map G5 • 020 850 2451 • www.hotelarena.nl*

2 Escape

One of Amsterdam's biggest and most exciting clubs, which can hold up to 2,000 people, has a huge dance floor, hi-tech lighting, a multi-media environment and, as you would expect, a stunning sound system. At weekends it attracts a big out-of-town crowd. *Rembrandtplein 11–15 • Map N6 • 020 622 1111 • www.escape.nl*

Odeon

3 Odeon

A stunning combination of historic Amsterdam and sophisticated modern style. The Odeon has it all from a café, restaurant, cocktail bar to a concert hall which doubles as a night club. The ultra-chic interior is within a building that dates back to 1662 by one of the city's loveliest canals. *Singel 460 • Map M5 • 020 521 8555 • www.odeontheater.nl*

4 Melkweg

As well as regular parties that take place throughout the various rooms of this multi-media venue, DJs play before and after the live bands that appear on both stages. Most Saturdays there is a late-night dance party *(see p57)*.

5 Sugar Factory

Whether its avant-garde performances, sultry jazz or German electro nights, this minimal club by the Leidseplein never fails to deliver an impressive international programme. *Lijnbaansgracht 238 • Map K6 • 020 627 0008 • www.sugarfactory.nl*

6 Jimmy Woo

With its opulent oriental theme (styled on an 18th-century Chinese opium den), state-of-the-art sound system and superb lighting, Jimmy Woo is Amsterdam's most glamorous club. *Korte Leidsedwarsstraat 18 • Map K6 • 020 626 3150 • www.jimmywoo.com*

Sugar Factory

7 Paradiso

Formerly a church, now predominantly a live music venue, DJs spin here after the bands have been on – with an emphasis on Alternative music. The programming for parties can be erratic – anything from Moroccan dance nights to cinema-club evenings *(see p105)*.

8 Panama

Monied 30-somethings with a penchant for champagne make the trek to this lavish, vaudeville theatre-style club with attached bar and restaurant on the east side of town. Entry is expensive and the drinks aren't cheap either. ✎ *Oostelijke Handelskade 4 • Map I13 • 020 311 8686 • www.panama.nl*

9 Exit

This hugely popular, multi-level gay club is open Wednesday to Saturday, when the dancefloor throbs with revellers. The trendy clientele is predominantly male and the music mostly house (with quieter bar music upstairs). ✎ *Reguliersdwarsstraat 42 • Map P6 • 020 625 8788*

10 Winston International

Eclectic and inspired programming give this small, rococo-style venue an edge on the city's other clubs. Easy-tuners with a taste for the unusual head here for Sunday's Vegas nights. An additional plus: it boasts the smallest art gallery in Amsterdam – in its toilets. ✎ *Warmoesstraat 131 • Map N3 • 020 623 1380 • www.winston.nl*

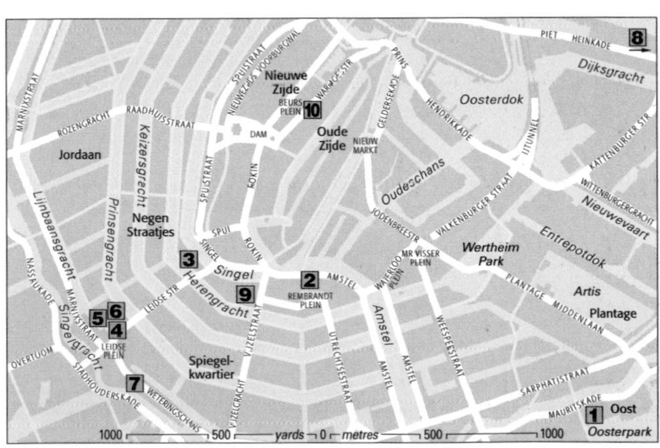

Left **Boom Chicago** Right **KIT Tropentheater**

TOP 10 Performing Arts Venues

1 Muziekgebouw aan 't IJ

Amsterdam's spectacular new concert hall for the 21st century occupies a unique position on a peninsular on the IJ, which gives it magnificent views. As well as a 735-seat main auditorium there is a smaller 125-seat hall, foyer decks overlooking the IJ and a café restaurant, the Star Ferry, with a waterfront terrace. The venue's impressive programme will concentrate mainly on contemporary works. *Piet Heinkade 1 • Map G2 • 020 788 2000 • www.muziekgebouw.nl*

2 Boom Chicago

On a daily basis, this US comedy crew puts on satirical shows whose targets are anything from Dutch "quirks" to topical news issues. Big on laughs and big on beer. The latter, served in huge pitchers, is a welcome respite from the tiny frothy-headed *pilsjes*. Star-watchers note: Burt Reynolds once popped in. *Leidseplein Theater, Leidseplein 12 • Map K6 • 020 423 0101 • www.boomchicago.nl*

3 Het Bethaniënklooster

The refectory of a former nunnery (dedicated to St Mary of Bethany) is now an intimate concert hall. The hall's size and acoustics are ideal for chamber music, and many leading international soloists and chamber groups perform here. *Barndesteeg 6B • Map P3 • 020 625 0078 • www.bethanienklooster.nl*

4 Carré

Originally built as a circus theatre in 1894, circus troupes still appear at this impressive landmark on the banks of the Amstel – along with anything from opera to ballet, magicians to music. Nothing beats sipping champagne on the balcony overlooking the river on a warm evening *(see p125)*.

5 Concertgebouw

The *crème de la crème* of international musicians and conductors appear at this palatial classical music venue – one of the world's most prestigious. Audrey Hepburn had a season ticket when she lived in Amsterdam after World War II, and it's not hard to understand why. Don't miss the free lunchtime concerts on Wednesdays *(see p115)*.

Concertgebouw

Stadsschouwburg

6 Melkweg

This multimedia centre (the Milky Way) occupies a former dairy behind the Stadsschouwburg. Opened in 1970, the venue offers a wide range of entertainment including live music, film, theatre and dance. ⓢ *Lijnbaansgracht 234A • Map K6 • 020 531 8181 • www.melkweg.nl*

7 Heineken Music Hall

Amsterdam's second biggest live music venue (the ArenA next door, home to Ajax football team, is the biggest). Some distance from the centre, but worth it to catch the likes of Garbage or The Chemical Brothers. ⓢ *Heineken Music Hall, ArenA Boulevard 590 • 0900 687 424 255 • www.heineken-music-hall.nl*

8 Tropentheater

Eclectic world music/theatre performances are appropriately staged in the theatre of the city's tropical museum *(see p127)*. Some world cinema is also to be had – though double-check the language the subtitles are in! ⓢ *Mauritskade 63 / Linnaeusstraat 2 • Map G5 • 020 568 8500 • www.kit.nl*

9 Het Muziektheater

The Dutch royals regularly pop in to catch shows at this comfortable – and once controversial – modern theatre, which is home to the Netherlands Opera and Ballet companies *(see p78)*. Tickets for shows – particularly opera – can sell out months in advance, so it's advisable to book before you travel if you want to go. Inspired programming gives contemporary culture vultures an occasional look-in. ⓢ *Amstel 3 • Map E4 • 020 625 5455 • www.muziektheater.nl*

10 Stadsschouwburg

This Neo-Renaissance building – both of whose predecessors burned down – houses the city's municipal theatre. Local groups as well as visiting companies tread the boards here. It's also host to the annual Julidans (July Dance) Festival. Regular English-language performances take place in the upstairs Bovenzaal. ⓢ *Leidseplein 26 • Map K6 • 020 624 2311 • www.stadsschouwburgamsterdam.nl*

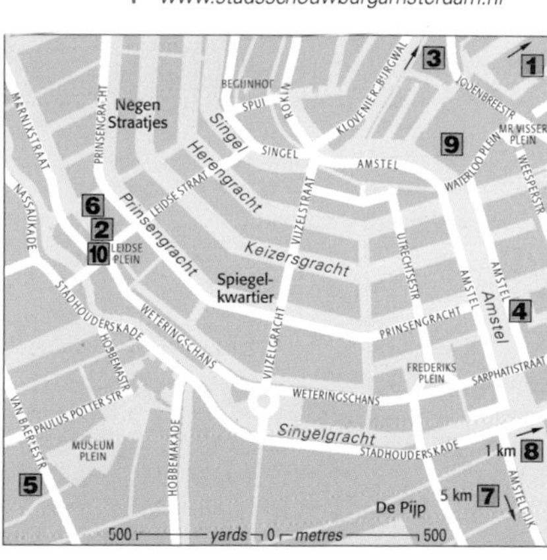

Left ***Patat* served with mayonnaise** Right ***Bitterballen***

Top 10 Culinary Highlights

1 Maatjes Haring

Fresh raw herring, with chopped onion or gherkin, is sold as a snack from street stalls. Traditionally, you take your herring by the tail and toss it whole down your throat, with your head held back – but the faint-hearted may prefer them on a plate or in a roll. Best in May, when the *groene* (new season's) herrings appear.

2 Gerookte Paling

A delicious Dutch speciality, *paling* (smoked eel) comes from the IJsselmeer. Served with white toast and a squeeze of lemon, it makes a perfect starter.

3 Kaas

In the Netherlands, a staggering 14 kg (31 lb) of cheese per person is consumed each year. Gouda and Edam are the best known, but there are others, such as *Friese nagelkaas*, a clove cheese which became popular when spices were first imported in the 17th century.

4 Bitterballen

Served much like tapas to accompany drinks in a café or bar, these deep-fried meatballs have a crunchy exterior and a soft meat filling. They are served with mustard.

5 Hutspot

The Dutch love affair with potatoes manifests itself in a variety of hearty winter dishes. *Hutspot* (meaning hotchpotch) is a stew of braised beef and potatoes mashed with carrots, while *stamppot boerenkool* consists of mashed potato and cabbage flecked with chopped bacon and served with smoked sausage.

6 Erwtensoep

Like raw herring, this pea soup is another Dutch favourite that some foreigners find hard to love, with a consistency akin to wallpaper paste. Try it at Dorrius, which serves genuine Dutch food. *Nieuwezijds Voorburgwal 5 • Map N1*

Erwtensoep

7 Rijsttafel

A delicious culinary after-echo of Holland's colonial past, Indonesian cuisine is usually eaten in the form of *rijsttafel* (rice table), a veritable feast consisting of as many as 25 little dishes of meat, fish, vegetables and sauces (some very hot), centred around a shared bowl of rice or noodles. Amsterdam has several good Indonesian restaurants, including Kantijl en de Tijger and Tujuh Maret *(see p61)*. *Kantijl en de Tijger: Spuistraat 291 • Map M4*

For Top 10 Restaurants **See pp60–61**

8 Appelgebak

Puddings are very popular, particularly the classic apple pie, accompanied by a large dollop of whipped cream *(slagroom)*. By common consent, the best *appelgebak* in Amsterdam is served at Winkel. *Winkel: Noordermarkt 43 • Map D2*

Pannenkoeken

9 Pannenkoeken

Pancake houses offer an astonishing variety of fillings – try the Pancake Bakery *(see p97)* for an excellent selection. The traditional Dutch favourite is a large pancake topped with a thick syrup called *stroop*. If you have room for more, there are delicious, sugary *poffertjes*, the mini pancakes sold in summer from brightly painted stalls and from permanent stands at Dam Square and Leidseplein.

10 Patat

Served from street stalls in a handy paper cone, chips (french fries) are ubiquitous, and very good indeed. They are generally made from whole (not pulped) Dutch potatoes, and fried in good, clean fat. Served with a large dollop of mayonnaise, they are definitely not for the diet-conscious. For the very best, go to Vleminckx. *Vleminckx: Voetboogstraat 33 • Map M5*

Top 10 Drinks

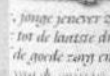

1 Pils

The national drink of the Netherlands is beer. *Pils* – top brands Heineken and Grolsch – is the lager-like beer served (with froth) in bars. The Dutch generally drink it from small glasses, so it remains ice-cold to the last drop.

2 Witbier

Wheat-brewed white beer is pale and cloudy – often served with a slice of lemon.

3 Bokbier

A brown, sweet, winter beer served in round glasses.

4 Jonge Jenever

Dutch gin is flavoured with juniper and drunk neat – usually downed in a swift gulp from a small glass. *Jonge* (young) *jenever* is colourless and sharp.

5 Oude Jenever

Smoother, more complex, and slightly yellow in colour. Both types are referred to in bars as *borrel* (a tot).

6 Kopstoot

Aptly named, a *kopstoot* (head knock) is a *pils* swiftly followed by a *jenever* chaser.

7 Naveltje Bloot

Literally, Naked Tummy Button: a fruit liqueur traditionally taken when a mother-to-be shows off her bump to family and friends.

8 Oranje Bitter

An orange-flavoured liqueur knocked back on *Koninginnedag* (30 April).

9 Bakkie

A cup of strong black coffee, the way the Dutch prefer it.

10 Koffie Verkeerd

If you like your coffee milky, "wrong coffee" is what to ask for.

Left **Café Roux** Right **Mamouche**

TOP 10 Restaurants

1 Supperclub

Putting a contemporary spin on hedonistic Roman banqueting, the seminal Supperclub sees guests recline on white beds whilst grazing leisurely on five creative Mediterranean courses. Live performances and DJs are laid on to ensure guests are kept thoroughly entertained. *Jonge Roelensteeg 21 • Map M3 • 020 344 6400 • €€€€€*

2 Van Vlaanderen

The décor may be plain, but the dishes are rich and elaborate at this gourmands' paradise, which for years was known only to insiders but recently acquired an international reputation when it picked up a long-deserved Michelin star. Expect to feast on goose-liver, suckling pig, pigeon breasts, sweetbreads and other delightfully wicked fare. *Weteringschans 175 • Map E5 • 020 622 8292 • €€€€*

3 Lof

Tantalizing aromas from the open-plan kitchen, clanging pans and cheery banter fill the air at this friendly, bistro-style local favourite. Amsterdammers in the know come for scrumptious, imaginative cooking, taking pot-luck from a set menu that changes daily. *Haarlemmerstraat 62 • Map D2 • 020 620 2997 • €€€*

4 Proeflokaal Janvier

Housed in an historic 17th-century wooden church, the creative chef at this upmarket restaurant conjures up exceptional classic French food with ingenious twists. *Amstelveld 12 • Map E5 • 020 626 1199 • €€€€*

5 Café Roux

One of Amsterdam's smartest hotels is home to this classic, long-time favourite. It's a realm of crisp linen, soft light and clinking glasses; the atmosphere is relaxed and the staff charming. Star chef Albert Roux inspires dishes with a fine French touch, such as brill with parsnip purée, salsify and thyme – and you can choose from a top-class wine list. (Albert Roux is not the resident chef here, only a behind-the scenes consultant.) *The Grand Hotel, Oudezijds Voorburgwal 197 • Map N4 • 020 555 3560 • €€€€*

Lof

For more restaurants **See pp80, 81, 86, 94, 95, 102, 103, 110, 111, 113, 118**

Proeflokaal Janvier

6 Bazar

A lofty, former church provides a stunning home for this fantastic Eastern-influenced restaurant. Located along Albert Cuypmarkt *(see p109)* and decorated with colourful tables and lanterns, Bazar is a great place to dine after a day browsing the myriad market stalls. Expect delicious North African, Iranian and Turkish delights *(see p111)*.

7 Tujuh Maret

Treating yourself to an Indonesian *rijsttafel* ('rice table') is an absolute must in Amsterdam – and this one is outstanding. Enjoy a feast of 18 deliciously spicy dishes, from mild to explosively chilli-filled, flavoured with coconut and ginger, peanuts and lemongrass, all served with mounds of rice. *Utrechtsestraat 42 • Map E5 • 020 625 9251 • €€€*

8 Mamouche

Join a super-fashionable crowd in super-chic surroundings to experience the very best of Moroccan cuisine. Familiar dishes like lamb tagine and couscous share the menu alongside the chef's much more elaborate and exotic creations, such as the delicious stewed rabbit and sesame with baked apricots and cinnamon seeds. *Quellijnstraat 104 • Map D6 • 020 673 6361 • €€€*

9 Fifteen

An offshoot of British celebrity-chef Jamie Oliver's famous London restaurant, Fifteen is housed in a gentrified waterfront warehouse and offers sleek, open-plan dining. Fare includes an Italian-inspired tasting menu that changes weekly and is accompanied by a wine tasting menu. There are also more modestly priced options from its trattoria. *Jollemanhof 9 • Map H2 • 0900 343 8336 • €€€€*

10 Hemelse Modder

Reservations are essential at this friendly, off-the-beaten track restaurant, renowned for its imaginative French- and Italian-influenced international cuisine and choice wine list. Besides attentive service, its best kept secret is its charming alleyway terrace. Fixed-price menus and vegetarian options available. *Oude Waal 11 • Map Q3 • 020 624 3203 • €€€€*

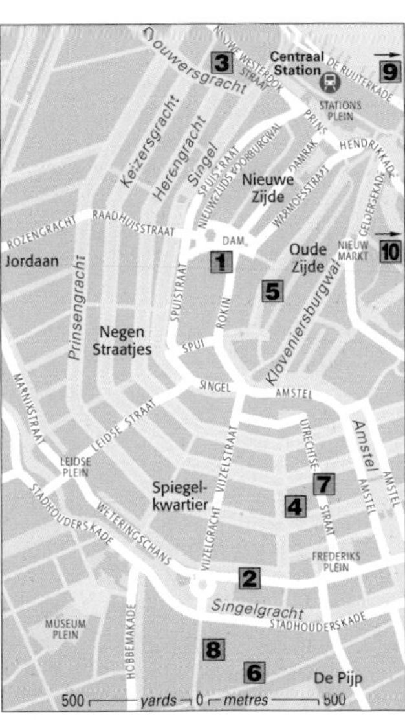

For a guide to restaurant prices See p81

Left **Bloemenmarkt** Right **Looiersmarkt**

Top 10 Shops and Markets

1 Albert Cuypmarkt

Amsterdam's largest general market runs all the way down this long street in the Pijp area, touting everything from fresh fish to footwear. Come here for fabrics, but don't come here for clothes *(see p109)*.

Albert Cuypmarkt

2 Albert Heijn

Albert Heijn is a rather upmarket supermarket chain – there's at least one in each area of town. A little pricey, but the selection is wide, the aisles are wide, and they're wide awake: unusually, several centrally located branches stay open until 10pm. *Various branches*

3 De Bijenkorf

Named "The Beehive" (which just about sums it up if you're here at the weekend), Amsterdam's prestigious department store caters for everyone from children to clubbers. Often described as the Dutch Harrods, prices ensure that it's only the well-honied that tend to part with their cash here. *Dam 1 • Map N3*

4 Bloemenmarkt

Amsterdam's famous floating flower market – the stalls still float, but now they are permanent *(see p108)*.

5 HEMA

This ubiquitous, cheap and cheerful department store chain started life in 1926 and has become something of a Dutch institution. The store offers affordable designer products, practical clothing, stationery, kitchen equipment and food products. It also stocks its own brand of items. *Various branches*

6 Boerenmarkt

Amsterdam's organic Saturday "farmer's market" is a treat rather than a routine shopping trip. Cruise the stalls to the accompaniment of some fine busking and sample free goats' cheese and other goodies – plus freshly-baked bread, flowers and a fabulous fungi selection. *Noordermarkt • Map D2*

7 Looiersmarkt

Burrow away to your heart's content in this highly browsable and perpetually intriguing indoor warren of antiques and collectibles. When you've dug out some bargains, there's also a café where you can put your weary feet up *(see p100)*.

8 Magna Plaza

Built between 1895 and 1899, this magnificent building – once derisively dubbed "post-office Gothic" by its critics – was designed by Cornelis Hendrik Peters (1874–1932) to house Amsterdam's head post office. Now a shopping mall, around 40 diverse stores are located over its four floors. There are two cafés. ✎ *Nieuwezijds Voorburgwal 182 • Map M3*

9 Noordermarkt

There has been a market on this site since 1627 – a fact you can contemplate as you fight over the bargains with the die-hard clubbers who arrive here after a night out, or with the locals who come for a more civilized Monday-morning rummage. Unbeatable for second-hand clothes and accessories *(see p92)*.

10 Waterlooplein

Whether your taste is exotic crafts and jewellery or vintage clothes, you can find them from Monday to Saturday at the city's best flea market – although it's a jumble at the best of times. When you can take no more, escape to the adjacent indoor markets. ✎ *Map Q5*

Magna Plaza

Top 10 Souvenirs

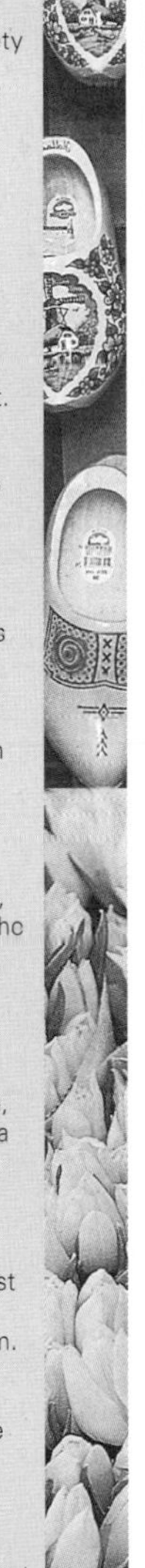

1 Beer
There's more to Dutch beer than Heineken. The Dutch make a fabulous variety of beers, and you will find many of them at De Bierkoning *(see p87)*.

2 Bulbs
Check your country's import regulations before packing this fabulous floral souvenir into your luggage.

3 Cannabis
Don't even think about it.

4 Cheese
If you don't have time to make it to an out-of-town cheese market, visit De Kaaskamer *(see p104)* for a mouth-watering selection that's guaranteed to impress more than Edam or Gouda.

5 Clogs
The quintessential Dutch footwear; be in fashion, and be heard.

6 Condoms
Novelty condoms galore, and in a variety of flavours; the city's infamous Condomerie will oblige *(see p81)*.

7 Delftware
If you don't manage to snag one of the dishy Dutch, at least you can take home a Dutch dish.

8 Diamonds
Definitely a girl's best friend, but possibly the worst nightmare of the poor guy who has to fork out for them.

9 Jenever
"The father of gin" – the real thing, in a variety of flavours and bottle types.

10 T-shirts/Postcards
No shortage of T-shirts and postcards portraying anything from the utterly sublime to the absolutely ridiculous.

For more shops **See pp81, 87, 104, 105, 112, 113, 119**

Left **The Jordaan from the tower of the Westerkerk** Right **Leidseplein by night**

TOP 10 Walks and Cycle Rides

1 Jordaan

Start at Westerkerk *(see p91)*, perhaps climbing its tower for a bird's-eye view of the area. Work your way north to picturesque Brouwersgracht *(see p92)*.

2 Shopping Walk

Beginning at Noordermarkt *(see pp63, 92)*, take Prinsengracht to the Negen Straatjes *(see p100)* with its quirky shops. Have a look at De Looier antiques market in Elandsgracht *(see p62)* before heading down Lijnbaansgracht to Leidseplein. Turn up Leidsestraat and make for Metz & Co, with its top-floor café *(see p99)* – then on to Bloemenmarkt *(see pp63, 108)*, ending at De Bijenkorf on Damrak *(see p62)*.

3 Nightlife Walk

Start at the entertainment hub, Leidseplein *(see p101)*, before moving to the bright lights around Rembrandtplein *(see p107)*. Wind down at the junction of Reguliersgracht with Herengracht, where you can see no less than 15 romantically lit bridges. Continue to Amstelkerk, finishing in Utrechtsestraat, with its many appealing cafés and restaurants *(see p61, 110, 111)*.

The Oudeschans

4 Around Oudeschans

From Centraal Station, discover a quiet part of the old city by taking Binnenkant, lined with fine houses, and then, passing Montelbaanstoren, walking along Oudeschans to reach the Rembrandthuis *(see p77)*. Pause at De Sluyswacht, the crooked café on the bridge *(see p80)*, before exploring the old Jewish quarter, Jodenbuurt *(see p48)*, or continuing to Nieuwmarkt *(see p77)*.

5 Herengracht

Shortest and most fascinating of the Grachtengordel *(see pp8–11)*, the Herengracht is lined with beautiful buildings, such as Bartolotti House *(see p91)*, the Bijbels Museum *(see p99)* and the mansions of the Golden Bend *(see p8)*.

6 To Ouderkerk aan de Amstel

For a tranquil cycle ride, follow the Amstel from the city centre (start near Blauwbrug) to Ouderkerk aan de Amstel *(see p128)*. The route passes Amstelpark and the De Rieker windmill *(see p127)* before entering attractive countryside. About 20 km (12 miles) round trip.

7 Plantage

With its distinguished villas, tree-lined streets, parks and gardens, Plantage *(see pp122–5)* is a calm district to explore by bike (with the exception of busy Plantage Middenlaan).

8 Prinsengracht

At 3 km (2 miles), the outermost canal of the Grachtengordel *(see p8)* is quite tiring on foot, but makes a very pleasant, fairly carfree cycle ride, with plenty of cafés at which to rest along the way.

9 Western Islands

Perhaps the most peaceful part of Amsterdam in which to walk or cycle lies to the north-west of Centraal Station. The islands of Prinseneiland, Bickerseiland and Realeneiland, together known as the Western Islands, have a remote, bracing quality, with well-worn boatyards and white drawbridges, as well as modern housing *(see p93)*.

10 Amsterdamse Bos

This attractive wooded park south of the city is ideal for cyclists, thanks to 48 km (30 miles) of cycle path; those on foot have no less than 160 km (100 miles) of footpath to stroll along. Perfect for a family picnic outing *(see p128)*.

Prinsengracht

Top 10 Tips for Cycling in Amsterdam

1 Stick to the Rules
Don't copy the locals, who frequently jump red lights and ride on sidewalks.

2 Stay in the Cycle Lanes
Amsterdam has an excellent integrated network of *fietspaden* (cycle lanes), with white lines, cycle signs and dedicated traffic lights.

3 Cross Tramlines with Care
If you have to, cross tramlines at an angle, to avoid your front wheel getting stuck.

4 Avoid Trams
They are bigger than you, and can't be steered; listen for their rattle and stay clear.

5 Watch for Pedestrians
It's usually tourists who mistakenly walk in cycle lanes; keep an eye out for parked cars, too.

6 Give Priority
Motorists and cyclists have priority when entering your road from the right.

7 Dismount at Busy Junctions
Unless you are really confident, it's better to negotiate these on foot.

8 Don't Cycle Two-Abreast
It's only allowed if you are not obstructing the traffic; otherwise, stay in single file.

9 Use Lights
By law, you must turn your lights on after dusk – you must also have reflector bands on both wheels.

10 Lock Your Bike
Bicycle theft is rife. Make sure that you always lock both front wheel and frame to an immovable object.

For information on bicycle hire **See p135**

Left **De Star Hofje** Right **Egelantiersgracht**

Top 10 Places for Peace and Quiet

1 De Star and Zon's Hofjes

These two charming courtyards, just a few paces from each other, offer the weary visitor a calm retreat from the crowds *(see p92)*.

2 Museum Van Loon

Behind Adriaan Dortsman's grand façade, the Van Loon family residence has a calm, welcoming feel. Lose yourself in the intimate, elegantly furnished rooms, or in the charming rose garden with its 18th-century coach house disguised as a Neo-Classical temple *(see pp30–31)*.

18th-century sledge, Museum Van Loon

3 Zandhoek

Only a few minutes away from the bustle of central Amsterdam, Zandhoek (on Realeneiland in the Western Islands) feels remote and slow-paced. Cobbles, white draw-bridges, 17th-century buildings and splendid old barges moored along the harbour front make a picturesque sight *(see p93)*.

4 Binnenkant

Bordering Waalseilandsgracht, an attractive side-canal dotted with houseboats, Binnenkant is lined with fine old merchants' houses. A couple of well-placed benches at the junction with Kalkmarkt allow you to sit and contemplate a charming stretch of the Oudeschans, site of the city's first shipyards, and the fortified Montelbaanstoren towering above it *(see p79)*. *Map Q3*

5 Café de Sluyswacht

A few steps down from busy Jodenbreestraat brings you to the crooked Café de Sluyswacht *(see p80)* with its spacious terrace, where tables and chairs are set out at the merest hint of fine weather. A surprisingly tranquil spot, from here you enjoy a different perspective of the Oudeschans.

6 Grimburgwal

This peaceful corner of the Oude Zijde at the convergence of three canals was a popular spot for medieval convents: appropriately, one of the side streets is called Gebed Zonder End (Prayer Without End). If you need to rest, there are benches on Oudezijds Voorburgwal, just beyond the Huis op de Drie Grachten. *Map N5*

7 Hortus Botanicus

A wild and verdant place dotted with tropical palmhouses and welcome benches, the small botanical garden on the east side of the city dates back to 1682, when an apothecary's herb garden was established here *(see p124)*.

8 Bijbels Museum Garden

Behind the Bible Museum is a tranquil formal garden that is full of plants mentioned in the Bible. The garden is a lovely spot to rest after visiting the museum; there is no café on site but you can help yourself to tea or coffee from the machine *(see p99)*.

9 Egelantiersgracht

The Westerkerk carillon might be the only sound to break the silence as you stroll along this pretty side-canal in the Jordaan bordered by artisans' dwellings. At Nos 107–14, St Andrieshofje, built in 1616, is one of the city's oldest and best preserved almshouses. A charming blue-and-white tiled passage leads from the street into the courtyard *(see p92)*. *Map J2*

10 Overloop-plantsoen

This sleepy little park nestles at the junction of two canals, Nieuwe Keizersgracht and Plantage Muidergracht. *Map R6*

Hortus Botanicus

Top 10 Vantage Points

1 Westerkerk Tower
Climb Amsterdam's tallest tower to see the attractive jumble of the Jordaan below *(see p91)*.

2 Zuiderkerk Tower
The top of the Zuiderkerk gives a vista of the former Jewish quarter *(see p42)*.

3 Oude Kerk Tower
See the medieval city and the red-light district from this tower *(see p29)*.

4 Metz & Co
The city's most impressive canal views are from the sixth-floor café and the cupola perched on top *(see p99)*.

5 Madame Tussaud's Scenerama
The round window on the top floor offers a terrific view of Dam Square *(see p35)*.

6 Amstelveld
From this peaceful square at the junction of Reguliersgracht and Prinsengracht, there are pretty stretches of the canal in both directions.

7 Magere Brug
Stand on this bridge at night for splendid views of the Amstel *(see p11)*.

8 Reguliersgracht and Herengracht
Put Thorbeckeplein behind you and count 10 bridges from this junction – a spectacular sight after dark.

9 OBA
The seventh-floor terrace of the Amsterdam Public Library on Oosterdokseiland offers superb city views *(see p134)*.

10 NEMO
Climb the broad outside stairs to the roof for a striking view across the Oosterdok to the city *(see p129)*.

Sign up for DK's email newsletter on traveldk.com

Left **Artis Zoo** Right **NEMO**

Children's Attractions

1 East Indiaman Amsterdam

A splendid replica of a Dutch East India Company ship that sank on its maiden voyage in 1749. Watch the sailors hoisting cargo and swabbing decks. It will be moored next to NEMO *(see p129)* during the Scheepvaart Museum's renovation from 2007 to 2010 *(see p123)*.

East Indiaman Amsterdam

2 Canal Bikes

Explore the canals at your own pace. Adults may well find these pedal boats energy-sapping, but children will love them. They seat either two or four people, and can be boarded at four different central locations *(see p135)*.

3 Tram Rides

Go to Haarlemmermeer railway station and then take a 20-minute ride in an old-fashioned tram with wooden seats, clanging bell and friendly conductor to Amsterdamse Bos, where you will find pancakes, peacocks, and plenty of leg-stretching space. *Electrische Museumtramlijn: Haarlemmermeer-station, Amstelveenseweg 264 • 020 673 7538 • www.museumtram.nl • Trams depart Apr–Oct: 11am–5pm Sun • Admission charge*

4 Puppet Shows

There has been a puppet theatre on Dam Square for over a hundred years. Puppet Theatre Misha Kluft performs every Wednesday, Saturday and Sunday afternoons from May to October. *Puppet Theatre Misha Kluft 023 532 3951 • Free*

5 NEMO

It's worth going to Amsterdam's science and technology centre just for the building alone – dubbed "Titanic" by locals – and for the superb views you can get from the top deck. Inside, enquiring minds will be kept alert with scores of fun, thought-provoking experiments and demonstrations of the world around us *(see p129)*.

6 Artis Zoo

Children really love this action-packed zoo, where they can pat the animals in the children's farm, brave the steamy reptile house, see the stars in the planetarium, and marvel at the fish in the vast aquarium *(see p123)*.

7 Vondelpark

This is the perfect place to go with kids on a summer day – it has a paddling pool, playgrounds, puppet shows and face-painting (at the Melkhuis café), as well as free performances in the open-air theatre *(see p115)*.

8 TunFun

This vast adventure playground occupies a disused car tunnel. Pre-teen kids will love the warren of tunnels, towering scaffolding and slides, while toddlers can romp in a special padded area. There are also sofas where parents can relax. *Mr Visserplein 7 • Map Q5 • 020 689 4300 • Open 10am–6pm daily • Closed 1 Jan, 30 Apr • Admission charge*

9 Tropenmuseum

Stroll through a highly realistic North African street, Indian village or Arab market – all at the Tropenmuseum. There is also a "hands-on" Kindermuseum (Children's Museum), which is open to 6- to 12-year-olds by appointment (guided tours in Dutch only) *(see p127)*.

10 Madame Tussaud's Scenerama

If you want to take a trip back into the days of the Golden Age, experience a moon landing, or meet Michael Jackson and a host of other stars, then this waxworks is the place. There's a great view of Dam Square from the round window, too *(see p35)*.

Kindermuseum

Top 10 Sights and Sounds for Free

1 Civic Guards Gallery

Huge portraits of the Civic Guard at the Amsterdams Historisch Museum *(see p26)*.

2 Begijnhof

A haven of peace and tranquillity right in the centre of the city *(see p22–3)*. For more delightful *hofjes* in the Jordaan, *see p92*.

3 Hollandsche Manege

Stylish 19th-century royal riding school *(see p117)*.

4 Rijksmuseum Garden

Architectural curiosities in a formal garden *(see p14)*.

5 Lunchtime Concerts

At the Concertgebouw every Wednesday at 12:30pm, September to June *(see p119)* and at the Boekmanzaal in the Stadhuis *(see p78)* on Tuesdays at 12:30pm, October to June.

6 Ferry across the IJ

Join the locals on the five-minute ferry ride from Centraal Station *(see p84)* to North Amsterdam or to the NDSM wharf (15 minutes).

7 Bloemenmarkt

Locals and tourists alike love the Singel's colourful floating market *(see p108)*.

8 Seven European Houses

See Europe in a minute at Roemer Visscherstraat 20–30a – a row of houses in the style of seven countries *(see p148)*.

9 Barrel Organs

A joyful feature of Amsterdam's streets – there are eight of them in all.

10 Church Bells

The carillons of the Westertoren, Zuidertoren and Munttoren unleash their glorious peals from noon–1pm on Tuesdays, Thursdays and Fridays respectively.

Left **Queen's Day bric-a-brac sale** Right **Queen's Day revellers**

TOP 10 Festivals and Events

1 Nationaal Museumweekend

Most of Amsterdam's state-run museums participate in this scheme, run by SMK (Stichting Museumkaart), to offer free or reduced-price entry for one weekend. Details are published through the Tourist Board in mid-March. *mid-Apr*

2 Koninginnedag

On the Queen's birthday, the whole city becomes a gigantic street party. The locals sell bric-a-brac from stalls outside their houses, there's a fair in Dam Square, and people dressed in monarchist orange throng the streets. Music blares, fireworks fill the night sky, and the party goes on till dawn. *30 April*

3 Bevrijdingsdag

The day after *Herdenkingsdag* (Remembrance Day), Liberation Day celebrates the end of the Nazi occupation with speeches, concerts and open-air markets in the Vondelpark, Leidseplein, Museumplein and Rokin. *5 May*

4 Holland Festival

An exciting programme of theatre, music, opera, ballet and art staged at various venues in the city, the Holland Festival has earned itself a prestigious reputation, attracting top-flight performers from the Netherlands and abroad. *020 530 7110 • www.hollandfestival.nl • Jan*

5 Open Monumentendagen

An exciting opportunity to see what lies behind the gabled façades and medieval doorways of some of the city's most historic buildings, which are open to the public for free over this weekend. *020 422 2118 • www.openmonumentendag.nl • Second weekend in Sep*

6 Open Tuinendagen

During Open Garden Days some 30 canal house gardens are open to the public. Visit the green spaces of several museums, like Van Loon *(see pp30–31)*, and take the rare opportunity to see many private gardens. A day ticket includes transport by canal boat to all houses. *Third weekend in Jun • www.canalmuseums.nl*

7 Grachtenfestival

National and international stars perform classical music concerts at 20 historic locations around the three canals of the Grachtengordel *(see p11)*. The

Traditional dancers at the Jordaan Festival

Prinsengrachtconcert, Grachtenfestival

highlight is a free piano recital given on a barge on Prinsengracht opposite the Pulitzer Hotel. Concerts are also held at Muziekgebouw aan't IJ *(see p56)*. ✆ *020 421 4542 • www.grachtenfestival.nl • 2nd or 3rd Wed–Sun in Aug*

8 Jordaan Festival

This picturesque district *(see p92)* makes an ideal setting for a low-key early-autumn festival. The local talent comes out of the woodwork for contests on Westermarkt, and there are concerts, street parties and fairs – like the one devoted to food in Noordermarkt *(see 92 & 97)*.

9 Sinterklaas' Parade

The Christmas festivities start here. St Nicholas – the Dutch Santa Claus – arrives near St Nicholaas Kerk by boat with his mischievous servants, *Zwarte Pieten* (Black Peters). Together, they distribute sweets and gifts to the children of Amsterdam. ✆ *Second or third Sat in Nov*

10 New Year's Eve

New Year's Eve starts slowly and explodes into life at midnight with firework displays (there's an organized one over the Amstel) and wild street-partying centred on Nieuwmarkt and Dam Square. As with all events of this sort, things can sometimes get out of hand. ✆ *31 Dec*

Top 10 Spectator Sports

1 Football

See Ajax at their remarkable 50,000-seater stadium. ✆ *Amsterdam ArenA, Bijlmer • Aug–Dec, Feb–May*

2 Cycling

The RAI Derny Race is Amsterdam's only criterium (road circuit). ✆ *Amsterdam RAI, Europaplein • mid-May*

3 Basketball

The top local team is Ricoh Astronauts. ✆ *Sporthallen Zuid • Sep–mid-May*

4 Korfbal

A cross between netball and basketball. Blauw Wit is the club to watch. ✆ *Sportpark Joos Banckersweg • Sep–Jun*

5 Hockey

Amsterdamsche Hockey & Bandy Club are the ones to watch. ✆ *Wagener Stadium, Amstelveen • Sep–May*

6 Ice Hockey

The city supports the popular Boretti Tigers. ✆ *Sporthal Jaap Edenhal, Radioweg 64 • Oct–late Mar*

7 American Football

If you can't get tickets to watch Ajax, the Amsterdam Admirals also play at the ArenA *(see above)*. ✆ *Mar–Jun*

8 Running

The Amsterdam Marathon began in 1976 and is now an annual event. ✆ *Olympisch Stadion Stadionplein • Oct*

9 Rowing

Popular among the numerous competitions is the Head of the Amstel River race. ✆ *Last week Mar*

10 Show-jumping

Jumping Amsterdam is a series of international indoor competitions. ✆ *Amsterdam RAI, Europaplein • Jan–Feb*

Sign up for DK's email newsletter on traveldk.com

Left **Haarlem** Right **Hortus Botanicus, Leiden**

TOP 10 Excursions

1 Aalsmeer Bloemenveilingen

Witnessed from an elevated viewing gallery, the world's largest flower auction is an astonishing sight. With flowers, speed is of the essence, and the atmosphere is frenetic. Bidding is highly automated, using the "backwards" Dutch clock system: the clock starts at 100, then counts down until the first bidder to press his button stops the auction and wins. *www.vba.nl*

2 Delft

Sleepy Delft was shaken by a gunpowder explosion in 1654, after which the town was rebuilt – as recorded in *A View of Delft* by Vermeer around 1660. Since then, little has changed. There are Delft tiles in the Museum Lambert van Meerten and the shops. In Het Prinsenhof are the bullet holes left by the murder of William of Orange; his mausoleum is in the Nieuwe Kerk. *www.delft.nl*

3 The Hague

Political capital of the Netherlands, Den Haag (The Hague) is a stately city, with many public buildings and lovely parks. Centred round the Gothic Ridderzaal, places of interest include the parliament buildings, the International Court of Justice and the Mauritshuis, elegant home of the superlative Royal Picture Gallery. The seaside resort of Scheveningen is not far away. *www.denhaag.nl*

4 Enkhuizen

The fortunes of this attractive former fishing port declined dramatically after the construction of the huge Afsluitdijk in 1932 created the freshwater IJsselmeer and cut it off from the North Sea. Today it is home to the wonderful Zuiderzeemuseum, which includes a reconstruction of a typical fishing village with costumed "inhabitants" and craftsmen at work.

5 Haarlem

Centred around the Grote Markt, with its buzzing pavement cafés and lovely buildings, the historic centre of this lively, well-heeled city is a delight. Highlights include the Frans Hals Museum, the Grote Kerk with its magnificent decorated Müller organ, and the Art Deco train station. The Teylers Museum has an excellent collection of science, technology and art exhibits. *www.vvvzk.nl*

Lime kilns, Zuiderzeemuseum, Enkhuizen

Visit the Aalsmeer flower auction website at www.vba.nl
Visit the Zuiderzeemuseum website at www.zuiderzeemuseum.nl

6 Keukenhof

Throughout spring, but climaxing in mid-April when the tulips flower, a drab coastal strip between Leiden and Haarlem bursts into colour. Among these commercial bulbfields is the wooded Keukenhof park, a dazzling and unforgettable sight between late March and late May. *www.keukenhof.nl*

7 Leiden

An easy-going university town, full of cycling students, Leiden offers plenty of canals, cafés and museums, as well as the lovely Hortus Botanicus. *www.hollandrijnland.nl*

8 Marken

Just 16 km (10 miles) from Amsterdam, this former island fishing community, now reached by a narrow causeway, makes a refreshing day trip. Its distinctive wooden houses are charming.

9 Paleis Het Loo

Built in 1686 by Stadholder William III as a hunting lodge, Het Loo, near Apeldoorn, was a royal summer residence until the 1960s. Behind a sober façade lies a sumptuous interior, with rooms decorated to reflect the different eras of occupation, from the 1680s to the 1930s. There are also superb formal gardens to enjoy.

Wooden house, Marken

10 Utrecht

Like Leiden, Utrecht is a university city with much to offer – notwithstanding the vast, unappealing Hoog Catherijne shopping complex. A major medieval religious centre, it still has many traces of its past, and a lovely historic town centre. *www.utrechtyourway.nl*

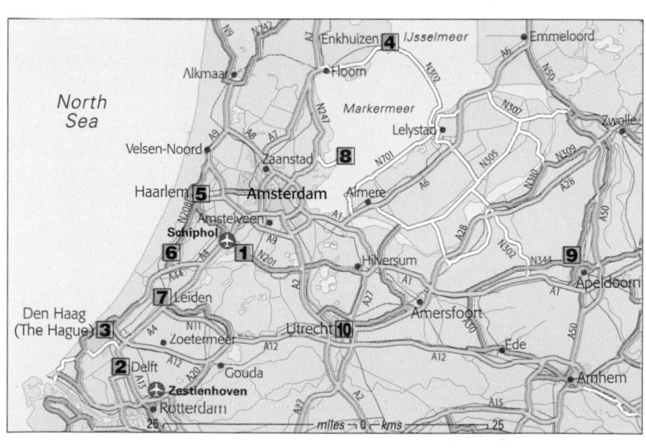

AROUND TOWN

Left **Stopera** Right **Museum Het Rembrandthuis**

Oude Zijde

THE STREETS OF THE OUDE ZIJDE (OLD SIDE) *are packed with historic and beautiful buildings, though many are buried in the seediest parts. As the name suggests, this is where Amsterdam has its roots; the city grew from a ribbon of land on the eastern bank of the Amstel between Damrak and Oudezijds Voorburgwal (which means "before the city wall"). Today, the Oude Zijde incorporates the medieval city, built around the Oude Kerk, and the area to the east, where development started in the 15th century and continued over the following two centuries to accommodate Jewish émigrés. An area of richness and contrasts, within its boundaries lie the Nieuwmarkt (dominated by the Waag, a 15th-century city gate turned weigh-house), the university quarter, Chinatown, the Red Light district, and what remains of the old Jodenbuurt* (see p48), *where four former synagogues have been combined to form the superb Joods Historisch Museum.*

Oude Kerk

Top 10 Sights

1. Oude Kerk
2. Nieuwmarkt
3. Museum Het Rembrandthuis
4. Zeedijk
5. Red Light District
6. Stopera
7. Joods Historisch Museum
8. Portugees-Israëlitische Synagoge
9. Hash Marihuana Hemp Museum
10. Montelbaanstoren

The Waag, Nieuwmarkt

1 Oude Kerk

The oldest church in Amsterdam has been altered and extended over the years, producing a heavenly jumble of architectural styles from medieval to Renaissance *(see pp28–9)*.

2 Nieuwmarkt

This vast open square has been a marketplace since the 15th century, and is still the scene of a Sunday antiques market in summer. Alone in the middle stands the bulky Waag (1488), bristling with turrets. The eastern gate in the city's defences, it was originally called St Antoniespoort. In the 17th century it became a weigh-house and home to numerous guilds, including the surgeons'. It was here that Rembrandt painted his famous *Anatomy Lesson of Dr Tulp*, now in the Mauritshuis, The Hague. There were few problems acquiring bodies for dissection, since public executions took place in the Nieuwmarkt. *Map P3*

3 Museum Het Rembrandthuis

Major refurbishment has recreated the interior as it might have been in Rembrandt's time. Of special interest are pictures by his master, Pieter Lastman. One room contains exotic collectibles of the day – busts of Roman emperors, spears and shells – as well as Rembrandt's precious art books and an inventory of his effects *(see p15)*. Look out for etching and paint-making demonstrations. *Jodenbreestraat 4 • Map Q5 • 020 520 0400 • www.rembrandthuis.nl • Open 10am–5pm Mon–Sat, 1–5pm Sun & public hols • Admission charge*

4 Zeedijk

Built in the early 1300s, the Zeedijk (sea dyke) was part of Amsterdam's original fortifications. As the city grew the canals were filled in and the dykes became obsolete. At No. 1 is one of the city's two remaining wooden-fronted houses, dating from the 16th century. It is not open to the public. Opposite is St Olofskapel, built in 1445 and named after the first Christian king of Norway and Denmark. *Map Q2*

5 Red Light District

The world's oldest profession aptly occupies Amsterdam's oldest quarter, de Walletjes ("the little walls"), bordered by Zeedijk, Kloveniersburgwal, Damstraat and Warmoesstraat. Today, the district is one of the city's greatest tourist attractions and a campaign to make the area a more attractive place is underway. The council is reducing the number of window-prostitutes and encouraging small creative businesses to open up shop. *Map P2, P3*

Red Light District

6 Stopera

With the Dutch penchant for clever wordplay, the Stadhuis-Muziektheater is better known as "Stopera" because it combines the *stadhuis* (town hall) with the headquarters of the city opera and ballet companies. A brutal design in red brick, marble and glass, it was built in 1987 amid intense controversy, since scores of medieval houses, among Jodenbuurt's few remnants, had to be destroyed in the process. In the passage between Stopera's two buildings, a bronze button indicates the exact NAP (*Normaal Amsterdams Peil*) water level. *Waterlooplein 22 • Map Q5 • Stadhuis: 14 020 • Open 8.30am–5pm Mon–Fri (Arcade open 24hrs daily) • Muziektheater: 020 625 5455*

7 Joods Historisch Museum

Abel Cahen's prize-winning design for the Jewish Historical Museum (1987) is a perfect marriage of old and new: the four synagogues that house it, built by Ashkenazi Jews during the 17th and 18th centuries, are linked by glass-covered internal walkways. Highlights of the exhibition are the Holy Ark (1791), focus of the Nieuwe Synagoge, the new Children's Museum, the exhibition on Dutch Jews in the 20th century and Elias Bouman's airy 17th-century Grote Synagoge *(see pp48–9)*. *Jonas Daniel Meijerplein 2–4 • Map Q5 • 020 531 0310 • www.jhm.nl • Open 11am–5pm daily • Closed Yom Kippur, Rosh Hashanah • Admission charge*

Modern-day Tolerance

In line with Amsterdam's long tradition of tolerance, the authorities generally overlook the possession and consumption of small quantities of cannabis or marijuana, although they are illegal. Their sale and use at regulated coffee shops *(see p51)* is officially accepted, but hard drugs and advertising are not. In 1990, brothels and the display of girls in their windows were legalized, although street prostitution remains illegal.

Joods Historisch Museum

8 Portugees-Israëlitische Synagoge

The Sephardic Jews, who settled in Amsterdam from the late 16th century, celebrated their new lives in a tolerant society a century later by commissioning Elias Bouman to build this imposing synagogue. It follows a traditional design with the Hechal (Holy Ark), facing Jerusalem, opposite the tebah, from where the cantor leads the service *(see p48)*. *Mr Visserplein 3 • Map R5 • 020 624 5351 • www.esnoga.nl • Open Apr–Oct: 10am–4pm Sun–Fri; Nov–Mar: 10am–4pm Sun–Thu, 10–3pm Fri • Closed Sat & Jewish hols • Admission charge*

9 Hash Marihuana Hemp Museum

Seen through a cloud of incense, exhibits in this tiny but fascinating museum chart the history of hemp (marijuana) from its earliest use some 8,000 years ago to the 20th-century drug wars. As *hennep*, it was used in Holland for making lace, linens, fishing nets and fabric for sails, and processed by special windmills called *hennepkloppers*. There are displays about smuggling, an array of hookahs and reefers, and a "grow room" where plants are cultivated. ⊗ *Oudezijds Achterburgwal 148 • Map P3 • 020 623 5961 • www.hashmuseum.com • Open 10am–10pm daily • Admission charge*

10 Montelbaanstoren

A fortified tower, the Montelbaanstoren was built in 1512 on the eastern edge of Amsterdam, just outside the city wall. Its original purpose was to defend the Dutch fleet; now, more prosaically, it houses the Amsterdam water authority. The open-work steeple was added by the ubiquitous Hendrick de Keyser in 1606, when the city fathers felt that they could at last afford the icing on the cake. It overlooks the lovely Oude Schans *(see p64)*, a canal that also dates from the early 16th century, dug to improve access for ships. ⊗ *Oude Schans 2 • Map R3*

Montelbaanstoren

A Day in the Oude Zijde

Morning

As the Oude Kerk does not open until 11am, start your day with a tour of the **Museum Ons' Lieve Heer op Solder** *(see pp20–1)*. Although in the Nieuwe Zijde, it is only a few steps from the **Oude Kerk** *(see pp28–9)*, which you can visit afterwards. Then walk to **Nieuwmarkt** *(see p77)* for a break at In de Waag (Nieuwmarkt 4), where you can sit, overlooking the square, in summer.

Afterwards, make your way to Oudezijds Achterburgwal for the **Hash Marihuana Hemp Museum**. Then follow the main drag of the **Red Light district** *(see p77)*, Oudezijds Voorburgwal, as far as Café Roux *(see p60)* for lunch.

Afternoon

Walk down to peaceful Grimburgwal and the House on the Three Canals. Agnietenkapel (now closed) is a few doors away. From here, head east to Oudezijds Achterburgwal and cut through Oudemanhuispoort (stone spectacles mark the entrance), browsing through the second-hand bookstalls as you go. Continue to Jodenbreestraat and the **Museum Het Rembrandthuis** *(see p77)*. After your tour – if it is a Monday, Wednesday, Friday or Saturday – pop into Pintohuis *(see p44)* for a glimpse of the painted ceiling. Revive yourself in Café de Sluyswacht *(see p80)*. From here there is a lovely canalside walk, past the **Montelbaanstoren**. Turn left and stroll along Binnenkant before heading back to your hotel.

Left **Wijnand Fockinck** Right **In 't Aepjen**

TOP 10 Restaurants, Cafés and Bars

1 Bird

Those in the know flock here for the tastiest Thai in town. Eat in their restaurant or duck out to their snackbar opposite for an utterly authentic experience. *Zeedijk 72 • Map P2 • 020 620 1442 • €€*

2 Café Cuba

An intriguing ode to the communist country, this long and narrow, darkly-lit bar serves fantastic cocktails and pitchers of sangria. There is a pool table at the back. *Nieuwmarkt 3 • Map P3 • 020 627 4919*

3 In 't Aepjen

This unusual bar is located in one of the oldest wooden houses in the city (1551). Sailors would pay for their stay in monkeys – hence the primate theme. *Zeedijk 1 • Map P2 • 020 626 8401*

4 De Bekeerde Suster

In 1544, the nuns at this cloister started making beer, a tradition revitalized a few years ago – and there's a fine restaurant. *Kloveniersburgwal 6-8 • Map P4 • 020 423 0112*

5 De Sluyswacht

Rembrandt sketched this leaning former lock-keeper's house. There's a peaceful canalside terrace at the back. *Jodenbreestraat 1 • Map Q4 • 020 625 7611*

6 De Engelbewaarder

Frequented by hi-brow locals, this convivial bar serves cheap and cheerful food and specialist beers on a peaceful canalside terrace. Live jazz on Sundays. *Kloveniersburgwal 59 • Map E4 • 020 6253772*

7 VOC Café

Housed in the city's oldest defence tower, the Schreierstoren *(see p10)*, this traditional-style bar has a "reading room" and two terraces overlooking the water. *Prins Hendrikkade 94 • Map Q1*

8 Wijnand Fockink

Barely looking a day older than its 1679 origins, this is the best *proeflokaal* (tasting house) in town. The hidden garden out back is only for use by guests of the Krasnapolski Hotel. *Pijlsteeg 31 • Map N3 • 020 639 2695*

9 Lime

One of the hippest and friendliest bars in the area, yet decidedly unpretentious. *Zeedijk 104 • Map P3*

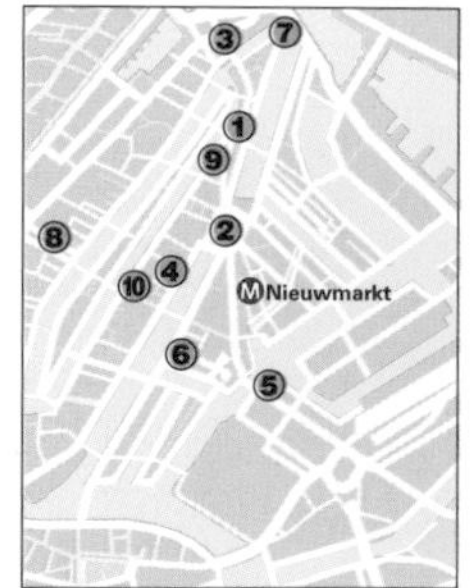

10 Blauw aan de Wal

An absolute treasure in the heart of the Red Light District, this Mediterranean restaurant should be savoured for hours. *Oudezijds Achterburgwal 99 • Map P4 • 020 330 2257 • €€€€*

Latei

Price Categories

For a three-course meal for one with half a bottle of wine (or equivalent meal), taxes and extra charges.

€	under €20
€€	€20–€30
€€€	€30–€45
€€€€	€45–€60
€€€€€	over €60

Top 10 Best of the Rest

1 Condomerie
A huge, hilarious range of (mostly) novelty condoms guaranteed to spice up the most jaded of love lives. Ⓢ *Warmoesstraat 141 • Map N3*

2 Fo Kuang Shan Temple
This nun-run Chinese Buddhist temple takes pride of place on this otherwise junkie-riddled street. Take a respectful peek one afternoon (you can keep your shoes on), or join a tour, held Saturday afternoon. Ⓢ *Zeedijk 118 • Map P3 • 020 420 2357 • €*

3 Himalaya
A veggie café at the back of this new age bookstore overlooking the water is a fantastic find in this hectically touristy area. Chill out, Zen-style. Ⓢ *Warmoesstraat 56 • Map P2*

4 Jacob Hooy & Co
Established in 1743, this chemist's store is simply the best place in town to pick up herbs, homeopathic remedies, tea and essential oils. Ⓢ *Kloveniersburgwal 12 • Map P3*

5 Joe's Vliegerwinkel
Colourful kites, quirky knick-knacks and kitsch bits for that perfect present to suit all ages. Ⓢ *Nieuwe Hoogstraat 19 • Map P4*

6 Latei
A delightful café cum bric-a-brac store. Ideal for a sandwich, fresh juice and decent-sized coffees. Ⓢ *Zeedijk 143 • Map P3*

7 Beestenwinkel
Toys, gadgets and games with an animal theme. From squirting fish to cuddly bars and rubber ducks that glow in the bath. Ⓢ *Staalstraat 11 • Map P5 • www.beestenwinkel.nl*

8 Droog Design
A group of young Dutch designers have joined forces to form Droog Design. Check out their shop for witty home accessories. Ⓢ *Staalstraat 7A/B • Map P5 • www.droogdesign.nl*

9 Tibet
Quite a find in the seedy surrounds of the Red Light District, this restaurant serves food until 1am. Ⓢ *Lange Niezel 24 • Map P2 • 020 624 1137 • €*

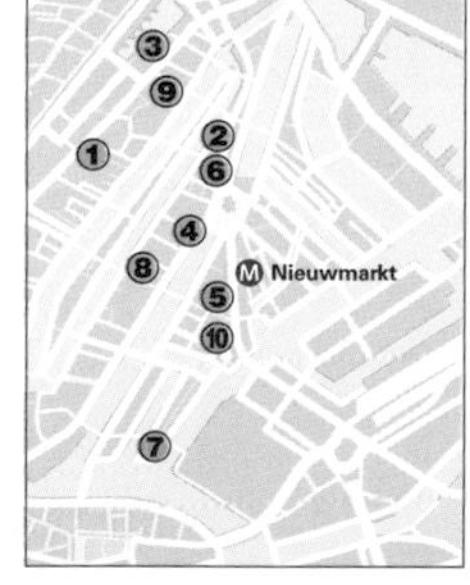

10 De Zuiderkerk
Built 1603–11 by Hendrick de Keyser, painted by Monet in 1874. Climb to the top for great views. Ⓢ *Zuiderkerkhof 72 • Map P4 • 020 552 7987 • Church open 9am–4pm Mon–Fri, noon–4pm Sat. Free • Closed public hols • Tower open noon–3:30pm Mon–Sat, Apr–Sep. Admission charge*

Left **Koninklijk Paleis** Right **View across Dam Square to the Nieuwe Kerk**

Nieuwe Zijde

DESPITE ITS NAME, THE NIEUWE ZIJDE (NEW SIDE), *together with the Oude Zijde, was at the centre of Amsterdam's early maritime settlement. From the boundary between the two districts, the Nieuwe Zijde extends west to the Singel. Its canal pattern once mirrored that of its neighbour, but over time it developed an entirely different character. The medieval city, with its wooden housing, was highly susceptible to fire, and much of the area was burnt down in 1452, necessitating extensive reconstruction. During the 19th century, most of its canals were filled in; the resulting thoroughfares, Damrak, Rokin and Nieuwendijk, are lively shopping streets, as is Kalverstraat, scene of a medieval market. Despite the changes, pockets of history survive – in the network of narrow 14th-century streets off Kalverstraat, the Begijnhof, the 17th-century orphanage that houses the Amsterdams Historisch Museum, and, at the heart of the district, Dam Square.*

18th-century monstrance, Museum Amstelkring

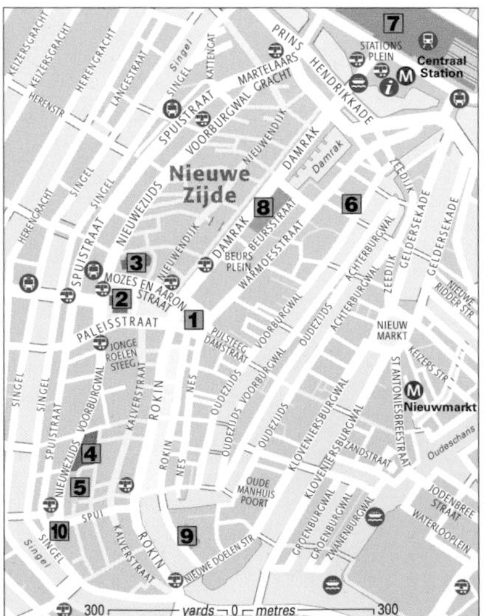

Top 10 Sights

1. Dam Square
2. Koninklijk Paleis
3. Nieuwe Kerk
4. Amsterdams Historisch Museum
5. Begijnhof
6. Museum Ons' Lieve Heer op Solder
7. Centraal Station
8. Beurs van Berlage
9. Allard Pierson Museum
10. Spui

Gilded cherub, Nieuwe Kerk

1 Dam Square

Amsterdam's main square is named after the dam on the River Amstel, around which the city grew. By the 17th century, it had become the focus of the Dutch trading empire *(see pp34–5)*.

2 Koninklijk Paleis

Supported by a staggering 13,659 wooden piles, Jacob van Campen's Classical building occupies one side of Dam Square. Designed as the *Stadhuis* (town hall), it was transformed into a Royal Palace in 1808 by King Louis Bonaparte. Although it is still used for official functions, such as the wedding reception of Crown Prince Willem-Alexander in February 2002 *(see p39)*, the present royal family live elsewhere. It is closed for renovation until 2008 *(see p34)*.

3 Nieuwe Kerk

Wealthy merchant banker Willem Eggert donated his orchard as a site for this Gothic church, as well as a large sum of money for its construction. It was consecrated to Our Lady and St Catherine, but has only ever been called the Nieuwe Kerk – to distinguish it from the Oude Kerk. When the town hall became the royal palace in the early 19th century *(see above)*, it was given the new, elevated title of national church of the Netherlands, and has been the setting for the coronation of every Dutch monarch since then *(see p34)*.

4 Amsterdams Historisch Museum

An excellent place to start a visit to Amsterdam, this museum chronicles how a tiny fishing village on the Amstel river grew into one of the wealthiest and most beautiful cities in the world *(see pp24–7)*.

5 Begijnhof

A charming and secluded courtyard of houses surrounding a tranquil garden in the centre of the city, the Begijnhof was established in the 14th century as a sanctuary for a lay Catholic sisterhood *(see pp22–3)*.

6 Museum Ons' Lieve Heer op Solder

This canal house turned museum, with its sober decoration and delightful secret Catholic church, plunges the visitor back into the Golden Age *(see pp20–1)*.

Amsterdams Historisch Museum collection

Centraal Station

7 Centraal Station

For many visitors, their experience of Amsterdam begins at Centraal Station, the transport hub of the city, where some 1,400 trains arrive and leave every day. It was built in the 1880s in Neo-Renaissance style by P J H Cuypers, who was also responsible for the Rijksmuseum *(see pp12–15)*, and A L van Gendt, designer of the Concertgebouw *(see p115)*. Before work on the building could start, three artificial islands had to be constructed and 8,600 wooden piles sunk to support them. The fact that the building blocked Amsterdammers' view of the sea caused much controversy at the time. The ornate red-brick façade depicts themes of travel, trade and city history, picked out in gold and other colours. If you have time, visit the station restaurant, 1e Klas *(see p51)*, to see its fine Art Nouveau setting. Major renovation works mean that parts of the building are closed until 2011. *Stationsplein • Map P1 • 0900 9292*

Amsterdam's Colonial Past

Acknowledged during the 17th century as the most powerful city in the Netherlands, Amsterdam turned its sights overseas. Expeditions established a spice trade out of Indonesia, and in 1602 the Dutch East India Company (VOC) was founded, followed in 1621 by the Dutch West India Company. Dutch colonies in Brazil and on Manhattan Island eventually succumbed, respectively, to Portuguese and English sea-power.

8 Beurs van Berlage

The innovative Stock Exchange building was derided when it was unveiled in 1903, but is now considered a key work of the period and almost universally admired. Designed by the pioneer of Dutch modern architecture, H P Berlage, its functional lines are softened by ornamental ironwork and tiled mosaics. The Stock Exchange has now moved next door, and Beurs van Berlage is the head office of the Nederlands Philharmonic Orchestra. It is used for exhibitions and contains a permanent display on the history of the Stock Exchange. Try to get a look at the amazingly light and spacious interior. *Damrak 277 • Map N2 • 020 530 4141 (exhibitions), 020 521 7575 (Nederlands Philharmonic box office) • www.berlage.com • Open only during exhibitions • Admission charge*

9 Allard Pierson Museum

Located in a stately Neo-Classical house built in the 1860s as a bank, this delightful small museum was named after the University of Amsterdam's first Professor of Classical Archaeology, and contains its archaeological collection. Fascinating exhibits conjure up vivid pictures of life in ancient civilizations; they include Egyptian mummies and sarcophagi, Coptic clothes, Cypriot jewellery, Greek geometric and red-figured pottery, Etruscan metalwork and Roman glassware and statuary. One of the museum's attractions is its size: even with an extra wing opened in 1994, it is possible to see everything in one visit. Oude Turfmarkt 127 • Map N5 • 020 525 2556 • www.allardpiersonmuseum.nl • Open 10am–5pm Tue–Fri, 1–5pm Sat, Sun & public hols • Closed 1 Jan, Easter Sun, Whitsunday, 30 Apr, 25 Dec • Admission charge

10 Spui

One of the most genial places in the city, this small square lined with cafés, bars and bookshops is generally quiet during the winter, but in summer, it bursts into life at lunchtime and again in the evening, when people spill out onto the pavement from bars. Cheek by jowl with university buildings, Spui has traditionally been a place where intellectuals gather to drink and debate. There is also a Friday book market. During the Provo riots of the 1960s *(see p39)*, the square was the scene of political protests and demonstrations, during which Carol Kneulman's twee statue of an urchin, *Het Lieverdje* (Little Darling) was frequently daubed with slogans. At No. 18, Café Hoppe *(see p50)* is a landmark brown café, in business for more than 300 years. Map M5

***Het Lieverdje*, Spui**

A Day in the Nieuwe Zijde

Morning

Spend the morning in the **Amsterdams Historisch Museum** *(see pp24–7)*, although a morning is scarcely enough. When you feel like a break, leave the main building and head for the Kalverstraat entrance, where the café-restaurant David and Goliath is on your left. Make sure that you keep your ticket so that you can re-enter the museum without having to pay again. The end of the tour brings you to the excellent museum shop.

Rather than leaving by one of the exits, cut through the Civic Guards' Gallery to the **Begijnhof** *(see pp22–3)*, and while away some time in this secluded place. Come out of the Gedempte Begijnensloot entrance and turn the corner into **Spui**, where you might lunch at Café Hoppe *(see p50)* or Café Esprit (Spui 10).

Afternoon

After lunch, walk down Kalverstraat, the district's main shopping street, to Dam Square, where you could visit the **Koninklijk Paleis** as well as the **Nieuwe Kerk** *(see pp34–5)*. Then take a break among the tiny shops built into the buttresses of the church in Gravenstraat; at No.18, De Drie Fleschjes is one of the oldest *proeflokalen* (tasting houses), dating from 1650.

When you are revived, walk down Damrak past the **Beurs van Berlage** to finish your day at the **Centraal Station**, where you can hop on a tram back to your hotel.

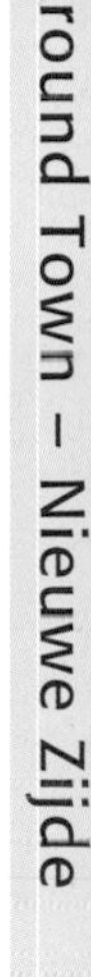

Left **De Jaren** Right **Supperclub**

TOP 10 Restaurants, Cafés and Bars

1 Green Planet
Bright, modern and full of greenery, this veggie café-restaurant is 90 per cent organic. Perfect for a drink, a quick snack or a hearty meal. *Spuistraat 122 • Map N2 • 020 625 8280 • €€*

2 Keuken van 1870
A local favourite, this former soup kitchen dishes up homely meat and vegetarian dinners at bargain prices. *Spuistraat 4 • Map N1 • 020 620 4018 • €*

3 Hoppe
Open since 1670, this historic brown café, with its lefty past and church pews, was a regular haunt of radical journalists, writers and intellectuals in the Provo-fuelled 1960s. *Spui 18 • Map M5 • 020 420 4420*

4 De Jaren
Formerly a bank, cash is the only currency at this modern grand-café. Simple sandwiches and soups downstairs, delicious meals upstairs. The waterside terrace is the place to be in summer. *Nieuwe Doelenstraat 20 • Map N5 • 020 625 5771*

5 Het Schuim
Art meets alcohol at this large, rustic-style bar, a popular hangout for creative types. Food served till 10pm. *Spuistraat 189 • Map M3*

6 Getto
This kitsch, New York-style gay bar and restaurant serves hearty meals to a mixed crowd. Cocktail Happy Hour runs from 5–7pm. *Warmoesstraat 51 • Map P2 • 020 421 5151 • €€€*

7 Greenwoods
Australian-run, typically English tearoom-style café that serves great breakfasts and high teas. Service can be painfully slow, but worth the wait. *Singel 103 • Map M1 • 020 623 7071*

8 Supperclub
There's a decadent lounge bar in the basement of this hip restaurant. Dress to impress if you want to get in. *Jonge Roelensteeg 21 • Map M3 • 020 344 6400*

9 Brasserie Harkema
A stylish establishment boasting a spacious dining room. Choose from the classic Parisian brasserie menu or come for late-night nibbles. Caters for large groups. *Nes 67 • Map N4 • 020 428 2222 • €€€*

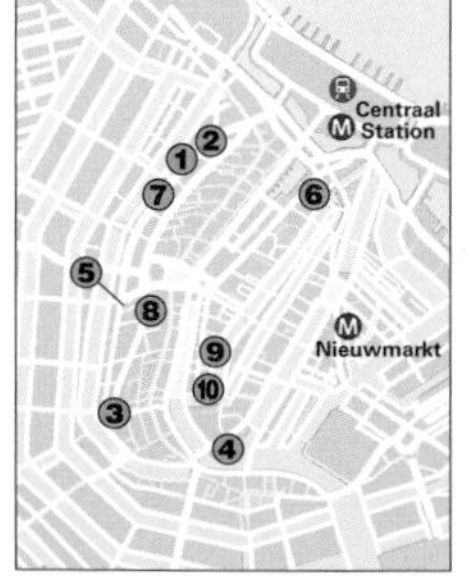

10 Kapitein Zeppos
Tucked away in a tiny alleyway, this charming restaurant serves French cuisine with Italian, Spanish and Moroccan influences. *Gebed Zonder End 5 • Map N4 • 020 624 2057 • €€€*

Recommend your favourite café on traveldk.com

De Bierkoning

Price Categories

For a three-course meal for one with half a bottle of wine (or equivalent meal), taxes and extra charges.

€	under €20
€€	€20–€30
€€€	€30–€45
€€€€	€45–€60
€€€€€	over €60

TOP 10 Best of the Rest

1 Absinthe

DJs spin and you might too, after sampling the *La Fée Verte* (The Green Fairy), the controversial wormwood-infused hallucinogenic this late-opening lounge bar takes its name from. *Nieuwezijds Voorburgwal 171 • Map M3*

2 Het Japanse Winkeltje

Japanese crafts centre selling beautiful lacquered and china bowls, sake decanters and kimonos. *Nieuwezijds Voorburgwal 177 • Map M3*

3 The American Book Center

Seven floors of books, magazines, newspapers and computer games. There are also art exhibitions, lectures and writers' workshops at the Treehouse annexe, a short walk away. *Spui 12 • Map M5*

4 De Bierkoning

"The Beer King" in the shadow of the Dam's Royal Palace has a fantastic range of beers – almost 1,000 of them – from all over the world. *Paleisstraat 125 • Map M3*

5 DOM-CK

Hypertrendy fashion and interior shop from Germany, selling anything from moose scarves to retro bead curtains. *Spuistraat 281a–c • Map M4 • www.dom-shop.com*

6 P G C Hajenius

Dutchman Hajenius fulfilled his 1826 pipe dream, and his store is now one of Europe's most famous cigar houses. A must for all cigar connoisseurs, but worth a peek just for the art deco interior. *Rokin 92–6 • Map N3*

7 Profiles Hair & Body Spa

For an afternoon of ultimate pampering, head to this spa where therapists work to Ayurvedic principles. Offers massage, herbal body wraps and skin treatments. *Spuistraat 330 • Map M5*

8 Puccini Bomboni

A chocoholic's paradise! Mouthwatering chocolates often with surprising fillings, such as nutmeg, lemongrass or pepper. Real junkies can also feast on big chunks of chocolate bars. *Singel 184 • Map M2*

9 Gastronomie Nostalgie

This charming shop sells elegant tableware for special occasions. Stock includes silverware, porcelain and crystal. *Nieuwezijds Voorburgwal 304 • Map M4*

10 Vrankrijk

Pop into the legalized bar of the city's most famous squat for a taste of Amsterdam's legendary squatting movement. *Spuistraat 216 • Map M4*

Left **Houseboat on Brouwersgracht** Right **De Star Hofje**

Western Canal Ring

FOR MANY, THE WESTERN CANAL RING *is the area of Amsterdam that perfectly encapsulates the city's relaxed yet stylish air. Construction of the Grachtengordel, Amsterdam's 17th-century ring of three fashionable canals (see p11), began here, with the marshy area just beyond reserved by city planner Hendrick Staets for workers and their unpalatable industries; Huguenot refugees who settled here – like others fleeing religious persecution – were said to have named it jardin (garden), later corrupted to Jordaan, and today it is one of Amsterdam's most fascinating – and bohemian – districts. Its narrow streets and oblique canals might seem random, but they followed the course of old paths and drainage ditches. North of the charming Brouwersgracht lies the recently revitalized district of Haarlemmerbuurt, and, further afield, the Western Islands, Bickerseiland, Prinseneiland and Realeneiland, created in the mid-17th century to provide much-needed warehousing.*

Huis met de Hoofden

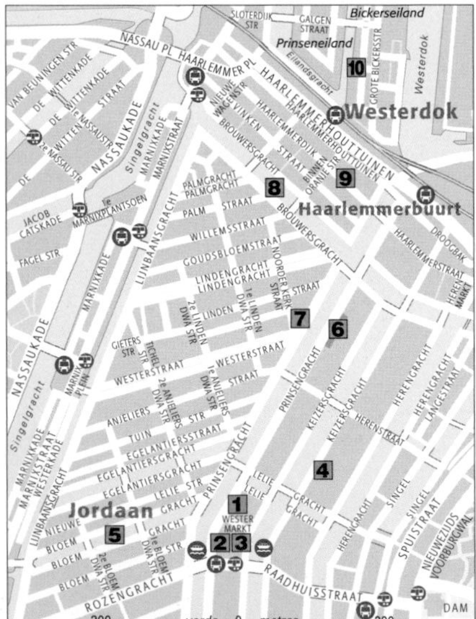

Top 10 Sights

1. Anne Frank Huis
2. Westerkerk
3. Homomonument
4. Huis met de Hoofden
5. Jordaan
6. Zon's Hofje and De Star Hofjes
7. Noordermarkt
8. Brouwersgracht
9. Haarlemmerbuurt
10. Western Islands

1 Anne Frank Huis

Recently enlarged, this thought-provoking museum encompasses the *achterhuis*, secret hideout of Anne Frank and her family, as well as background information on the plight of Amsterdam's Jews and racial oppression *(see pp32–3)*.

2 Westerkerk

An exacting climb to the top of the soaring tower of Westerkerk, a landmark close to the heart of every Amsterdammer, rewards you with a thrilling view *(see p67)*. Designed by Hendrick de Keyser and completed in1631, its austere interior is unadorned, except for the ornate organ and its lively painted shutters. A memorial to Rembrandt reminds us that he was buried here, although the precise burial site is unknown. Outside the church, notice the poignant, diminutive statue of Anne Frank and Homomonument, the pink granite triangle which commemorates persecuted homosexuals. *Prinsengracht 281. Map L2. 020 624 7766. www.westerkerk.nl • Church: open Easter–Sep: 11am–3pm Mon–Fri (Jul–Aug also Sat). Free • Tower: open Apr–Oct: guided tours every hour from 10am–6pm Mon–Sat (for further information call 020 689 2565) Admission charge*

Westerkerk

3 Homomonument

This first memorial in the world to gay men and women who lost their lives during World War II, also pays tribute to homosexuals who are still being oppressed today. The memorial was designed by Dutch artist Karin Daan and was erected in 1987. It consists of three

Homomonument

equilateral triangles made of pink granite, one level with the street, one protruding into the Keizersgracht and one slightly raised – symbolising the past, present and future. The pink triangle, originally a badge gay men were forced to wear in the World War II concentration camps, became a symbol of gay pride in the 1970s and 80s. *Westermarkt (between Westerkerk and Keizersgracht) • Map L2 • Tram 13, 14, 17 • www.homomonument.nl*

4 Huis met de Hoofden

An eye-catching extravaganza, the House with the Heads is named for the six heads on its elaborate step-gabled façade representing Classical gods – Apollo, Ceres, Mars, Minerva, Diana and Bacchus. Built in 1622 for a successful merchant, its Dutch Renaissance design is attributed to Hendrick de Keyser. The ground floor has scarcely changed. *Keizersgracht 123 • Map L2 • Closed to the public except on Monumentendagen (see p70)*

Hazenstraat, Jordaan

5 Jordaan

Quirky and characterful, with an intimate, easy-going atmosphere all its own, the Jordaan is a dense patch of small-scale streets and canals peppered with interesting shops and galleries, charming *hofjes* and inviting brown cafés. Bounded by Prinsengracht and Lijnbaansgracht to east and west, and Brouwersgracht and Looiersgracht to north and south, it was built for workers at the same time as the Grachtengordel *(see p11)*. ✎ *Map K3*

6 Zon's and De Star Hofjes

These two delightful *hofjes* are close to one another on Prinsengracht. At Zon's Hofje, a stone plaque depicting Noah's Ark is a clue that it was built on the site of a clandestine church known by that name. The De Star – officially Van Brienen – Hofje is named after a brewery that stood on this site. Merchant Jan Van Brienen is said to have built it in gratitude for his release from a vault in which he had accidently been locked. ✎ *Zon's Hofje: Prinsengracht 159–171. Map D2. Open 10am–5pm Mon–Fri • De Star Hofje: Prinsengracht 89–133. Open 6am–6pm Mon–Fri, 6am–2pm Sat*

7 Noordermarkt

By the entrance to the Noorderkerk *(see p42)*, a still-flourishing Protestant church, a sculpture commemorates the *Jordaanoproer* (Jordaan riot) of 1934, in which seven people died during demonstrations against cuts in unemployment benefits. Today the tranquil surrounding square, a market site since 1627, comes to life during the Monday flea market and the Saturday bird market and *boerenmarkt*, selling organic produce. ✎ *Map D2 • Flea market: 9am–1pm Mon • Boerenmarkt: 9am–4pm Sat*

8 Brouwersgracht

If you stand at the breezy junction of Brouwersgracht and Prinsengracht you will get terrific views in all directions, and a sense of the sea not far away. Today, Brouwersgracht, with its pretty bridges and picturesque houseboats, is a romantic delight, but a 17th-century brewery (*brouwer*) worker would be astonished to find that the spout-gabled warehouses of this once reeking industrial canal had now been converted into the smartest of private housing – particularly fine examples of which you can see at Nos 188–194. ✎ *Map D1*

Hofjes

Secretive and intimate, Amsterdam's *hofjes* – almshouses for the needy built by wealthy merchants in the 17th and 18th centuries – are part of the city's charm. Unobtrusive street entrances lead to pretty houses (sometimes still used for their original purpose) around a flower-filled garden or courtyard. Visitors are usually admitted, but they are asked to respect residents' privacy.

9 Haarlemmerbuurt

In recent times, the bustling streets of this stalwart residential neighbourhood have seen the arrival of all manner of shops, mixing bric-a-brac with *haute couture*, New Age with funky furniture and specialist food with local groceries. On Haarlemmerstraat is Westindisch Huis, once the headquarters of the Dutch West India Company *(see p45)*. To the west is Haarlemmerpoort, a gateway – now converted into flats – built in 1840 for the entry of William II. Beyond it lies peaceful Westerpark, and Westergasfabriek, former gasworks turned arts centre. *Map D1*

10 Western Islands

Despite being very much part of the city, the man-made Western Islands have a remote, bracing quality. Comprising Bickerseiland, Prinseneiland and Realeneiland, they were created in the early 17th century to accommmodate shipyards and warehouses. In recent years, large-scale development has taken place, and modern housing now co-exists in harmony with white wooden drawbridges. Don't miss Zandhoek on Realeneiland, with its row of charming 17th-century houses, or atmospheric Prinseneiland with its boatyard and old shuttered warehouses. *Map D1*

Boatyard, Prinseneiland

Exploring the Western Canal Ring

Morning

Beat the queues and be first to arrive at the **Anne Frank Huis** *(see pp32–3)*, which opens at 9am. Afterwards, you could take a contemplative walk along Prinsengracht to the Western Islands, perhaps first climbing the tower of **Westerkerk** *(see p91)*. On the way, drop in on two peaceful *hofjes*, **Zon's** and **De Star** *(see facing page)*. For refreshment, visit Papeneiland, a tiny brown café founded in 1642, at the junction of Prinsengracht and Brouwersgracht.

On the **Western Islands**, stroll round Prinseneiland and along Zandhoek on Realeneiland, where you could lunch very well at De Gouden Reael (Zandhoek 14). If you are with children, visit Dierencapel, the children's farm on Bickerseiland.

Afternoon

En route to the Jordaan, hardened shoppers will first want to stop in **Haarlemmerbuurt**, with its mix of shops, both smart and tatty. Don't miss a peak at over-the-top Café Dulac (Haarlemmerstraat 118), and the world's narrowest restaurant, De Groene Lanteerne (Haarlemmerstraat 43).

Spend a couple of hours exploring the endlessly picturesque **Jordaan**, then join today's breed of young Jordaanese in one of the trendy cafés around Noordermarkt – Finch or Proust, or the wildly kitsch Café Nol in Westerstraat. If it's dinner time, head for Manzano *(see p95)*, for good tapas and sangria.

Left **'t Smalle** Right **Finch**

Bars and Cafés

1 't Arendsnest

Over 130 types of Dutch beer are served at this specialist bar – with several on tap. On the last Sunday of each month, sample 10 different kinds in their informal tasting sessions. *Herengracht 90 • Map M1 • 020 421 2057*

2 Duende

Release the inner gypsy in this small, busy tapas bar in the Jordaan. Authentic atmosphere, value for money, and regular live music. Olé! *Lindengracht 62 • Map C2 • 020 420 6692 • €€*

3 Finch

This small watering-hole on the edge of a scenic square can get decidedly crowded. In summer, the hip local clientele spills out onto the square. *Noordermarkt 5 • Map D2 • 020 626 4461*

4 P96

This peaceful bar opens around 8pm in the evenings and stays open later than most. The premises extend in the summer to an outdoors terrace on a fairy-lit barge. *Prinsengracht 96 • Map L1 • 020 622 1864*

5 Harlem

This rustic café serves wholesome "soul food" plus hearty sandwiches and fruit shakes. *Haarlemmerstraat 77 • Map D2 • 020 330 1498*

6 Stout!

Minimalist café drawing a hip crowd who come for the latest trends in international cuisine and the fine wines. *Haarlemmerstraat 77 • Map D2 • 020 616 3664 • €€€*

7 't Smalle

Originally a liquor distillery, this split-level brown bar is now a discerning wine-café. A must-see. *Egelantiersgracht 12 • Map L1*

8 Sound Garden

Don't let the tattoos, piercings and grunge factor put you off. This huge bar has a great atmosphere and some unusual beers on tap, too. *Marnixstraat 164–166 • Map J3 • 020 620 2853*

9 Tabac

Tabac used to be a brown café but has recently succumbed to the lounge trend. Locals notice, visitors may not. *Brouwersgracht 101 • Map D2 • 020 622 4413*

10 Twee Zwaantjes

Open from mid-afternoon until the early hours, The Two Swans is an authentic Jordaan bar where you will hear live – mostly accordion – music unique to this once working-class district. *Prinsengracht 114 • Map L2 • 020 625 2729*

Spanjer & Van Twist

Price Categories

For a three-course meal for one with half a bottle of wine (or equivalent meal), taxes and extra charges.

€	under €20
€€	€20–€30
€€€	€30–€45
€€€€	€45–€60
€€€€€	over €60

Top 10 Restaurants

1 Balraj

The sister of Beatrix, Queen of the Netherlands, is a regular diner at this well-priced restaurant offering some of the best Indian food in town. *Haarlemmerdijk 28 • Map D1 • 020 625 1428 • €€*

2 De Belhamel

The charm and ambience of this canalside restaurant make up for the somewhat variable quality of the food. *Brouwersgracht 60 • Map D2 • 020 622 1095 • €€€*

3 De Bolhoed

Undoubtedly one of the most charming restaurants in the area. Delicious, well-priced vegetarian (and vegan) food with a wicked dessert selection. *Prinsengracht 60 • Map L1 • 020 626 1803 • €€*

4 Christophe

This restaurant's one-Michelin star owner-chef may have moved on, but its renowned quality has not diminished. Expect gastronomic French fare and an excellent wine list. *Leliegracht 46 • Map L2 • 020 625 0807 • €€€€€*

5 Foodism

A great little place tucked away in this narrow street. Delicious, healthy food, including a wide range of vegetarian options. *Oude Leliestraat 8 • Map M2 • 020 427 5103 • €*

6 Werck

A few doors down from the Anne Frank Huis *(see pp32–3)*, this lounge-style establishment serves creative international dishes. *Prinsengracht 277 • Map K2 • 020 612 3021 • €€€*

7 Manzano

Reached through a courtyard, this authentic Spanish tapas bar offers a good, inexpensive menu and copious sangria. *Rozengracht 106 • Map K3 • 020 624 5752 • €€*

8 Spanjer & Van Twist

The perfect place to rest those weary feet. Hole yourself up for the afternoon in the second-floor window seat. *Leliegracht 60 • Map L2 • 020 639 0109 • €€*

9 Toscanini

Despite its quiet location and deceptive size (it's huge inside), this superb Italian restaurant gets quickly booked up. The cooks create delicious dishes from an open kitchen. *Lindengracht 75 • Map C2 • 020 623 2813 • €€€*

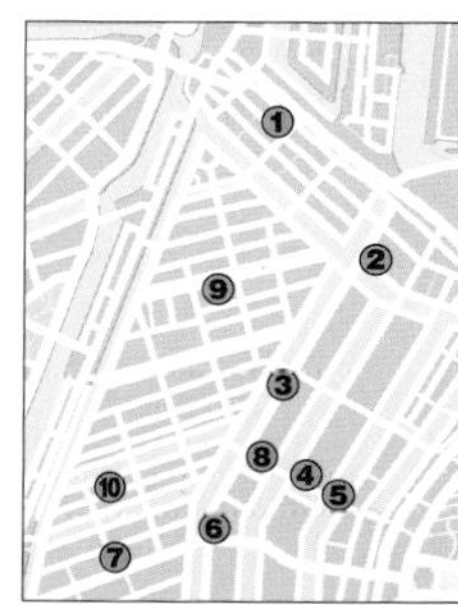

10 De Vliegende Schotel

Slow service, but infinitely worth it for the huge portions of delicious vegetarian food. House wine is the only alcohol served. *Nieuwe Leliestraat 162 • Map K2 • 020 625 2041 • €€*

Recommend your favourite restaurant on traveldk.com

Left **Donald E Jongejans** Right **Mechanisch Speelgoed**

Top 10 Shopping

1 Back Beat
Jools Holland and even Mick Jagger have popped into this new and second-hand record/CD shop specializing in jazz, soul, funk and R&B. Rare collector's items to be had. *Egelantiersstraat 19 • Map L1*

2 De Belly
Unable to wait for Saturday's organic market? Then head to this friendly organic store. Pulses, grains, candles, soaps, fresh fruit and vegetables, plus a good selection of wine and beer. *Nieuwe Leliestraat 174 • Map K2*

3 Big Shoe
Fashionable footwear for folk with big feet. *Leliegracht 12 • Map L2*

4 SPRMRKT
Spacious and perpetually intriguing, this store is an absolute must for style aficionados who have a discerning eye for retro clothing and accessories, furniture and fabrics. *Rozengracht 191–193 • Map J3*

5 Donald E Jongejans
Vintage frames specialist selling a fascinating selection of eyewear dating from the 1800s onwards. If it's shut, just check out the window display. *Noorderkerkstraat 18 • Map D2*

6 Unlimited Delicious
Savour the signature hot chocolate, bonbons and sublimely-flavoured pastries at this popular patisserie and chocolatier. *Haarlemmerstraat 122 • Map D2*

7 Kitsch Kitchen
Ample to spice up your kitchen and accessorize the cooks. Pop across the nearby Rozengracht to number 183, where "Kitsch Kitchen Kids" has a range for the little people. *Rozengracht 8–12 • Map K3*

8 Mechanisch Speelgoed
A fascinating, nostalgia-inducing collection of mechanical toys and good old-fashioned children's playthings. Simply put: life before Gameboy. *Westerstraat 67 • Map D2*

9 Pasta Panini
A fabulous Italian deli. Great for freshly-filled ciabattas at lunchtime or hand-made pasta for supper. Plus a tantalizing range of cookies, soup, sauces and wine. *Rozengracht 82 • Map K3*

10 papabubble
The caramel artisans in this store produce their unique, hand-crafted candy on site. Tahitian lime and bergamot are just some of the flavours used. *Haarlemmerdijk 70 • Map D1*

Left **GO Gallery** Right **Pancake Bakery**

TOP 10 Best of the Rest

1 Avondverkoop Dolf

In a town which doesn't quite have the 24/7 American mentality, this late-night store can be a Godsend – even if it is a little pricey. General groceries and a good range of alchohol. *Willemstraat 79 • Map D1*

2 Architectura & Natura

Bookshop and publisher specialising in architecture, gardening and natural history. Knowledgeable staff and a wide selection of English-language books. *Leliegracht 22 • Map L2*

3 't Geveltje

Beginners and pros jam together in the Jordaan's famous jazz bar for musicians and jazz aficionados alike. Pros play every Friday. Closed Saturdays and Sundays. *Bloemgracht 170 • Map J2*

4 GO Gallery

Friendly neighbourhood gallery hosting shows with figurative and abstract art by international artists. *Prinsengracht 64 • Map L1*

5 Meeuwig & Zn.

Stockists of a prodigious range of olive oils selected from small farmers around the Med. Also, vinegars, mustards and spices. *Haarlemmerstraat 70 • Map D2*

6 Jordaan Festival

The "Jordaaners" are fiercely proud of the accordion-laden oompah songs unique to this area. Over one weekend mid-September, stages are set up on this filled-in canal, and the beer and bellowing flow. *Westermarkt • Map L2 • 020 626 5587 • www.jordaanfestival.nl*

7 Petticoat

Vintage clothing and accessories including a great collection of 1950s dresses and petticoats. *Lindengracht 99 • Map D2*

8 Pancake Bakery

Although unashamedly touristy, you could do a lot worse than this restaurant in a former 17th-century warehouse named "Hope" to sample the local fare. *Prinsengracht 191 • Map L1*

9 Paradox

A paradox in itself, this coffeeshop shows few traces of serving "the herb". Fresh fruit and veg shakes, healthy food and a bright interior make it a perfect place for breakfast or lunch. *Eerste Bloemdwarsstraat 2 • Map K2*

10 Small World

Simply the best quick-stop for sandwiches, carrot cake and other delicious offerings. *Binnen Oranjestraat 14 • Map D1*

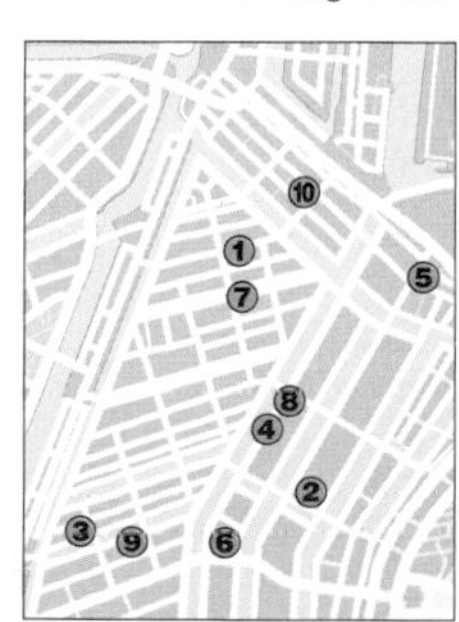

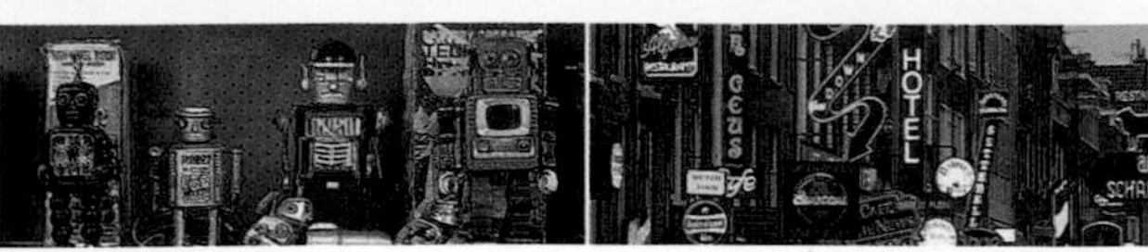

Left **Vintage robots for sale at the Looier Kunst an Antiekcentrum** Right **Leidseplein at night**

Central Canal Ring

AMSTERDAM'S THREE GREAT CANALS, *Herengracht, Keizersgracht and Prinsengracht, are at their most impressive in this central section of the Grachtengordel (see p11), which culminates in the stretch known as the Golden Bend, where the wealthiest Amsterdammers built stately houses in the 1660s. Designed and decorated by the best architects of the day, such as Philips Vingboons, the mansions built here were often twice the width of standard canal houses. Nowadays, many of these buildings are occupied by institutions. In contrast, the intimate cross-streets that run between the three canals, known as De Negen Straatjes (The Nine Streets) enticingly display the city's talent for creative retail. Another magnet for shoppers is Metz & Co, which provides a bird's-eye view of the whole area from its top-floor café. Cutting through this elegant district is the main thoroughfare, Leidsestraat, which culminates in the brash and lively entertainment hub, Leidseplein. Architectural highlights include the Paleis van Justitie and the American Hotel.*

1891 turret, Metz & Co

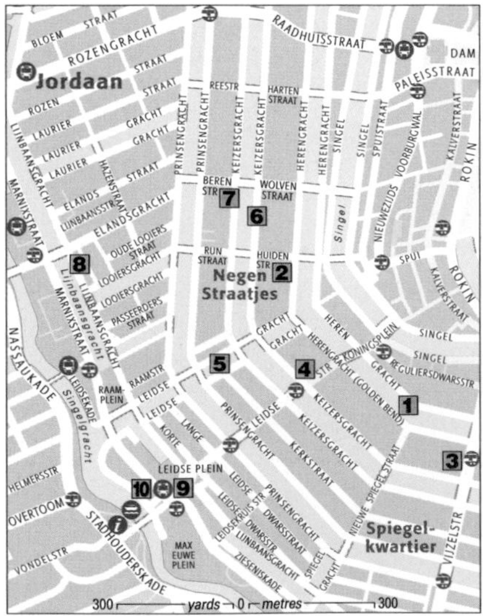

Top 10 Sights

1. Golden Bend
2. Bijbels Museum
3. Stadsarchief
4. Metz & Co
5. Leidsegracht
6. Negen Straatjes
7. Felix Meritis Building
8. Looier Kunst en Antiekcentrum
9. Leidseplein
10. American Hotel

Model of Temple Mount, Jerusalem, Bijbels Museum

1 Golden Bend

So named because of the concentration of wealth amongst its first residents, this stretch of the Herengracht between Vijzelstraat and Leidsestraat feels grand but bland, unless you pick out eye-catching details as you stroll. Look out for Louis XIV-style No. 475, said to be Amsterdam's most beautiful house; and No. 476, elegantly restyled in the 1730s and topped with an eagle. No. 497 is open to the public, but you have to like cats: it's the Kattenkabinet, a unique museum devoted to cats in art. Be careful not to trip over one of the many feline attendants. *Kattenkabinet: Herengracht 497 • Map M6 • 020 626 5378 • www.kattenkabinet.nl • Open 10am–2pm Tue–Fri, 1–5pm Sat–Sun • Admission charge*

2 Bijbels Museum

Far lovelier than the Golden Bend is the stretch of Herengracht between Huidenstraat and Leidsestraat, particularly Nos 364–70, four houses built by Philips Vingboons in 1662. Two of them house the Bible Museum, where apart from biblical artifacts you can admire the early-18th-century interior and take a stroll in the peaceful garden. *Heren-gracht 366–368 • Map L5 • 020 624 2436 • www.bijbelsmuseum.nl • Open 10am–5pm Mon–Sat, 11am–5pm Sun • Closed 1 Jan, 30 Apr • Admission charge*

3 Stadsarchief

The Stadsarchief, which houses the city's municipal archives, has moved from its old location in Amsteldijk and now occupies a monumental building designed by the Amsterdamse School architect De Bazel. It was completed in 1926 and is full of original features. One of the largest buildings in the city centre, it was originally the headquarters of the Netherlands Trading Corporation (now ABN Amro). *Vijzelstraat 32 • Map 4 F2 • Tram 16, 24, 25 • 251 1510 • www.stadsarchief.amsterdam.nl • Open 10am–5pm Tue–Sat, 11am–5pm Sun • Closed public holidays*

4 Metz & Co

The great attraction of this pondorous late-19th-century building (apart, of course, from the five floors of luxury goods on sale) is its sixth-floor cupola and café, with superb views of the canal ring below. Originally built for an insurance company in 1891, it was taken over by Metz & Co in 1908. Gerrit Rietveld added his splendid glass cupola in 1933. In 1973, Liberty of London bought the business, renovated the building and commissioned Cees Dam to design the sixth-floor café. *Leidsestraat 34–36 • Map L6 • 020 520 7020 • Open 11am–6pm Mon, 9:30am–6pm Tue–Sat, noon–5pm Sun*

The Stadsarchief

5 Leidsegracht

For dream canal houses in pristine condition, look no further than sophisticated Leidsegracht, one of the city's most sought-after addresses. At Herengracht 394, on the corner with Leidsegracht, notice the fine wall plaque depicting characters from a medieval legend – the four *Heemskinderen* on their horse Beyaart. Another plaque, at No. 39, shows Cornelis Lely, who drew up the original plans for draining the Zuiderzee. *Map K6*

6 Negen Straatjes

Nestling in the centre of the canal ring are these three parallel rows of cross-streets bordered by Singel and Prinsengracht to east and west, and Raadhuisstraat and Leidsegracht to north and south. Known collectively as the Nine Streets, these charming, largely car-free roads were once a centre for the leather trade. Today they are packed with amusing, imaginative and sometimes eccentric shops like De Witte Tandenwinkel, devoted to toothbrushes *(see p104)*. In Gasthuismolensteeg, don't miss the Brilmuseum at No. 7, an enchanting museum and shop devoted to spectacles old and new (open noon–5pm Wed–Sat). *Map L4*

Houseboats

Around 2,500 houseboats are called "home" in Amsterdam, but it was only after World War II, when there was a severe housing shortage, that they became popular. Though linked to the electricity and water supplies, they use the canals (which are flushed out nightly) for sewage disposal. Visit the Woonbootmuseum (Houseboat Museum) opposite Prinsengracht 296 to find out more.

Felix Meritis Building

7 Felix Meritis Building

The splendid Neo-Classical façade of this building comes as a surprise on gabled Keizersgracht. Designed in 1787 by Jacob Otten Husly as a science and arts centre (the name Felix Meritis means "happiness through merit"), it flourished until the late 19th century. Later, it became headquarters of the Dutch Communist Party (CPN), and in the 1970s was home to the avant-garde Shaffy Theatre Company. Today, it houses the European Centre for Arts and Sciences – its arts complex and Summer University courses mean it is always humming. *Keizersgracht 324 • Map L4 • 020 623 1311 • www.felix.meritis.nl*

8 Looier Kunst en Antiekcentrum

If the smart shops of the Spiegelkwartier *(see p112)* are too expensive and rarified, try searching for more affordable antiques in this warren of stalls occupying a vast network of ground-floor rooms in a block of houses near the Looiersgracht (tanners' canal). Taken together, this is the largest collection of art and antiques in the Netherlands. The stall-holders have a lively community spirit, hosting bridge sessions which are open to all. *Elandsgracht 109 • Map J5 • Open 11am–5pm Sat–Thu • www.looier.com*

9 Leidseplein

The city's tourist hub. Sophisticated it is not, tacky and fun (and, at night, often raucous) it is, especially in summer, when buskers and street performers, from family pop groups to lone fire-eaters, keep the milling throngs amused. Despite its rambling, dog-leg shape, Leidseplein is a natural gathering place, packed with fast food stalls, cafés and smoking coffee shops. Nightspots De Melkweg, Paradiso, and Holland Casino are close at hand, while for a more reflective diversion you can play chess on a giant outdoor chessboard in adjacent Max Euweplein, or stroll in the tiny Leidsebos park. *Map C5*

10 American Hotel

Leidseplein's most famous landmark is this one-off Dutch interpretation of Art Nouveau by Willem Kromhout (1902), which foretold the Amsterdam School of architecture. Only the exterior is of interest: the interior is as bland as any other chain hotel (in this case, Crowne Plaza). The exception is the hotel's famous Café Americain, with its stained-glass windows and glass parasol lampshades. The literati who once inhabited it may have disappeared, but it's a welcome haven from the rigours of Leidseplein. *Map C5*

Looking towards the American Hotel

Exploring the Central Canal Ring

Morning

This compact area is focused on Amsterdam's most famous canals, so why not start the day with a canal tour. Amsterdam Canal Cruises start and end on Singelgracht, opposite the Heineken Brewery. From here, it's a short walk to **Leidseplein** and welcome refreshment at the **Café Americain**.

Leaving the hubbub of Leidseplein, walk along Prinsengracht (passing the Paleis van Justitie, once the city orphanage) to elegant **Leidsegracht**. If there's time, investigate the antiques market, **Looier**, in Elandsgracht. For lunch, try brown cafés Van Puffelen or Het Molenpad, or designer hang-out Het Land van Walem *(see p102)*.

Afternoon

Plunge into the **Negen Straatjes** for some serious shopping in its frivolous shops. You may not be able to resist the cakes and chocolate on offer at Chocolaterie Pompadour *(see p104)*. Pop into the Woonbootmuseum, moored on Prinsengracht opposite Elandsgracht, to marvel at how a bargeman and his family could have lived in such a tiny space. Then cross to Herengracht, which you will have seen earlier from the water, and stroll along, admiring its architectural gems around the **Bijbels Museum** and **Golden Bend** *(see p99)*. If it's before 6pm (9pm on Thu, 5pm on Sun), end the afternoon with a bird's eye view of your day's exploration from the sixth-floor café at **Metz & Co** *(see p99)*.

For more on canal tours **See pp10 and 136**

Left **The Bar With No Name** Right **Van Puffelen**

Top 10 Bars

1 De Admiraal
One of the smarter *proeflokalen* (tasting houses) in the city – and unlike the rest, it closes late. Collapse on the couches and knock back the liquors and *jenever*. ✎ *Herengracht 319 • Map L4 • 020 625 4334 • €€€*

2 The Bar With No Name
Known to the locals as Wolvenstraat, this 1970s-style lounge bar-restaurant is the haunt of young advertising darlings and other affluent beings. Open from breakfast to bedtime, it serves imaginative sandwiches, soup and pan-Asian cuisine. ✎ *Wolvenstraat 23 • Map L4 • 020 320 0843 • €€*

3 De Pels
A low-key, easygoing neighbourhood bar – locals read the papers at the big table by the window. A great place to recover from a hangover on a Sunday (breakfast is served until 1:30pm). ✎ *Huidenstraat 25 • Map L5*

4 Het Land van Walem
One of the city's original designer bars, this was the creation of renowned Dutch architect, Gerrit Rietveld. Inside, it's bright and minimalist; outside, there are charming terraces. ✎ *Keizersgracht 449 • Map L6*

5 Lux
Split-level, late-opening designer bar. DJs spin every night. ✎ *Marnixstraat 403 • Map K6*

6 Het Molenpad
A charming brown bar between the city's main library and the Leidsestraat – equally suitable for bookworms and the shopped-out. ✎ *Prinsengracht 653 • Map K5 • 020 625 9680 • €€*

7 Vyne
Wine bar-cum-Italian delicatessen with trademark interior by architect firm Concrete. ✎ *Prinsengracht 411 • Map K4*

8 Saarein II
Once an infamous women-only bar, now men are welcome. Quiet during the week, rowdy at weekends. Pool table, good bar food. ✎ *Elandsstraat 119 • Map K4*

9 Van Puffelen
The rich and beautiful flock to this elegant haunt – the biggest brown bar in town. ✎ *Prinsengracht 377 • Map K3 • 020 624 6270 • €€*

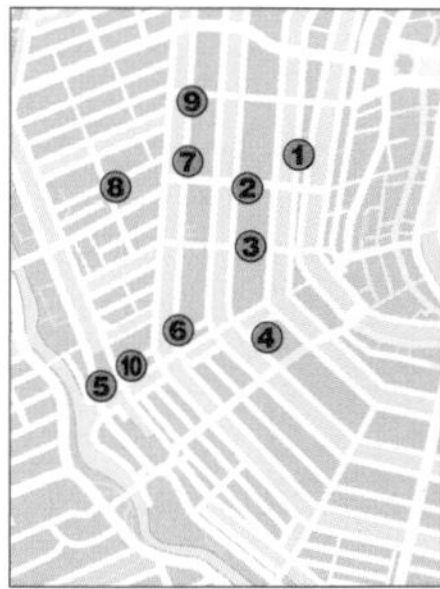

10 De Zotte
This Belgian bar (appropriately named "Drunken Fool") has a huge range of beers. Delicious food helps soak it all up. ✎ *Raamstraat 29 • Map K6 • 020 626 8694 • €€*

Recommend your favourite bar on traveldk.com

Price Categories

For a three-course meal for one with half a bottle of wine (or equivalent meal), taxes and extra charges.

€	under €20
€€	€20–€30
€€€	€30–€45
€€€€	€45–€60
€€€€€	over €60

Wagamama

Top 10 Restaurants

1 The Dylan

Save this restaurant located in Anoushka Hempel's upmarket hotel for a special occasion. The food is a fusion of French and eastern – highly creative, but at a cost *(see p144)*. *€€€€€*

2 Bojo

Inexpensive, informal and Indonesian – head here after most of the city's restaurants have gone to bed. *Lange Leidsedwarsstraat 49–51 • Map D5 • 020 622 7434 • €*

3 Goodies

A culinary delight in the heart of the Nine Streets. Healthy soups, salads and sandwiches by day; the perfect pasta by night. *Huidenstraat 9 • Map L5 • 020 625 6122 • €€*

4 Los Pilones

This Mexican cantina is small, but size isn't everything. Savour the authentic home cooking, between slams of tequila. *Kerkstraat 63 • Map L6 • 020 320 4651 • €€€*

5 Vuong

A member of the Jimmy Woo family *(see p54)*, this French-Vietnamese brasserie offers innovative Asian fusion cuisine and exquisite coffee. *Korte Leidsedwarsstraat 51 • Map K6 • 020 530 5577 • €€€*

6 Balthazar's Keuken

Book ahead for this unique, homely restaurant. Set three-course menu served Wednesday to Friday. *Elandsgracht 108 • Map K4 • 020 420 2114 • €€€*

7 Nomads

This late-night restaurant is the ultimate in decadent dining. Lounge on mattresses while food is served from bronze platters. DJs enhance the Arabian experience at weekends. *Rozengracht 133 • Map J3 • 020 344 6401 • €€€€*

8 Rakang

Totally authentic Thai; one of the best of its kind in the city. Those in the know load up at their cheaper, equally delicious take-away next door. *Elandsgracht 29–31 • Map K4 • 020 620 9551 • €€€*

9 Envy

This is one of Amsterdam's finest offerings. The chefs expertly combine flavours to create superb mediterranean delicacies. *Prinsengracht 381 • Map K4 • 020 344 6407 • €€€*

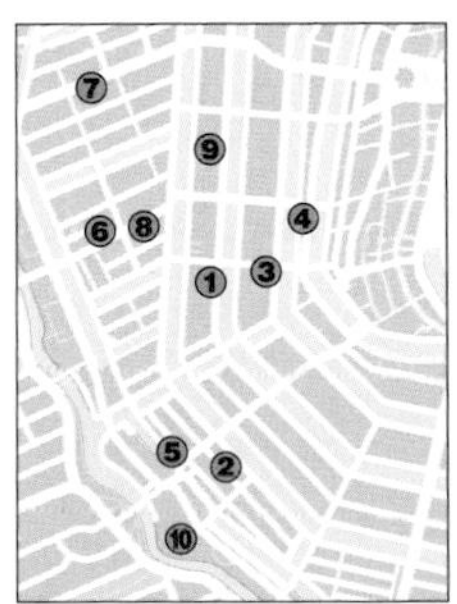

10 Wagamama

Fast food, slow service – but you could do worse for a quick lunch. Don't miss the king-size chess action taking place on the giant board outside. *Max Euweplein 10 • Map C5 • 020 528 7778 • €€*

Left **Pontifex** Right **Skins Cosmetics Lounge**

Top 10 Shopping (Nine Streets)

1 Bakkerij Paul Année

Where can you find the best bread in Amsterdam? At this organic baker's outlet, selling a delicious range of wholemeal bread and croissants, pizza, tofu *broodjes* and sugar-free oatcakes. *Runstraat 25 • Map K5*

2 Skins Cosmetics Lounge

An exclusive range of perfumes and cosmetics are on offer in this stark and laboratory-like shop. *Runstraat 9 • Map K5 • www.skins.nl*

3 De Kaaskamer

For cheese with a capital C, try "The Cheese Chamber", where there are over 200 different kinds of one of Holland's best exports. If it isn't here, it probably doesn't exist. *Runstraat 7 • Map K5*

4 Van Ravenstein

Exclusive boutique selling designer wear by well-known Dutch and Belgian couturiers including Dries van Noten. *Keizersgracht 359 • Map L5*

5 Brilmuseum/Brillenwinkel

This fascinating spectacles museum and shop, housed in a 1620 building, explores the history of glasses and sells vintage frames as well as contemporary models. *Gasthuismolensteeg 7 • Map L3*

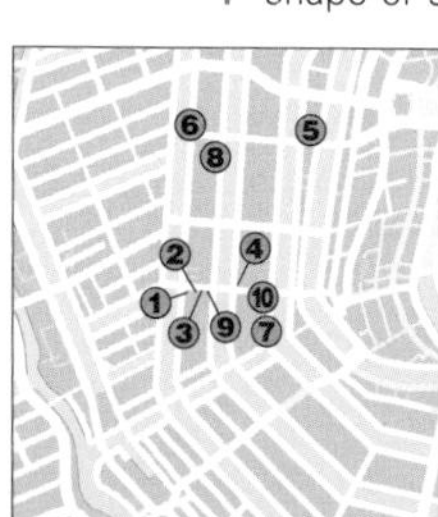

6 Pontifex

This tiny waxworks gives Madame Tussauds a run for their money, with a colourful range of candles of every type imaginable. Adjoining are the premises of the rather spooky doll doctor, Kramer. *Reestraat 20 • Map K3*

7 Chocolaterie Pompadour

You can pile on the calories just staring at the window display of this chic chocolaterie. Try the famous home-made chocolates or Pompadour's exquisite tarts. *Huidenstraat 12 • Map L5*

8 Fifties-Sixties

Iconic toasters, chrome ashtrays and lamps aplenty are just some of the retro gems from the 1950s and 1960s waiting to be discovered in this browsable shop. *Reestraat 5 • Map L3*

9 De Witte Tandenwinkel

A veritable ode to the tooth, this shop specializes in every shape or size of toothbrush imaginable, and is sure to take your (bad) breath away. Mouthy Mick Jagger has even dropped by. *Runstraat 5 • Map L5*

10 Zipper

Immaculately displayed vintage second-hand clothes and accessories. *Huidenstraat 7 • Map L5*

Left **Frozen Fountain** Right **Melkweg**

TOP 10 Best of the Rest

1 Bagels & Beans
American-style freshly-baked cookies and cheesecake, freshly-squeezed juices and (rare in Amsterdam) decent-sized cups of coffee. *Keizersgracht 504 • Map L5*

2 Ben & Jerry's
Forget the nearby Häagen-Dazs parlour – ice cream never tasted this good. *Leidsestraat 90 • Map K6*

3 Frozen Fountain
Arguably, Amsterdam's most important designer store and exhibition space for furniture and household products. A revered international reputation for its cutting-edge designs and fresh talent makes it a must-see. *Prinsengracht 629 • Map K5*

4 Urban Home & Garden Tours
Garden designer André Ancion gives English-language walking tours delving behind the façades of some of the city's most impressive canal houses. *020 688 1243 • www.uhgt.nl*

5 Melkweg
Known in the 1970s as an alternative clutural meeting place, today this former milk factory hosts live music events. Plus there's a cinema, theatre, gallery, café-bar, upstairs bar and video room (*see p57*).

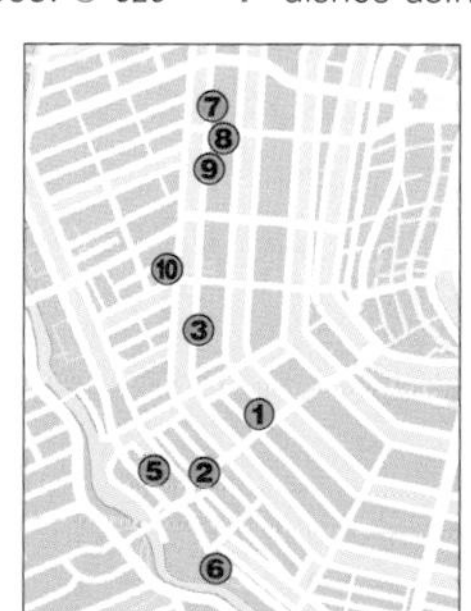

6 Paradiso
One of Amsterdam's bestloved live music spots. Velvet Underground and Macy Gray have played here. The upstairs hall often has unknowns before they go big. *Weteringschanss 6-8 • Map C5 • 020 626 4521 • www.paradiso.nl*

7 Hotel Pulitzer
August, at this prestigious hotel, is the time when hampers and champagne come out in full force and a floating stage is set up out front for the unmissable Grachtenfestival's open-air classical concerts. *Prinsengracht 315–331 • Map K3*

8 Cortina Papier
A wonderful selection of beautiful, handbound books and albums, printed and marbled wrapping papers, and inks in all colours. *Reestraat 22 • Map K3*

9 Raïnaraï
An utterly charming Algerian deli producing delicious, authentic dishes using spices imported from the North African country. Takeaway, but also a few seats inside. *Prinsengracht 252 • Map K3*

10 La Tertulia
A mother and daughter run this bright, split-level canalside coffeeshop. *Prinsengracht 312 • Map K5*

Left **Munttoren** Right **Dray horses at the Heineken Experience**

Eastern Canal Ring

BEGUN IN THE EARLY 17TH CENTURY, *the Grachtengordel* (see p11) *was extended further east to reach the Amstel in the 1660s, making new plots of land available for wealthy merchants to build their luxurious if sober town houses. Among the highlights of the area are two such patrician mansions, the Museum Van Loon and the Museum Willet-Holthuysen. Medieval Amsterdam is recalled at the Munttoren, whose base was once part of the Regulierspoort, a gate in the city wall; by contrast, you can see the modern city in full swing in lively Rembrandtplein, formerly a butter market. There are diverse opportunities for shopping among the antiques of the Spiegelkwartier, at the colourful Bloemenmarkt, and at vibrant Albert Cuypmarkt; or you could catch a movie at Abraham Tuschinski's extraordinary 1921 cinema, now lovingly restored and offering six screens. And to refresh the parts that other beers may or may not be able to reach, you can visit the original Heineken Brewery for a guided tour and a free beer.*

Tuschinski Theatre

Top 10 Sights

1. Museum Van Loon
2. Museum Willet-Holthuysen
3. Amstel River
4. Rembrandtplein
5. Tuschinski Theatre
6. Munttoren
7. Bloemenmarkt
8. Spiegelkwartier
9. Heineken Experience
10. Albert Cuypmarkt

1 Museum Van Loon

A chance to see inside a private canal house, whose grand yet approachable 18th-century interior recreates a bygone age *(see pp30–31)*.

2 Museum Willet-Holthuysen

Though it lacks the lived-in feel of the Museum Van Loon, this 17th-century canal house has its own special atmosphere. An air of stiff formality tinged with melancholy pervades its stately rooms: the Ballroom; the Blue Room, reserved for the men of the house, with painted ceiling by Jacob de Wit; the glittering Dining Room; and the delicate Garden Room, with views over the formal garden. The collections of its last owners, Sandrina Holthuysen and her husband, Abraham Willet, are displayed throughout – paintings, glass, ceramics, silver. The top floors are used for temporary exhibitions. It was the widowed Sandrina who left the house and its contents to the city. She died a lonely death in 1885. *Herengracht 605 • Map P6 • Tram 4, 9, 14 • 020 523 1822 • www.museumwilletholthuysen.nl • Open 10am–5pm Mon–Fri, 11am–5pm Sat & Sun • Closed 1 Jan, 30 Apr, 25 Dec • Admission charge*

Museum Willet-Holthuysen

Magere Brug

3 Amstel River

No visit to Amsterdam is complete without a walk along the banks of the Amstel, the river whose mouth spawned a fishing settlement in the 12th century *(see p38)*. In 1222 the river was dammed, and Amsterdam turned from fishing to trade – the beginning of its expansion. Commercial barges still ply the river, passing Blauwbrug (Blue Bridge), inspired by the *belle époque* Pont Alexandre III in Paris, the muchloved Magere Brug *(see p11)*, and the Amstelsluizen (sluice gates), which help to pump millions of gallons of fresh water into the canals to keep them from stagnating. *Map P5 • Tram 4, 7, 9, 10, 14*

4 Rembrandtplein

This former butter market has what you might call a split personality. In its centre is a 19th-century statue of Rembrandt set in a tranquil garden, but around its sides are neon-lit, low-brow and – at night – high-octane bars and cafés, packed with Amsterdammers and visitors alike. This is a great place for an early evening drink; you might choose grand cafés Schiller *(see p113)* and De Kroon *(see p50)*, as popular at the turn of the 20th century as they are now. *Map N6 • Tram 4, 9, 14*

5 Tuschinski Theatre

Amsterdam's – perhaps the world's – most elaborate cinema was the extraordinary creation of a self-made Jewish tailor from Poland. Obsessed by film and the belief that it could change lives, he built this cinema, in 1921, in a slum known as Devil's Corner. He was later to perish in Auschwitz, but his wonderful creation – loosely Art Nouveau, but termed Tuschinski Style for its unique mixture of influences – lives on. In 2002 it reopened, after a multi-million dollar renovation. In the process, hitherto unknown paintings of Vogue-style ladies were uncovered, and the theatre has been returned to its former glory. Buy a ticket for Screen One to admire the main theatre before the lights go down. *Reguliersbreestraat 26–28 • Map N6 • Tram 4, 9, 14*

6 Munttoren

Take a close look at the Mint Tower (it was briefly used as the city mint in 1673). Its bottom half is the remnant of a gate in the medieval city wall. When the gate burned down in 1618, Hendrick de Keyser slapped one of his clock towers *(see p42)* on top of the remains. The carillon of 1699 rings every 15 minutes.

Flower Power

The Dutch adore flowers, particularly tulips. They are everywhere, on window boxes, in houses, in shops and markets. You can buy bulbs at the Bloemenmarkt, visit the vast flower auction at Aalsmeer and the spring spectacle at Keukenhof *(see p72-3)*, and cycle through the bulbfields near Leiden. But you won't find the mythical black tulip: it doesn't exist, though breeders are getting very close to it.

Blooms at the Bloemenmarkt

Today, there is a gift shop on the ground floor. *Map N5 • Tram 4, 9, 14, 16, 24, 25*

7 Bloemenmarkt

Undoubtedly one of Amsterdam's most picturesque sights, the flower market is a magnet for tourists. There are local shoppers too, buying armfuls for their houses, while visitors arrange for bulbs to be mailed home. Vendors once sailed up the Amstel from their nurseries to this spot on the Singel, selling their wares directly from their boats. Nowadays the stalls are still floating, though you wouldn't know it as they feel firmly fixed. *Map M5 • Tram 1, 2, 4, 5, 9, 14, 16, 24, 25*

8 Spiegelkwartier

In the late 19th century, specialist antique dealers with an eye for an opportunity began to set up shop on Nieuwe Spiegelstraat, leading to the newly opened Rijksmuseum. There are more than 80 of them in the area now, making it a sparkling, elegant place in which to stroll. Content yourself with looking longingly at the gleaming displays of antique furniture, porcelain and glass, or treat yourself to a faded old Delft tile for just a few euros from Kramer *(see p112)*. *Map D5 • Tram 1, 2, 5, 16, 24, 25*

9 Heineken Experience

The biggest draw to Heineken's former brewery, which ceased production here in 1988, must be the free beer at the end of the tour (if you are over 18). On the way, you will learn the story of Holland's most famous brewery, walk through the brewhouse with its huge copper stills, and visit the stables. Dray horses are still seen carting beer, but only for publicity purposes. Recent additions include a mini-brewery and tasting bar. *Stadhouderskade 78 • Map D6 • Tram 16, 24 • 020 523 9666 • www.heinekenexperience.com • Open 10am–6pm (box office 5pm) Tue–Sun Closed 1 Jan, 25 Dec • Admission charge*

10 Albert Cuypmarkt

Shabby but vibrant, De Pijp is a district where a wide mix of immigrants, artists, students and young couples create a heady atmosphere. Albert Cuypmarkt, which has been trading since 1904, is its bustling hub. The street it occupies, once a canal, was named after Dutch landscape painter Albert Cuyp. With around 350 stalls, backed by all manner of shops and ethnic restaurants, it's an unmissable experience. Typically Dutch food stalls – cheese, fish, waffles – jostle merrily with clothes, fabrics, shoes and bags. *Albert Cuypstraat • Map D6 • Tram 4, 16, 24, 25 • Open 9:30am–5pm Mon–Sat*

Smoked fish in Albert Cuypmarkt

Exploring the Eastern Canal Ring

Morning

On a fine stretch of the **Amstel River**, dainty Magere Brug makes a good spot to begin. Walking north, follow the river's curve, pausing at Amstel 104 and its equally crooked neighbours. Reaching **Munttoren**, wander along the **Bloemenmarkt**, then head out to Reguliersbreestraat to check out the incredible **Tuschinski Theatre** a little further along the street. Classic films are shown in the main theatre every second or third Sunday at 10:30am, Sep–Jul.

Chic Utrechtsestraat, with its appealing selection of restaurants, cafés, delicatessens, boutiques and galleries, is perfect for both shopping and lunch. The best Indonesian *rijsttafel* in town is served at Tujuh Maret *(see p61)*.

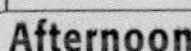

Afternoon

From Utrechtsestraat cross to Amstelveld, where the wooden Amstelkerk lends a countrified air, and Reguliersgracht *(see p8)* intersects picturesquely with Prinsengracht. Make your way along Prinsengracht, cross Vijzelstraat, and dive into Weteringbuurt. On the other side of Prinsengracht, admire elegant Deutzenhofje (Nos 855–99), erected in 1695 for destitute women.

From here, it's only a short walk to the **Museum Van Loon** *(see pp30–31)*, or a little further to **Museum Willet-Holthuysen** *(see p107)*, after which you can wind down with a drink in jolly Rembrandtplein. Best cafés are Schiller *(see p113)* and De Kroon *(see p50)*.

Check out new photography museum Foam at Keizersgracht 609.

Left **April** Right **Soho**

Top 10 Bars

1 April
A large, modern, comfortable gay bar that's great for reading a newspaper in the day or meeting up for drinks pre-clubbing. Unusual feature: the circular back bar revolves when it gets busy. *Reguliersdwarsstraat 37 • Map M6*

2 Sappho
This arty, "multisexual" bar has a DJ booth and small dance-floor. Open mic every Tuesday night. *Vijzelstraat 103 • Map D5*

3 De Duivel
Cypress Hill and The Roots have joined the boisterous baggy brigade at Amsterdam's small but legendary hip hop bar. These days, the hip hop is melted down with anything from funk to disco. *Reguliersdwarsstraat 87 • Map N6*

4 De Huyschkaemer
A corner-located, split-level designer bar popular with a young arty crowd. Great atmosphere and friendly staff. *Utrechtsestraat 137 • Map E5 • 020 627 0575*

5 Helden
Knock back the cocktails while a DJ spins chillout music and upbeat house at this lounge bar-cum-restaurant serving international cuisine. *Eerste van der Helststraat 42 • Map D6 • 020 673 3332 • €€€*

6 Kingfisher
With its modern take on the brown bar style, this large bar is one of the best watering-holes in the Pijp. Imaginative world cuisine. *Ferdinand Bolstraat 24 • Map D6 • 020 671 2395 • €*

7 Lellebel
Amsterdam's infamous – and only – dragshow bar, the complete antithesis of the testosterone-fuelled Rembrandt-plein nearby. At first glance it's unremarkable, but when Shirley Bassey is turned up on the soundsystem, the bar staff perform quite some routine. *Utrechtsestraat 4 • Map P6*

8 Mulligans
If you're tired of the Rembrandtplein, pop round the corner to this authentic Irish bar for some good *craic*. *Amstel 100 • Map P6*

9 Onder de Ooievaar
More of a wintertime bar, "Under the Stork" is warm, wooden and spacious. *Utrechtse-straat 119 • Map E5*

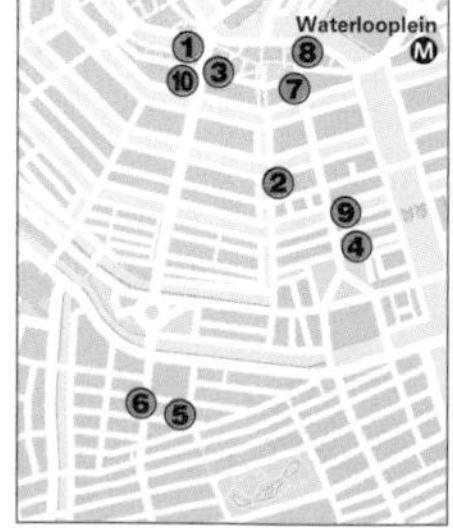

10 Soho
The "English pub formula" worked so well that Soho has become the biggest pint- and punter-puller on Amsterdam's trendy gay street. *Reguliers-dwarsstraat 36 • Map M6*

Zushi

Price Categories

For a three course meal for one with half a bottle of wine (or equivalent meal), taxes and extra charges.

€	under €20
€€	€20–€30
€€€	€30–€45
€€€€	€45–€60
€€€€€	over €60

Top 10 Restaurants

1 Eufraat

The décor leaves a little to be desired, but the fresh food at this Assyrian café makes it perpetually popular. A favourite haunt of revered (and feared) Amsterdam food critic Johannes van Dam. *Eerste van der Helststraat 72 • Map D6 • 020 672 0579 • €*

2 The Golden Temple

Vegetarian restaurant run by American Sikhs offering a range of Indian, Middle Eastern and Mexican food with a home-cooked feel. *Utrechtsestraat 26 • Map E5 • 020 626 8650 • €*

3 De Waaghals

This restaurant serves organic vegetarian food as well as locally-brewed organic wine and beer. *Frans Halsstraat 29 • Map D6 • 020 679 9609 • €€€*

4 Bazar

Cheap and flavourful North African cuisine in the heart of Amsterdam's largest outdoor market, Albert Cuypmarkt *(see p61 & p109)*. *Albert Cuypstraat 182 • Map E6 • 020 675 0544 • €€*

5 Janvier

Enjoy excellent New Dutch cuisine in this friendly relaxed restaurant with outside tables. *Amstelveld 12 • Map E5 • 020 626 1199 • €€€*

6 Rose's Cantina

This Mexican cantina has Tex-Mex down to a tee – the food is varied and delicious, and the margaritas are served in pitchers! *Reguliersdwarsstraat 38 • Map M6 • 020 625 9797 • €€€*

7 Bouchon du Centre

Hanneke cooks fresh produce she's bought from the markets that day, and serves you from her open kitchen. One of the city's best kept secrets. *Falckstraat 3 • Map E5 • 020 330 1128 • €€€*

8 Utrechtsedwarstafel

Pick a number of courses, choose a range from simple to gastronomic, and leave the rest to the wine connoisseur and cook duo who run this unusual eaterie. *Utrechtsedwarsstraat 107-109 • Map E5 • 020 625 4189 • €€€€*

9 Beddington's

The menu at Jean Beddington's new restaurant is truly international, offering exciting dishes with hints of Japan, the Mediterranean and England. *Utrechtse-dwarsstraat 141 • Map E5 • 020 620 7393 • €€€€*

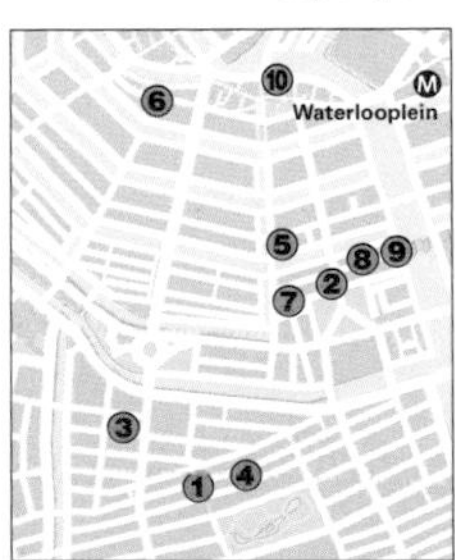

10 Zushi

Hyper-modern and hyped-up, this is the place to be if you like your sushi with a zing. *Amstel 20 • Map P6 • 020 330 6882 • €€*

Recommend your favourite restaurant on traveldk.com

Left **Tóth-Ikonen** Right **Aalderink**

TOP 10 Antique Shops

1 Aalderink
Aalderink is the oldest and most reputable dealer of Asian Art and Ethnographics in the Netherlands, specializing in fine Japanese *netsuke* and *okimono*. *Spiegelgracht 15 • Map D5*

2 Aronson Antiquairs
David Aronson opened this prestigious gallery around 1900; now it is run by his great-and great-great-grandsons. Early Delftware, continental 17th-and 18th-century furniture, plus Chinese *famille verte* and *famille rose* porcelain – much of it rare. *Nieuwe Spiegelstraat 39 • Map D5*

3 E H Ariëns Kappers / C P J van der Peet BV
A huge range of mid-16th- to mid-20th-century prints, including a remarkable selection of Japanese woodblock prints. *Nieuwe Spiegelstraat 32 • Map D5*

4 Staetshuys Antiquairs
A curiosity shop selling odd scientific instruments, globes and other unusual objects. *Nieuwe Spiegelstraat 45A • Map D5*

5 Frans Leidelmeijer
A testament to taste, this decorative arts shop was featured in an issue of *Wallpaper** not so long ago. *Lijnbaansgracht 369H • Map D5*

6 Eduard Kramer
Decorative Dutch tiles, Blue Delftware, antique books, prints, pewter, candlesticks and lamps. *Nieuwe Spiegelstraat 64 • Map D5*

7 Thom & Lenny Nelis
A fascinating collection of medical instruments dating from the early 18th to the early 20th century. Dissection kits, dental tools, apothecary accoutrements and much more! *Keizersgracht 541 • Map M6*

8 Tóth-Ikonen
The only icon specialist in the Spiegelkwartier, and the oldest in Amsterdam. Behold a dazzling array of 16th-to 19th-century Russian icons – including a large collection of brass travelling icons. *Nieuwe Spiegelstraat 68 • Map D5*

9 Marjan Sterk
An exquisite selection of antique, Art Deco and Art Nouveau jewellery, plus 18th- and 19th-century Dutch silver. *Nieuwe Spiegelstraat 63 • Map D5*

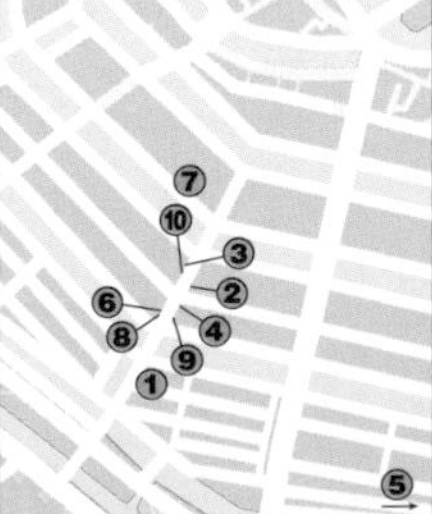

10 Van Dreven Antiquair
Alive with the sound of ticking, this shop proffers an eclectic selection of clocks from the early 17th century to the 1930s, plus a treasured collection of music boxes. *Nieuwe Spiegelstraat 38 • Map D5*

Left **NH Schiller** Right **Bloemenmarkt**

Top 10 Best of the Rest

1 Backstage
A bizarre café-cum-crochet store run by Gary, one half of the legendary "Christmas Twins", a US cabaret duo. Pop in here for some "foam in rome" (cappucino), a spontaneous horoscope reading by Gary, or simply for cake and gossip. *Utrechtsedwarsstraat 67 • Map E5*

2 Bloemenmarkt
The legendary floating flower market *(see p108)*.

3 Concerto
Simply the best record store in town; new and secondhand. *Utrechtsestraat 52–60 • Map E5*

4 Soup en Zo
This one-stop modern soup kitchen is just a short walk from the Rijksmuseum. Great for take-aways, but some seats are available. Over half the soups are vegetarian. *Nieuwe Spiegelstraat 54 • Map D5*

5 Hemp Hotel
Little escapes being hempified at this small, family-run hotel – from the hemp futons to the fresh hemp muffins served at breakfast, and the hemp beer served in the late-opening Hemple Temple Nightbar. *Frederiksplein 15 • Map E5 • 020 625 4425*

6 Heineken Experience
If you're here for the beer, this self-guided tour of the original Heineken brewery is a must. Entrance includes three glasses of the famous brew *(see p109)*.

7 Magere Brug
The city's best-known bridge – worth a wander for perfect photo opportunites, the stunning views, or simply to watch the drawbridge in action. Romantic at night when it's all lit up *(see p11)*.

8 The Otherside
For a perfectly pink joint, head to the city's only gay coffeeshop – a bright, modern, friendly place. *Reguliersdwarsstraat 6 • Map M6*

9 NH Schiller
The bar and restaurant are a gorgeous Art Nouveau escape from touristic Rembrandtplein. Owned for the best part of the last century by painter Frits Schiller, it was a regular meeting place for artists, and still has something of that atmosphere. Schiller's paintings are displayed throughout the premises *(see p146)*.

10 Village Bagels
Delicious bagels and fresh juices are served at this New York-style bagel shop. *Vijzelstraat 137 • Map D5*

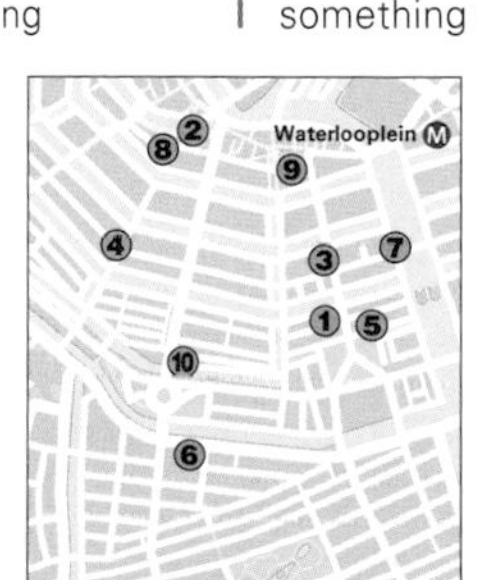

Left **Concertgebouw** Right **Café Vertigo, Filmmuseum**

Museum Quarter

UNTIL THE LATE 19TH CENTURY, *the Museum Quarter lay outside the city limits, a region of small farms and market gardens. Then the city council designated it an area of art and culture, and plans were conceived for the first of Amsterdam's celebrated cultural institutions. With its great museums of art, an internationally renowned concert hall, the city's largest park and a clutch of exclusive shopping streets, the Museum Quarter is today one of Amsterdam's most impressive areas.*

TOP 10 Sights

1. Rijksmuseum
2. Van Gogh Museum
3. Stedelijk Museum
4. Concertgebouw
5. Vondelpark
6. Coster Diamonds
7. Museumplein
8. Filmmuseum
9. Hollandsche Manege
10. P C Hooftstraat

Rijksmuseum

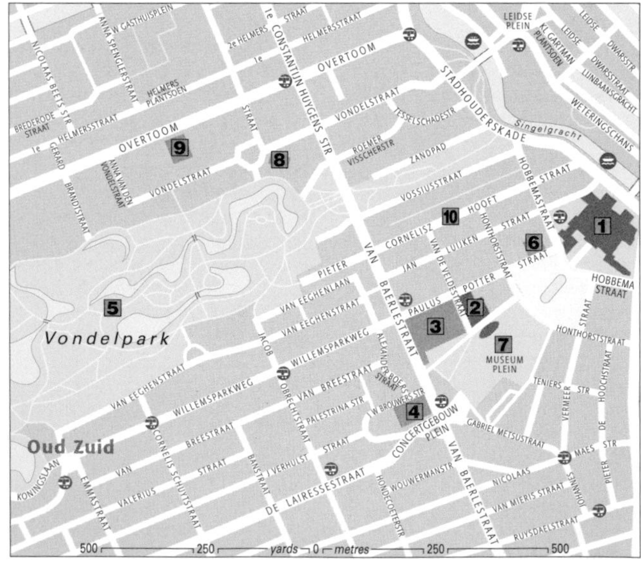

1 Rijksmuseum

Established by King Louis Napoleon in 1808 along the lines of the Paris Louvre, the Rijksmuseum collection has grown in the intervening years to nearly seven million works of art. It has moved twice since its beginnings in the Royal Palace on the Dam. Since 1885 it has been housed in P J H Cuypers' ornate Neo-Gothic building *(see pp12–15)*.

2 Van Gogh Museum

The uncompromisingly modern building by De Stijl architect Gerrit Rietveld was specially designed to display the nation's collection of this disturbed yet brilliant artist's work *(see pp16–19)*.

3 Stedelijk Museum

Devoted to modern art from the mid-19th century to the present day, this invigorating museum is undergoing a total renovation. The main building and stunning new addition, designed by Van Benthem Crouwel, will open in winter 2009 *(see p40)*. *Paulus Potterstraat 13 • Map C6 • Tram 2, 3, 5, 12 • 020 573 2911 • www.stedelijk.nl*

4 Concertgebouw

One of the world's great concert halls, the Concertgebouw was built in 1888, designed by A L Van Gendt in Neo-Dutch Renaissance style with a colonnaded Neo-Classical façade. In the 1980s, the building was discovered to be in danger of collapse. In time for the centenary of both the concert hall and its world-famous orchestra, new foundations were laid, and the building was restored and enlarged. Amazingly, all this took place without its having to close. *Concertgebouwplein 2–6 • Map C6 • Tram 3, 5, 12, 16, 24 • 020 671 8345 • www.concertgebouw.nl • Box office open 10am–8:15pm daily*

5 Vondelpark

Founded in 1864 by a group of philanthropic citizens, this congenial park was later named after the 17th-century poet Joost van den Vondel. Landscaped on informal English lines in 1865 – and enlarged in 1877 – by father and son J D and L P Zocher, with wide green vistas, a profusion of trees and lakes, a rose garden and a bandstand, it became a mecca for hippies in the late 1960s and 1970s. It is still a lively place on summer Sundays, when people flock to hear concerts and plays in the open-air theatre, glimpse the occasional juggler or fire-eater, jog, rollerblade or play football. There are many different species of plants, trees and wildlife. A distinctive landmark, looking a little like a neat boater turned upside-down, is the round Blauwe Theehuis (teahouse), built by H A J Baanders in 1936 in the New Functionalist style *(see p50)*. *Stadhouderskade • Map A6 • Tram 1, 2, 3, 5, 12*

Bandstand in Vondelpark

Share your travel recommendations on traveldk.com

Diamonds

Amsterdam has been a centre of diamond cutting, polishing and trading since the 16th century, when Jews, fleeing the Spanish Inquisition, brought the business to the city. The trade flourished in the late 19th century with the influx of Jews from Antwerp, many of them skilled in the industry, and with the import of diamonds from South Africa.

6 Coster Diamonds

Founded in 1840 and now occupying three grand villas, Coster is one of a handful of diamond workshops offering guided tours. About 30 minutes in length, they give you the opportunity to observe stone graders, cutters and polishers at work. In 1852, the *Koh-i-Noor* (mountain of light) diamond was re-polished here for the British Crown Jewels, and a replica of the crown that contains it – incorporating a copy of the fabulous blue-white stone – is displayed in the entrance hall. There are diamonds and jewellery for sale here as well as at the Diamond Museum next door. *PaulusPotterstraat 2–8 • Map C5 • Tram 2, 5 • 020 305 5555 • www.costerdiamonds.com • Open 9am–5pm daily • Free*

Coster Diamonds

7 Museumplein

The city's largest square was first landscaped in 1872, but it was ruined in 1953 when a hair-raising stretch of road – which locals nicknamed "the shortest motorway in Europe" – was built across it. Completely redesigned between 1990 and 1996, it is now a great swathe of green, still more functional than beautiful, but giving an uninterrupted view from the Rijksmuseum to the Concertgebouw. It has children's play areas and a pond that is frozen over to form an ice-rink in winter. Various events are staged here – from circuses to political demonstrations – and it is the setting for *Hel van Vuur* (Hell of Fire), a monument to all gypsies persecuted by the Nazis, as well as the Ravensbrück Memorial *(see p49)*. The district is one of the wealthiest in Amsterdam, with broad streets lined by grand houses. *Map C6 • Tram 2, 3, 5, 12, 16, 24*

8 Filmmuseum

"Museum" is a slight misnomer for this institution, as the Filmmuseum no longer has an exhibition. What it does have is an archive of more than 30,000 films, ranging from classic to art-house, a selection of which is screened here throughout the year. Part of the collection is housed in a glorious 19th-century pavilion at the edge of the Vondelpark. The building, designed by the architects P J Hamer and his son W Hamer, opened in 1881 as a fashionable teahouse. It has since undergone two major renovations, the first in 1947 and the second in 1991. *Vondelpark 3 • Map B5 • Tram 1, 3, 12 • Box Office: 020 589 1400. www.filmmuseum.nl • Library: Vondelstraat 69–71, 020 589 1435, Open 1–5pm Mon–Fri*

Hollandsche Manege

9 Hollandsche Manege

Magnificent and quite unexpected, concealed behind an unexceptional façade, A L van Gendt's Hollandsche Manege is a vast Neo-Classical indoor riding school, built in 1881. (It was commissioned to replace the original Dutch Riding School building, which was situated on Leidsegracht.) Based on the Spanish Riding School in Vienna, it sports elegant plasterwork, sculpted horses' heads, and a stunning open ironwork roof rising high above the sand arena. The school was threatened with demolition in the 1980s, but public outcry saved it. If there is a lesson in progress, you can stay and watch. There is also a decent café. *Vondelstraat 140 • Map B5 • Tram 1 • 020 618 0942 • Open 9am–midnight Mon–Fri, 9am–6pm Sat & Sun • Free*

10 P C Hooftstraat

This elegant shopping street is to Amsterdam what Bond Street is to London. All the names in international fashion are here – Tommy Hilfiger, Hugo Boss, DKNY, Gucci, Mulberry, Emporio Armani – although well-heeled locals tend to favour friendlier Cornelis Schuytstraat nearby. *Map C5 • Tram 1, 2, 3, 5, 12*

A Day in the Museum Quarter

Morning

Depending on your taste in art, start the day either in the **Rijksmuseum** *(see pp12–15)* or the **Van Gogh Museum** *(see pp16–19)*. If you choose the former, be selective, and do bear in mind that from late 2003, the main building will be closed for restoration, *(see p12)*. Whichever museum you visit, you should aim to spend the whole morning there. The Van Gogh Museum has a useful ground floor café, and you can end your visit with a browse in the museum shop next to the main entrance.

Next, cross **Museumplein** to the **Concertgebouw** *(see p115)* and pop in for a look. Make your way to Art Deco Brasserie van Baerle (Van Baerlestraat 158) for lunch. It has a lovely shady garden and is popular, so it's worth booking a table.

Afternoon

Head back to Paulus Potterstraat and **Coster Diamonds**, where you could take one of the half-hour tours. Afterwards, walk along Hobbemastraat until you reach the elegant shops of **P C Hooftstraat**. Turn left and window-shop your way along the street.

If your feet are up to it, spend an hour or so strolling around the Vondelpark, finishing either at the Blauwe Theehuis *(see p50)* or the **Filmmuseum's** Café Vertigo, which has a lovely terrace overlooking the park. You could end with a visit to the **Hollandsche Manege**, which opens till midnight on weekdays.

Price Categories

For a three-course meal for one with half a bottle of wine (or equivalent meal), taxes and extra charges.

€	under €20
€€	€20–€30
€€€	€30–€45
€€€€	€45–€60
€€€€€	over €60

Bakkerswinkel van Nineties

Top 10 Food and Drink

1 Bakkerswinkel van Nineties

This bakery with seats inside is an ideal spot for breakfast, lunch or high tea – but beware, it can get crowded. *Roelof Hartstraat 68*

2 The College Hotel

This elegant restaurant serves classic Dutch dishes with a contemporary twist. *Roelof Hartstraat 1 • 020 571 1511 • €€€€*

3 Brasserie van Baerle

This polished contemporary brasserie is popular with Dutch celebs for its well-reputed wine list, imaginative French cuisine, languishing lunches and hedonistic Sunday brunches. *Van Baerlestraat 158 • Map C6 • 020 679 1532 • €€€€*

4 CoBrA Café

Designer café on Museumplein created as an ode to the members of the CoBrA art movement. Wine and dine in the restaurant, or go Japanese at the stylish sushi bar. *Hobbemastraat 18 • Map C6 • 020 470 0111 • €€*

5 Café Ebeling

A relaxed, spacious bar popular with a younger, trendier crowd. *Overtoom 52 • Map C5*

6 Le Garage

The famous and beautiful of Amsterdam fill their tummies and empty their wallets here. The food is a delicate fusion of French with international cuisine. *Ruysdaelstraat 54–56 • Map C6 • 020 679 7176 • €€€€*

7 The Mansion

Contemporary Chinese dishes are on the menu at this über-chic establishment, which also boasts three cocktail bars and a basement nightclub. *Hobbemastraat 2 • Map C5 • 020 616 6664 • €€€€*

8 Vertigo

Resembling a wine cellar, Vertigo serves up soups and sandwiches as well as a full international menu. *Vondelpark 3 • Map C5 • 020 612 3021 • €€€*

9 Café Toussaint

This charming, relaxed café-bar has an open kitchen from which delicious lunches and dinners are served. *Bosboom Toussaintstraat 26 • Map J6 • 020 685 0737 • €€€*

10 Pasta di Mamma

Wafts of freshly-baked bread and other delights will lead you to this rustic, upmarket trattoria and espresso bar, located on the city's most luxurious shopping street. *PC Hoofstraat 52 • Map C5 • 020 664 8314*

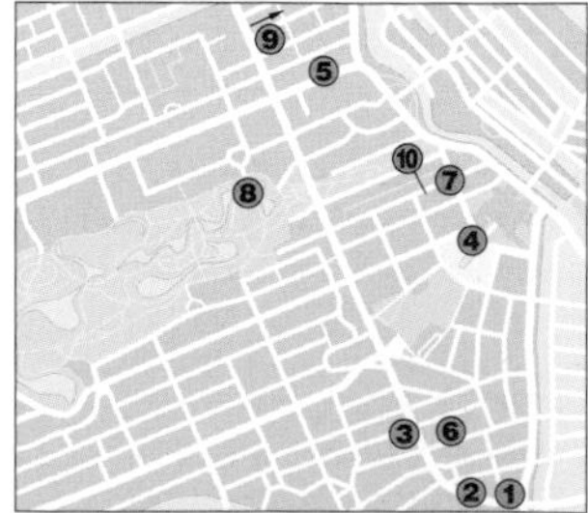

Left **Filmmuseum terrace** Right **Concertgebouw**

TOP 10 Best of the Rest

1 Van Altena Zeebanket
One of the best places in town to try the traditional Dutch custom of slipping a raw herring down your gullet. The less brave can settle for a salmon sandwich. *Stadhouderskade 41 • Map D5*

2 Het Blauwe Theehuis
This teahouse in the Vondelpark is one of the city's best-kept secrets, despite its central location. *Vondelpark • Map B6*

3 Broekmans & Van Poppel
Founded in 1914, this store has one of the largest collections of sheet music in the world. *Van Baerlestraat 92–94 • Map C6*

4 Concertgebouw
Every Wednesday at 12:30pm (except in summer) there are free lunchtime concerts here. Atmosphere informal, quality unsurpassed; queue early *(see p115)*.

5 Filmmuseum
Don't miss the live musical performances to silent classics, or the open-air screenings from the historic building's balcony in summer *(see p116)*.

6 Friday Night Skate
Join this huge group of skaters for a free, two-hour, 15 km (9 mile) tour of the city. Anyone who is reasonably proficient can join in. Gather from 8pm. *Vondelpark (Roemer Visscherstraat entrance) • Map C5*

7 Hollandsche Manege
One of the more unusual places to stop for a drink in town. The upstairs café of this stables overlooks the sand arena below as classes are being held *(see p117)*.

8 De Peperwortel
Just two minutes from the Filmmuseum, this charming traiteur is ideally placed for picnicking in the park. Delicious quiches, pasta, salads and soup, with vegetarians particularly well catered for. Plus a choice selection of wine. *Overtoom 140 • Map B5*

9 Vondelpark Openluchttheater
Catch a bit of drama, flamenco, puppetry or pop in the Vondelpark's open-air theatre. *Vondelpark • Map B6 • end May–end Aug: Wed–Sun*

10 Zuiderbad
This recently restored Art Nouveau swimming pool, dating from 1911, is the city's most stylish place to bathe. *Hobbemastraat 26 • Map D6*

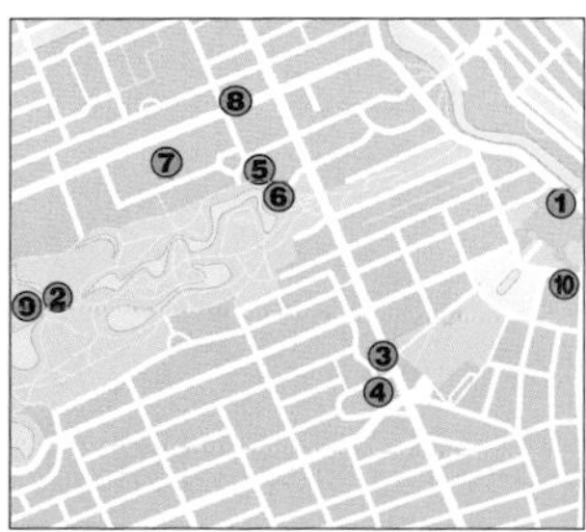

For more information on the Friday Night Skate, visit www.fridaynightskate.com

50 tulpen
€ 5,-
3 pakken
€ 10,-

Left **Koninklijk Theater Carré** Right **Werf't Kromhout Museum**

Plantage

VISITORS FLOCK TO AMSTERDAM'S EXCELLENT ZOO, but the rest of this distinguished residential district, with its elegant villas and broad, tree-lined streets, is often overlooked. Most of the villas appeared in the 19th century, many of them occupied by Jews who had prospered in the diamond industry, and the neighbourhood's strong Jewish tradition is reflected in its numerous memorials. Plantage means plantation: this was a rural area until the final extension of the Grachtengordel in 1638. Despite its tranquillity, there is no shortage of places to visit and sights to see.

Sights

1. **Nederlands Scheepvaart Museum**
2. **Artis**
3. **Entrepotdok**
4. **Werf 't Kromhout Museum**
5. **Verzetsmuseum**
6. **Hortus Botanicus**
7. **De Burcht**
8. **Hollandsche Schouwburg**
9. **Koninklijk Theater Carré**
10. **Hermitage**

Entrepotdok

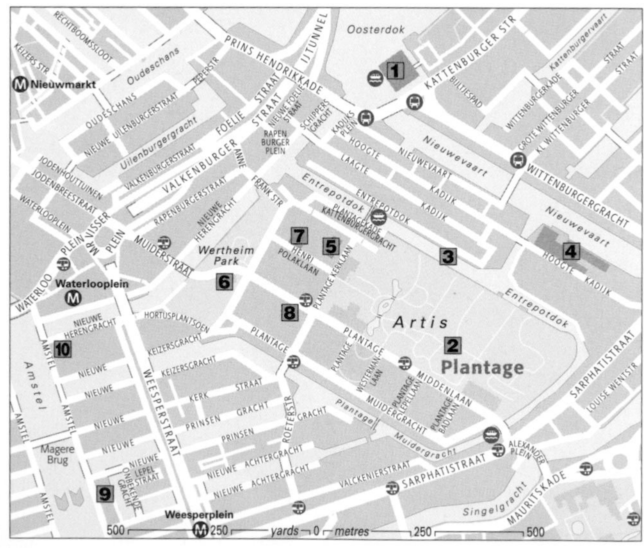

1 Nederlands Scheepvaart Museum

For anyone who loves ships, the maritime museum is a must. Where sails, ropes, guns and munitions were once stored is now an Aladdin's Cave of nautical treasures *(see pp41 and 68)*. During renovation the East Indiaman Amsterdam will be moored outside NEMO *(see p129)*. *Kattenburgerplein 1 • Map G3 • 020 523 2222 • www.scheepvaart-museum.nl • Museum: closed for renovation until 2010 • Amsterdam: Oosterdok 2. Open Sep–May: 10am–5pm Tue–Sun; Jun–Aug: daily; also open 10am–5pm Mon during school holidays. Closed 1 Jan, 30 Apr, 25 Dec • Admission charge*

2 Artis

If you want to give human culture a break, the zoological garden makes a terrific contrast. About 900 species are kept in reasonably naturalistic surroundings, including a recently created African landscape. Watch the Japanese monkeys grooming one another, the reptiles slithering in their steamy jungle, or the polar bears lazing with menacing unconcern. There are plenty of places where you can shelter from the rain, including the Planetarium, Geological and Zoological museums, and the Aquarium, home to more than 2,000 mesmerizing fish. *Plantage Kerklaan 38–40 • Tram 9, 14 • Map G4 • 020 523 3400 • www.artis.nl • Open Apr–Oct: 9am–6pm daily (till sunset Jul–Aug); Nov–Mar: 9am–5pm daily • Guided tour 11am Sun • Admission charge*

3 Entrepotdok

The flat brick façades of these typical 19th-century warehouses, punctuated by shuttered, arched windows, seem to stretch endlessly along the dockside. When owned by the Dutch East India Company (VOC), they were declared part of a free port, and no duties were levied here on cargoes in transit. Now they have been converted into offices and apartments, served by pleasant cafés and restaurants with tables outside in summer. *Tram 9, 14, bus 22, 32 • Map G4*

4 Werf 't Kromhout Museum

In the 18th century, the Eastern docklands were packed with shipyards. Today this recently restored working yard is one of the few remaining. It has survived by moving with the times – concentrating on restoration when shipbuilding declined, producing the diesel engine that powered most inland waterways craft, and doubling as a museum. Its displays include tools, machinery, steam engines, photographs and an exhibition on 300 years of shipbuilding in the area. *Hoogte Kadijk 147 • Tram 9, 14; bus 22, 32 • Map G4 • 020 627 6777 • www.machinekamer.nl • Open 10am–3pm Tue • Groups by appointment • Admission charge*

Artis Planetarium

The Dutch East India Company (VOC)

Amsterdam's wealth in the 17th century was in no small measure due to the success of the VOC. Founded in 1602, it had a trading monopoly east of the Cape of Good Hope. Its legendary fleet of "East Indiamen" *(see p68)* carried much of Europe's spice imports until it folded in 1791.

5 Verzetsmuseum

Following the development of the Dutch Resistance movement from the German invasion in May 1940 to the liberation in May 1945, this exhibition shows how the Dutch people courageously faced the occupation. Its fascinating and evocative displays relate private stories of individual heroism and place them in their historical context. Among the memorabilia are forged identity papers, old photographs and underground newspapers. *Plantage Kerklaan 61 • Map G4 • Tram 9, 14 • 020 620 2535 • www.verzetsmuseum.org • Open 10am–5pm Tue–Fri, noon–5pm Sat, Sun & public holidays • Closed 1 Jan, 30 Apr, 25 Dec • Admission charge*

6 Hortus Botanicus

About 8,000 different species of plants, flowers and trees, rock and herb gardens and numerous

Hortus Botanicus

De Burcht

glasshouses are crammed into this small botanical garden. Most of the exotic plants were collected by the VOC in the 17th and 18th centuries. Highlights are a 300-year old Cycad palm, the three-climates glasshouse and a coffee plant, Europe's first, smuggled out of Ethiopia in 1706. There is a lovely café here. *Plantage Middenlaan 2A • Map R5 • Tram 9, 14 • 020 625 8411 • www.dehortus.nl • Open Feb–Nov: 9am–5pm Mon–Fri, 10am–5pm Sat, Sun & public holidays (Jul–Aug: until 9pm daily); Dec–Jan: 9am–4pm Mon–Fri, 10am–4pm Sat, Sun & public holidays • Closed 1 Jan, 25 Dec • Admission charge*

7 De Burcht (Vakbondsmuseum)

Nicknamed "the castle" because of its crenellated façade, this is the oldest Trades Union building in the Netherlands, built in 1900 by H P Berlage of Beurs fame *(see p84)* for the General Dutch Diamond Workers' Union (ANDB). Go inside for the stunning tiled entrance hall and staircase, and murals by Richard Roland Holst of the Amsterdam School. *Henri Polaklaan 9 • Map F4 • Tram 9, 14 • 020 624 1166 • www.deburcht.org • Open 11am–5pm Tue–Fri, 1–5pm Sun • Admission charge*

8 Hollandsche Schouwburg

During the Nazi occupation, this former theatre was used as an assembly-point for thousands of Jews. Behind an intact façade, a garden has been created around a basalt monument on the site of the auditorium. The names of 6,700 Dutch Jews are engraved in a memorial hall to the 104,000 who were exterminated. There is an exhibition upstairs. *Plantage Middenlaan 24 • Map F4 • Tram 9, 14 • 020 531 0340 • www.hollandscheschouwburg.nl • Open 11am–4pm daily • Closed Yom Kippur, Rosh Hashanah • Free*

9 Koninklijk Theater Carré

It is hard to believe that the magnificent Carré Theatre, superbly set beside the Amstel, was built at break-neck speed in 1887 to house Oscar Carré's circus. A copy of his other circus in Cologne, it has a fine Neo-Renaissance frontage, some splendid ironwork, and is decorated appropriately with the heads of clowns and dancers. Today, it hosts pop concerts, dance shows, lavish musicals, and even the occasional circus. *Amstel 115–25 • Map F5 • Tram 7, 9, 10, 14 • 0900 252 5255 • www.theatercarre.nl • Box office open 4pm–9pm daily • Guided tours*

10 Hermitage

When this sober *hofje*, the Amstelhof, was completed in 1683, it was the widest building in Amsterdam. The site now houses the Hermitage Amsterdam, a satellite of the Hermitage, St Petersburg. The light, modern interior has six exhibition galleries and an educational studio for children. There is also a café near the entrance and a museum shop. *Nieuwe Herengracht 14 • Map Q6 • Tram 4, 9, 14 • www.hermitage.nl • Open 10am–5pm daily. Closed 1 Jan, 30 Apr, 25 Dec • Admission charge*

A Day in the Plantage

Morning

Start your day among the cannons, models, figure-heads, maps and instruments of the **Nederlands Scheepvaart Museum** *(see p123)*, then revive yourself at the pleasant ground-floor café. If you secretly hanker after a ship-in-a-bottle, a cutlass paper knife or other objects with a nautical theme, visit the museum shop before you leave. Outside, take a look around the Amsterdam, the full-size replica of an 18th-century East Indiaman, manned by actors.

If it is a Tuesday and you haven't yet had your fill of boats, take a short detour to the **Werf 't Kromhout Museum** *(see p123)* to see some shipbuilding in progress or, at the very least, the exhibition about it. Lunch at one of the cafés in **Entrepotdok** – such as Café 't Kromhout at No. 36.

Afternoon

After lunch, you could make your way to Plantage Kerklaan and the **Verzetsmuseum** *(see facing page)*. A visit here is definitely worthwhile, if harrowing. Afterwards, blow the cobwebs away by spending an hour or two at **Artis** *(see p123)*. For a few euros, the excellent zoo plan gives you feeding times, as well as pinpointing the two museums and the revamped Aquarium. Head back towards the main entrance, where there is a café, and a shop selling goods with a wildlife theme. If there is time, you could finish your explorations with a quick dash around the solar system at the Planetarium.

Left **De Rieker Windmill, Amstelpark** Right **Ouderkerk aan de Amstel**

Further Afield

CENTRAL AMSTERDAM HAS MORE THAN ENOUGH *to keep any visitor occupied, but if time permits, it's certainly worth taking the trouble to explore the outskirts, where a diverse selection of sights is on offer. Football fans will want to make a beeline for the city's stunning new stadium, Amsterdam ArenA, home of legendary soccer club Ajax. There are fascinating exhibits on view at the Cobra Museum, the Tropenmuseum and NEMO. If you are interested in architecture, make sure that you see the innovative 1920s buildings of the De Dageraad housing estate. If it's peace and quiet you want, there are several choices, including the small, historic town of Ouderkerk aan de Amstel – older than Amsterdam itself – and the wide open spaces of Amsterdamse Bos. The city's excellent transport system makes all these sights easily accessible, and some of them are not far from the centre – or from each other.*

TOP 10 Sights

1. **Tropenmuseum**
2. **De Dageraad Housing**
3. **Amstelpark**
4. **Ajax Museum**
5. **Ouderkerk aan de Amstel**
6. **Amsterdamse Bos**
7. **Cobra Museum**
8. **Eastern Docklands**
9. **NEMO**
10. **Frankendael**

De Dageraad Housing

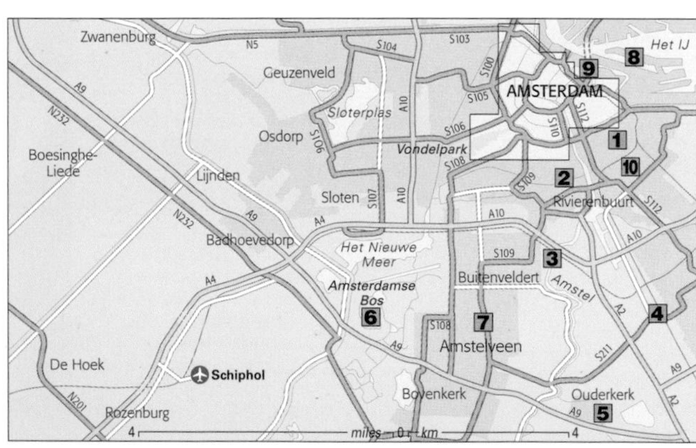

Tropenmuseum

1 Tropenmuseum

Originally conceived to celebrate Dutch colonialism but now redeployed to educate visitors about the developing world. Reconstructions – whether of an Arabian bazaar, an African village or an Indian slum – are vividly brought to life with the help of soundtracks and even smells. The separate Tropenmuseum Junior is strictly for 6–12-year-olds (no admission to an adult unless accompanied by a child), by appointment, with guided tours in Dutch. *Linnaeusstraat 2 • Tram 9, 10, 14; bus 22 • Tropenmuseum: 020 568 8215 • Tropenmuseum Junior: 020 568 8233 • www.tropenmuseum.nl • www.tropenmuseumjunior.nl • Tropenmuseum: Open 10am–5pm daily • Tropenmuseum Junior: Opening times contact for details • Admission charge*

2 De Dageraad Housing

A housing estate seems an unlikely tourist attraction, but the complex built for the De Dageraad (Dawn) housing association from 1918–23 is well worth a visit – especially for anyone interested in the Amsterdam School of Architecture. Piet Kramer and Michel de Klerk designed sculptural buildings of great originality, with tiled roofs that undulate in waves, and brick walls that billow and curve. The project was part of an initiative to provide better housing for poorer families, in the wake of the revolutionary Housing Act of 1901. *Pieter Lodewijk Takstraat • Tram 4, 12, 25*

3 Amstelpark

This welcome green space to the south of the city has a rose garden, a maze and an art gallery, as well as pony rides, farm animals and a miniature steam train for children. At its southernmost tip is the well-preserved De Rieker windmill. Built in 1636, it was a favourite of Rembrandt, whose statue stands nearby, and is now a private home. *Europaboulevard • Metro RAI; Tram 4; Bus 66, 199 • Open dawn–dusk*

4 Ajax Museum

Football fans will want to pay their respects to the brilliant Ajax club at their impressive stadium, Amsterdam ArenA. Visit the interactive museum, which brings the club and its greatest moments to life, and tour the state-of-the-art 50,000-seat stadium. There are usually six tours a day in summer, four in winter, except on event days; phone ahead for times. *Arena Boulevard 1 • Metro to Strandvliet or Bijlmer, train to Bijlmer • 020 311 1333/020 311 1336 • www.amsterdamarena.nl • Open Apr–Sep: 11am–6pm daily (last tour 5pm); Oct–Mar: 11am–5pm Mon–Sat (last tour 4:30pm) • Ajax Museum: Open Oct–Mar: 9:30am–5pm Mon–Sat; Apr–Sep: 9:30am–6pm Mon–Fri, 10am–5pm Sat–Sun • Admission charge*

Ajax Museum

5 Ouderkerk aan de Amstel

There was no church in town until 1330 *(see p28)*, so people came instead to this picturesque riverside village to worship at the 11th-century Oude Kerk that stood here until it was destroyed by a storm in 1674. Convivial waterside cafés and restaurants are the chief lure these days, but you can also walk in the wooded garden of an 18th-century house, Wester Amstel, and visit an unexpected site: the Beth Haim Jewish cemetery. Amsterdam's Jews have been buried here since 1615, when they were forbidden burial in the city. *Metro or train to Bijlmer, then bus 175, 300*

6 Amsterdamse Bos

Just a short bus, oldfashioned tram *(see p68)* or bike ride away, this attractive woodland park is a wonderful contrast to the city. Laid out on reclaimed land in the 1930s with the dual purpose of creating jobs for the unemployed and providing more recreation space, the park has woods and meadows, lakes and nature reserves. There is plenty to do: hire bicycles, go boating, eat pancakes, visit the bison and the goats and the Bos Museum, which describes the park and how it was built. *Amstelveenseweg • Bus 142, 144, 166, 170, 171, 172 • Open permanently*

City of Cyclists

Cycling comes as naturally to Amsterdammers as walking, royal family included. There are about 600,000 bikes in the city – almost one per person. Theft is endemic, so snazzy models are avoided. Look out for: the huge bike shed at Centraal Station; bikes being dredged up from canals; the eight-man "conference bike" and the heart-shaped "love bike".

Amsterdamse Bos

7 Cobra Museum

This museum of modern art in residential Amstelveen is dedicated in part to the influential Dutch movement conceived in 1948. Its founders, including Dutchman Karel Appel *(see p47)* amalgamated the names of their home cities – Copenhagen, Brussels and Amsterdam – to create its name: CoBrA. They wanted to promote art that was spontaneous and inclusive, and were inspired by the work of primitives, children and the mentally ill. Paintings in the permanent collection are shown in changing thematic displays, augmented by temporary exhibitions. The light, spare building, by Wim Quist, opened in 1995. *Sandbergplein 1–3, Amstelveen • Tram 5 to Binnenhof • 020 547 5050 • www.cobra-museum.nl • Open 11am– 5pm Tue–Sun • Closed 1 Jan, 30 Apr, 25 Dec • Admission charge*

8 Eastern Docklands

A mecca for architecture aficionados, this former docklands area to the east of Centraal Station has been transformed by ambitious urban regeneration plans. Spend a few hours admiring the bridge, inspired by a lizard, or the apartment block that resembles a whale. Also here is a row of houses, each designed by a different architect, and some inspired public art. Nearby are shops and cafés. *Ferry from Centraal Station or Bus 41, 42; tram 10, 26*

Catch the Electrische Museumtramlijn at Haarlemmermeerstation (No.16 tram from Centraal Station).

9 NEMO

The most arresting feature of this interactive science and technology centre – the largest in the Netherlands – is the building itself. Designed by Renzo Piano, its harbour location (in the Eastern Islands) gave the impetus for a green copper structure resembling a ship. The views from the top deck will certainly appeal, even if the hands-on games, experiments and demonstrations, designed to entertain and educate both children and adults, do not. *Oosterdok 2 • Bus 22, 42, 43 • 0900 919 1100 • www.e-nemo.nl • Open 10am–5pm Tue–Sun, also Mon during school holidays • Closed 1 Jan, 30 Apr, 25 Dec • Adm charge*

10 Frankendael

The elegant Louis XIV-style Frankendael is the last survivor of an enclave of exclusive early 18th-century houses, which were built south of Plantage Middenlaan on reclaimed land called the Watergraafsmeer. The ornamental fountain by Ignatius van Logteren (1686–1732), and the house and coach buildings are worth seeing. The main building hosts temporary exhibitions and one of the coach houses is now a restaurant. There is also a formal garden and English-style park beyond with rare trees. *Middenweg 72 • Bus 41; tram 9 • 774 4480 • Garden open dawn–dusk*

NEMO

A Day Out with the Kids

Morning

Start by taking tram 7, 9, 10 or 14 to the **Tropenmuseum** *(see p127)*, a fascinating ethnographic museum which explores various non-Western cultures from around the world. Afterwards, enjoy an exotic lunch in the museum's café-restaurant, Ekeko, and don't forget to pop into the museum's shop to pick up a postcard or ethnic gift.

Afternoon

Outside the Tropenmuseum, pick up tram 7 or 10 to the Leidseplein and from there walk through the Max Euweplein to the **Vondelpark** *(see p115)* where you can take in a music, dance or puppetry show at the open-air theatre. Nearby is the KinderKookKafé where supervised children cook and serve up simple meals (closed in August).

If park life is a big hit, head to the **Amsterdamse Bos** *(see p128)*. Be sure to stop at the visitor centre by the main entrance for a map of this sprawling woodland park. Rent bikes, canoe, horse-ride or take a ride on a historic tram. Don't miss the ferry on Sundays that sails from the north of the park to a pancake house in the south or the working farm where children can feed the animals.

If there is time, take bus 170, 171 or 172 to Amstelveen and end the day with some modern art at the **Cobra Museum** *(see p128)*. Tram 5 or metro 51 will take you back to the city centre.

KinderKookKafé: 020 625 3257, www.kinderkookkafe.nl

STREETSMART

Left **Euro notes** Right **Umbrellas on a rainy day**

Top 10 Planning Your Trip

1 Choosing an Area

Most tourist hotels are to be found in one of three areas: the historic centre, the Museum Quarter and the atmospheric *Grachtengordel* (Canal Ring) with its gabled canal houses. Many business-oriented hotels are located a little further afield in the *Nieuw Zuid* (New South).

2 What to Pack

Be prepared for all weathers, and bring an umbrella, a waterproof jacket and a sweater – even in summer. Comfortable walking shoes are essential. Amsterdammers' dress style is casual and often creative. Few places insist on formality – casinos are an exception – but you can dress up for concerts and smart hotels and restaurants.

3 Passports and Other Documents

You must have a valid passport to enter the Netherlands. Citizens of EU countries, the USA, Australia and New Zealand need no visa as long as the stay is for less than three months. Passports must be valid for at least three months beyond the end of your stay. Citizens of other countries should consult their Dutch embassy or consulate for information. Everyone over 14 must carry valid means of identification at all times.

4 Customs

Apart from offensive weapons, plants and perishable foods, there are few limits on what EU nationals can import for personal use. Non-EU citizens can buy duty-free goods up to the current limit. Cats and dogs are allowed, provided they have a certificate of inoculation against rabies. Flower bulbs may be exported from the Netherlands; for the USA, a certificate of inspection from the Plant Protection Service is required. Bulbs are best mailed home; the dealer should carry out all the paperwork.

5 Currency

For security, bring a cash card or traveller's cheques. Make sure that your cash withdrawal card is accepted in the Netherlands – most are. Bring some euros to pay for immediate needs on arrival. There is no limit on how much currency you can bring in or take out of the country.

6 Driving

If you are planning to drive your own car, you must bring an EU or International Driver's Licence, valid insurance documents, proof of registration, road safety certificate and international identification disc. To hire a car, you must be 21 or over, with a valid driving licence and a credit card.

7 Electricity

The electricity supply in the Netherlands is 220 volts AC. British visitors should bring a two-pin adaptor for their three-pin plugs. Americans need to convert their equipment or buy a transformer, as Dutch wall sockets require a larger plug.

8 Time Difference

The Netherlands is on Central European Time, one hour ahead of GMT. Like the rest of the EU and the USA, it observes Daylight Saving Time, so it remains one hour ahead of the UK and six hours ahead of New York all year round.

9 Children's Needs

If you have very young children, it is best to carry them in baby slings; pushchairs are difficult to manoeuvre on the cobbled streets, and almost impossible to get on and off crowded trams and canal boats. Most places accept children, except for some expensive restaurants.

10 Public Holidays

Public holidays are as follows: New Year's Day (1 Jan); *Tweede Paasdag* (Easter Monday); *Koninginnedag* (30 Apr); *Bevrijdingsdag* (5 May); *Hemelvaartsdag* (Ascension Day); *Pinksteren* (Whitsun); *Eerste Kerstdag* (Christmas Day); *Tweede Kerstdag* (26 Dec).

Left **Train at Centraal Station** Right **Arriving by road**

TOP 10 Arriving in Amsterdam

1 Schiphol Airport

Amsterdam's airport (official name Amsterdam Airport Schiphol) is efficient, modern and easy to use, with an incredible range of facilities from golf to gambling. There is a single terminal, with one level for Arrivals and another level for Departures. Signs are colour-coded: yellow for transfer desks and gates, green for amenities. *Flight information: 0900 0141 • www.schiphol.com*

2 From Schiphol by Train

The best and cheapest method of getting from the airport to the city is by rail – access is by escalator from the shopping plaza where the tickets are on sale. Trains run direct to Centraal Station every four to seven minutes from 6am to midnight, then every hour. Journey time is 20 minutes.

3 From Schiphol by Bus

Instead of the train, you can take the smart Connexxion Airport-Hotel Shuttle (www.airporthotel shuttle.nl) from outside the main exit. It stops at over 100 hotels, leaving every 30 minutes between 6am and 9pm. You can also take a taxi, but it's hardly worth the expense, considering the ease of public transport.

4 Arriving by Train

You will arrive at Centraal Station. Its best feature is the Eerste Klas café *(see p51)*; otherwise, it's crowded and prone to pickpockets and drug pushers, so head directly for the main entrance and Stationsplein. Here you will find the Amsterdam Tourist Board (VVV) and tram stops to the left and right, bus stops to the left. *Eurostar enquiries and reservations: 08705 186 186 • www.eurostar.com*

5 Arriving by Road

Drive on the right. Speed limits are 100 kph (60 mph) or 120 kph (75 mph) on motorways, 80 kph (50 mph) outside cities, and 50 kph (30 mph) in built-up areas. From the A10 ring road, the S-routes (marked by blue signs) take you to the centre of Amsterdam. *(See Driving p132.)*

6 Parking

Best to stay in a hotel with secure parking, or leave your car in the park-and-ride facility at Amsterdam Arena, at Sloterdijk Station Olympisch Stadion Zeeburg, or in a covered public car park (indicated by a white P on a blue background). *Muziektheater Parking: Waterlooplein 28. Map Q5 • Byzantium: Tesselschadestraat 1G. Map C5 • Europarking: Marnixstraat 250. Map J5 • www.naaramsterdam.nl*

7 Arriving by Ferry

From London, the boat-train service, the Dutchflyer, offered by Stena Line via Harwich and the Hook of Holland departs twice daily and takes about 8 hours, and you will end your journey at Centraal Station. P&O ferries cross from Hull to Rotterdam or Zeebrugge and Dover to Calais, and DFDS Seaways has overnight crossings from Newcastle to IJmuiden. *DFDS: 08715 229955 • www.dfds.co.uk • P&O: 08716 645645 • www.poferries.com • Stena Line: 08705 455455 • www.dutchflyer.co.uk*

8 Bus and Coach

From London's Victoria Coach Station, National Express coaches go via the Channel Tunnel or the ferry, taking between 9 and 12 hours to reach Amstel Station. *National Express: 08717 818181 • www.nationalexpress.com*

9 Car Hire

For the best rates, try Dutch firms such as Diks or Kuperus. *(See Driving p132.)* *Diks: 020 662 3366 • Kuperus: 020 668 3311 • Ouke Baas: 020 679 4842*

10 Left Luggage

At Schiphol there is a staffed counter, open from 7am–10.45pm (6012443), as well as lockers. At Centraal Station there are 24-hour lockers.

Left **Amsterdam Tourist Board** Right **Reference books in an Amsterdam library**

Top 10 Sources of Information

1 Amsterdam Tourist Board

Still universally known by its old name, VVV, the Tourist Board has three offices in the city *(see below)*. At these you will find free maps, and leaflets on just about everything – including walks, canal tours, sights, exhibitions, transport and accommodation. Multi-lingual staff will give advice, change money, arrange excursions and – for a fee – book tickets and hotels. Here you can also buy the popular 1 Amsterdam card and *Museumkaart* *(see p136)*. *0900 400 4040 • www.visitamsterdam.nl www.amsterdamtourist.nl*

2 Tourist Offices

There are three VVV offices in Amsterdam itself: at Centraal Station (Platform 2), at Stationsplein 10 (in front of the station), and at Stadhouderskade (next to Canal Bus ticket booth). There is another office at Schiphol Airport (Holland Tourist Information Arrivals 2).

3 NBTC (Netherlands Board of Tourism and Conventions)

You can pick up the NBTC's own maps, information leaflets and brochures at any of its offices throughout the world. Visit your nearest branch before you travel. *www.holland.com*

4 Amsterdam Hotel Service

The friendly staff at this independent organization will make hotel reservations (even last-minute ones), book excursions and proffer helpful advice. *Damrak 7 • Map P1 • 020 520 7000 • www.amsterdamhotelservice.com*

5 Websites

The Amsterdam Tourist Board has two official websites: www.amsterdamtourist.nl and www.visitamsterdam.nl, which is linked to the NBTC website, www.holland.com. The City of Amsterdam has its own English-language website, www.iamsterdam.nl. All of these have useful, up-to-date information on accommodation, events, exhibitions, shopping and travel (you can also book hotel rooms online).
To find out what's on, visit www.uitburo.nl/amsterdam. The majority of the city's museums and attractions have their own websites.

6 Accommodation

To book hotels before you travel, contact the Amsterdam Reservation Center, a branch of the Amsterdam Tourist Board. *PO Box 3901, NL–1001 AS Amsterdam • 0900 400 4040 • reservations@atcb.nl or www.amsterdamtourist.nl*

7 Publications

The best listings magazine in Dutch is *Uitkrant*. Published monthly, it is free and widely available. The Tourist Board publishes *Day by Day*, a monthly listings magazine in English (on sale in newsagents and free in hotels and restaurants). *Amsterdam Weekly* is in English and free (www.amsterdamweekly.nl)

8 AUB Ticketshop

For information on plays and concerts, or to make reservations (for a small fee), contact Amsterdam Uitburo. Between noon–7:30pm, tickets are sold for same-day shows at reduced prices. *Leidseplein 26 • www.uitburo.nl/amsterdam • Map C5 • 0900 0191*

9 Newspapers

You will find the best selection of foreign daily and Sunday newspapers at Athenaeum Nieuwscentrum, Waterstone's and the American Book Center. *Athenaeum Nieuwscentrum: Spui 14–16. Map M5 • Waterstone's: Kalverstraat 152. Map M5 • American Book Center: Spui 12. Map M5*

10 Libraries

Only residents can borrow, but anyone can visit. The OBA (Amsterdam Public Library) is handy, with foreign-language books and newspapers. *Oosterdokskade 143 • Map R2 • 0900 242 5468 • Open 10am–10pm daily.*

For alternative listings, check out the excellent www.underwateramsterdam.com

Left **Bicyles secured in a bike rack** Right **Trams**

TOP 10 Getting Around

1 Trams
Trams run from 6am (6:30am on Saturday and Sunday) till midnight. Most start at Central Station. For routes, see the map on the back cover of this book. You can buy tickets in advance from the GVB *(see below)*, or on board the tram itself.

2 Buses
Most buses start at Centraal Station. A few follow similar routes, but buses also go to areas not covered by trams; again, see the map at the back. Buses have the same ticketing system as trams. The red and white Stop/Go bus runs every 12 minutes, daily, down Prinsengracht (Oosterdokskade to Waterlooplein) and can be hailed anywhere on route. A limited night service runs from midnight to 4am.

3 Metro
Serving more remote parts of the city, the metrohas only four lines, all terminating at Centraal Station. There are four other stations in the central area: Amsterdam CS, Nieuwmarkt, Waterlooplein and Weesperplein. It is best to avoid taking the metro at night.

4 Tickets
The *OV Chipkaart* (Public Transport Smartcard) is a new card that allows you to travel with any means of public transport throughout the Netherlands. Three cards are available - Personal (reloadable with credit or a season ticket), Anonymous (reloadable with credit only) and Disposable (fixed credit). When boarding, hold the card up to the card reader (either built into the gate or on a free-standing yellow pillar). At the end of the journey, hold the card up to the reader again. *GVB: Stationsplein 14 • Map P1 • 0900 9292 • www.gvb.nl • www.ov-chipkaart.nl*

5 Taxis
You can try to hail taxis in the street, but finding one in the centre is usually easy, as there are plenty of taxi ranks: at Centraal Station, Dam Square, Elandsgracht, Leidseplein, Muziektheater, Nieuwmarkt and Rembrandtplein. There is also a 24-hour phone service, Taxicentrale. *Taxicentrale: 020 777 7777*

6 Driving
The city centre has a complex one-way system, its roads are dominated by trams and cyclists, and parking is limited – and expensive. All of these are good reasons to avoid driving. If you have to, park in a car park *(see p133)* or on a meter (most allow you up to two hours).

7 Bicycle Hire
You will never be very far from a bicycle hire shop in this city of cyclists: Bike City, Holland Rent-a-Bike and Take-a-Bike are all conveniently central. Bike theft is rife, so secure your bike carefully when you park it. *Bike City: Bloemgracht 70. Map K2. 020 626 3721 • Holland Rent-a-Bike. Damrak 247. Map N2. 020 622 3207 • Macbike: Stationsplein 12. Map P1. 020 620 0985*

8 Canal Bikes
These two- or four-person pedaloes provide a fun way of getting around. There are four moorings in central Amsterdam, where you can collect or leave the bikes all year round. *Canal Bike: Weteringschans 24 • Map D5 • 020 623 9886 • www.canal.nl*

9 Trains
Nederlandse Spoorwegen, the Dutch national rail company, is renowned for its clean, punctual trains and reasonable fares. Contact the OVR (Openbaar Vervoer Reisinformatie) for information. *OVR: 0900 9292 • www.ns.nl*

10 Walking
Amsterdam is a great city for walking *(see pp64–5)*. The main pedestrian hazards are bicycles, trams and cobbled streets, so keep clear of cycle lanes, take care crossing tram tracks, and wear comfortable, flat shoes.

Left **Canal tour** Right **Yellow bicycle riders**

TOP 10 Sightseeing

1 I Amsterdam card

Available from hotels and Amsterdam Tourist Board offices *(see p134)*, the I Amsterdam card represents good value for money, at €33, €43 and €53 for one, two and three days respectively. It entitles the holder to free public transport, free admission to many museums, a free canal tour, and discounts at a variety of restaurants and other attractions.

2 Museumkaart

Most of the top museums are covered by the Amsterdam Pass *(see above)*. If you want to visit more, you need the *Museumkaart* (Museum Card), which buys a year's admission to over 400 museums throughout the Netherlands. You will recoup the cost after about three visits. Available from Amsterdam Tourist Board offices and all participating museums.

3 Cultureel Jongeren Passport (CJP)

The CJP gives under-26-year-olds discounted admission to theatres, museums and other attractions. It is available from offices of the Amsterdam Tourist Board and the AUB Uitburo ticketshop *(see p134)*.

4 Canal Tours

Cruises can either be booked direct with the operator or through the Amsterdam Tourist Board. Many operators start from Centraal Station. Amsterdam Canal Cruises start on Singelgracht, and Kooij from Rokin, near the Munttoren. ✆ *Lovers: Prins Hendrikkade 26. Map P1. 020 530 1090. www.lovers.nl • Amsterdam Canal Cruises: Nicolaas Witsenkade 1a. Map D6. 020 626 5636. www.amsterdamcanalcruises.nl • Kooij: Rokin 125. Map N5. 020 623 3810. www.rederijkooij.nl*

5 City (S)hopper

The City (S)hopper allows you to get on and off at any of seven different points to visit the major museums and shopping areas. The day ticket also entitles you to discounted admission. A boat comes by each stop once every 30 minutes between 9:55am and 4:45pm daily. ✆ *Stationsplein 8 • Map P1 • 020 530 1090 • www.lovers.nl*

6 Canalbus

Another frequent hop-on, hop-off canal boat, with discounts included in the ticket price. Choose one of three routes, with a total of 14 stops. A one-day All Amsterdam Transport Pass entitles you to unlimited use of metro, bus, tram and Canalbus. ✆ *Weteringschans 24 • Map D5 • 020 623 9886 • www.canal.nl*

7 Water Taxi

More private cruisers than taxis. The cost is around €100 an hour for an 8-seater. ✆ *Stationsplein 8 • Map P1 • 020 535 6363 • www.water-taxi.nl*

8 Koetstaxi

Sightseeing by horse-drawn carriage. Tours start at Dam Square and last 20–60 minutes, or use their taxi service and order a taxi to take you to town. ✆ *020 691 3478 • www.koetstaxi.nl*

9 Bicycle Tours

Yellow Bike offers two guided bicycle tours for up to 12 people: a three-hour city tour and a six-hour countryside tour. You can book direct through Yellow Bike, or through the Amsterdam Tourist Board. ✆ *Yellow Bike: 020 620 6940*

10 Walking Tours

The Amsterdam Tourist Board offers a range of walking tours. Urban Home & Garden Tours visit private and public canal houses. Mee in Mokum give fresh in sights into historic Amsterdam. Architectour/Archivisie concentrate on architecture. Amsterdam City Walks focus more on history. ✆ *Urban Home & Garden Tours: 020 688 1243. www.uhgt.nl • Mee in Mokum: 020 625 1390. www.gildeamsterdam.nl • Architectour/Archivisie: 020 625 8908 •Amsterdam City Walks: 061 825 7014. www.amsterdamcitywalks.com*

Sign up for DK's email newsletter on traveldk.com

Left **Street stall selling herring** Right **Street performer**

Top 10 Amsterdam on a Budget

1 Hostels and Camping

There are several popular youth hostels *(see box)*. Vondelpark is especially recommended, with private rooms as well as dormitories. Vliegenbos is a designated youth campsite. The Amsterdamse Bos campsite also has wooden cabins for hire, and, like Gaasper, is suited to families. *(See also Budget Hotels, p149.)*

2 Discount Cards

Under-26-year-olds can apply for a CJP for bargains on some performing arts tickets *(see p136)*. The Amsterdam Pass represents good value for money. The *Museumkaart* allows free admission to more than 400 museums in the Netherlands *(see p136)*.

3 OBA

The new main branch of the Amsterdam public library (OBA) is a great place to hang out on a rainy afternoon. Read a magazine, check your email free of charge or just take in the view of the city *(see p134)*.

4 Markets

The outdoor markets of Albert Cuypmarkt, Waterlooplein and Noordermarkt, and the indoor bargain basement Rommelmarkt, are all places where you can find food, clothing and bric-a-brac for next to nothing *(see p62)*.

5 Free Sights

Special places that can be visited free of charge include: the Civic Guards Gallery of the Amsterdams Historisch Museum *(see p26)*; *hofjes (see p92)*; the Begijnhof *(see p22)*; Hollandsche Manege *(see p117)*; the Rijksmuseum Garden *(see p14)*; and Bloemenmarkt *(see p109)*.

6 Free Music

There is plenty of music in the air, from the carillons of the Westertoren, Zuidertoren and Munttoren, to barrel organs, street performers and live bands in late-night bars. Free lunchtime concerts are held from September to early June at the Concertgebouw (Wed), Stopera (Tue in winter) and Thomaskerk (alternate Tuesdays).

7 Free Film and Theatre

There are free performances at the Vondelpark's open-air theatre, and free screenings in summer at the Filmmuseum *(see p116)*.

8 Tickets

To see what's on, consult *Uitkrant*, *Day by Day* and *Amsterdam Weekly*. The best place to book tickets is AUB in Leidseplein *(see p134)*.

9 Parks

Amsterdam's parks offer endless free entertainment, from theatre and concerts in the Vondelpark to the miniature train in Amstelpark, or just feeding the goats in Amsterdamse Bos.

10 Cheap Eats

You can keep hunger at bay without entering a restaurant in Amsterdam, with its many food stalls selling raw herring, smoked fish, chips with mayonnaise, *belegde broodjes* (filled bread rolls), waffles, pancakes and delicious, sugary *poffertjes* – and there are plenty of cheap cafés.

Hostels and Campsites

Hans Brinker
Kerkstraat 136 • 020 622 0687 • www.hans-brinker.com

The Bulldog
Oudezijds Voorburgwal 218–220 • 020 620 3822 • www.bulldog.nl

Flying Pig Palace
Vossiusstraat 46 • 020 400 4187 • www.flyingpig.nl

Stayokay Vondelpark
Zandpad 5 • 020 589 8996 • www.stayokay.com

Amsterdamse Bos Camping
Kleine Noorddijk 1, Amstelveen • 020 641 6868

Gaasper Camping
Loosdrechtdreef 7 • 020 696 7326

Vliegenbos Camping
Meeuwenlaan 138 • 020 636 8855 • www.vliegenbos.com

Left **Cheese on a stall in the Albert Cuypmarkt** Right **Tulips at Amsterdam's Bloemenmarkt**

TOP 10 Shopping Tips

1 Areas

Each shopping area has its own special character. De Negen Straatjes, the Jordaan and Haarlemmerbuurt have bric-a-brac and speciality shops. The Spiegelkwartier and Rokin are the places for art and antiques. Most chain stores are in Kalverstraat and Nieuwendijk. Leidsestraat and Utrechtsestraat have more upmarket boutiques, and PC Hooftstraat is the home of designer fashion.

2 Hours

Shops are generally open from 9am–6pm Tue, Wed and Fri, from 9am–9pm on Thu, from 9am–5pm on Sat, and from 1–6pm on Mon (although most department stores open at 11am). Many shops also open from noon to 6pm on Sun. By city law, shopkeepers can trade between 7am and 10pm daily.

3 Tax-free Shopping

Most marked prices include 19 per cent VAT. Global Refund entitles non-EU residents to a percentage back over a minimum figure of €50 (more you spend, the higher the percentage), bought at one shop on the same day and exported within 90 days. If the shop has 'Tax-free' status, collect a Global Refund Cheque, have it stamped by Customs on your departure, and claim your refund when you leave the EU.

4 Sales

January and July are the traditional months for end-of-season sales, when you are likely to find some great bargains. Some shops have an almost permanent sale rail. *Korting* means reductions are being offered. The Dutch for sale is *uitverkoop*.

5 What to Buy

Amsterdam shopping is very cosmopolitan. It spans designer fashion and off-beat second-hand clothes, valuable antiques and colourful Indonesian beads. For a flavour of the city, you might be tempted by Dutch chocolate, cheese, *haring* (raw herring), beer or *jenever* or, for something less ephemeral, Delftware or diamonds.

6 Department Stores and Malls

Compared to its speciality shops, Amsterdam's department stores seem run-of-the-mill. On the corner of Dam Square and Damrak, De Bijenkorf is the most famous. More exclusive, however, are Maison de Bonneterie and Metz & Co. The city's first mall, Magna Plaza, has several floors of boutiques and cafés in a converted post office.

7 Speciality Shops

It is these quirky little shops devoted to specific items – from candles to toothbrushes – that make shopping in Amsterdam such a joy. Although they crop up throughout the city, they are thickest on the ground in De Negen Straatjes *(see p104)*.

8 Art and Antiques

The Spiegelkwartier is the heart of the art and antiques trade. Here, a host of dealers specialize in a variety of objects from Delftware and glass to icons and tribal art *(see p112)*.

9 Diamonds

The shops listed below guarantee quality and give expert advice. *Amsterdam Diamond Center: Rokin 1. Map N3. 020 624 5787 • Coster Diamonds: Paulus Potterstraat 2–6. Map C5. 020 305 5555 • Gassan Diamonds: Nieuwe Uilenburgerstraat 173–5. Map Q4. 020 622 5333 • Van Pampus: Damrak 97: Map N3. 020 638 2422*

10 Bulbs and Flowers

The Dutch love flowers. For the best selection of cut flowers and bulbs, visit Amsterdam's famous floating market, Bloemenmarkt *(see p108)*. Depending on the harshness of the winter, bulbs are usually available between June and late December, but it is a good idea to check your own country's import regulations before exporting *(see p132)*.

For shops, markets and souvenirs **See pp62–3**

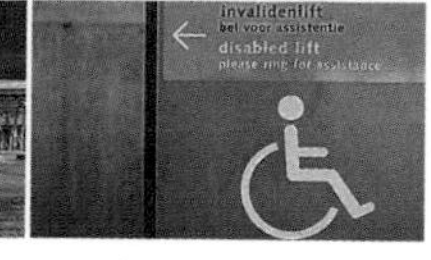

Left **Boonstra taxi service** Right **Disabled access sign**

TOP 10 Amsterdam for the Disabled

1 Organizations

Amsterdam's narrow, cobbled streets, uneven pavements, and old buildings with small entrances and steep stairs, make it a difficult city for disabled people to get around. For general information and advice, contact TTFA (Travel & Tourism for All) or SGOA (Stichting Gehandicapten Overleg Amsterdam). *TTFA: Postbus 121, 6658 2K, Beneden-Leeuwen. 0900 040 1410. www.toegankelijk.com • SGOA: Plantage Middenlaan 14l, 1018 DD. Map F4. 020 577 7955. www.sgoa.nl*

2 Leaflets

Useful leaflets on hotels, restaurants, museums and attractions, guided tours and excursions for people with disabilities are available from the Amsterdam Tourist Office and the AUB (Amsterdam Uitburo) *(see p104)*. You can also pick up an excellent booklet called Rail Travel for the Disabled from Centraal Station.

3 Accommodation

For such a progressive city, Amsterdam's hotels are remarkably cavalier about the needs of disabled people; very few have special facilities. Some modern hotels have adapted rooms, but old buildings and converted canal houses often have steep staircases and no lift. The accommodation booklet of the Amsterdam Tourist Office lists hotels with disabled facilities, but be sure that they meet your needs before you make a reservation.

4 Public Transport

Most trams are accessible for wheelchair users, with central doors at pavement level. The metro is wheelchair-friendly, with lifts at every station. For the visually impaired, there is a conductor who announces every stop. The NS (Dutch Railway) offers assistance when travelling by train (call 030 235 7822). Avoid public transport at rush hour.

5 Taxis

A folded wheelchair will fit into most taxis, but Amsterdam has a private service, Boonstra, specially designed for wheelchair users. It costs the same as a regular cab, but you need to book at least 24 hours in advance. *Prins Bernhardkade 1, Halfweg • 020 613 4134 • 9am–6pm Mon to Sat*

6 Museums

Most of the city's principal museums have adequate facilities for disabled people, including wide entrances, ramps, lifts and adapted toilets, although canalhouse museums like the Ons' Lieve Heer op Solder, Van Loon and Willet-Holthuysen have no upper-floor wheelchair access. Staff are usually very helpful, but it's always a good idea to telephone before you visit.

7 Restaurants

It's possible to get a wheelchair into most ground-floor restaurants, but only a handful have disabled toilet facilities. Again, phone ahead.

8 Wheelchair Hire

You can rent a wheelchair from Beumer de Jong for €20 per week, but you have to arrange for your hotel to collect it. Book well in advance, particularly in the holiday season. *Haarlemmermeerstraat 49–51 • 020 615 7188*

9 Guided Tours

Tours and Travel Services offer bus tours around Amsterdam and day-trips throughout Holland using buses suitable for wheelchairs. The Dutch Red Cross (Rode Kruis) runs a specially adapted tram around the city. *Tours & Travel Services: TT Melissaweg 15, 1033 SP Amsterdam. 020 635 31 10. www.tandts.nl • Rode Kruis: 020 622 6211.*

10 Impaired Sight

Audio tours of museums and other tourist attractions are increasingly available. The Dedicon has magazines etc. for the partially sighted. *0486 486 486 • Dedicon: www.dedicon.nl • public transport: 0900 9292*

Left **Pedestrian-free cycle lane** Right **Queue at Rijksmuseum**

Top 10 Things to Avoid

1 Street Crime

Beware pickpockets in crowded places like Centraal Station, the Red Light District, Damrak and Leidseplein. Never keep money in your back pocket, or leave your handbag exposed. At night, avoid the junkie-riddled fringes of the Red Light District, especially around sleazy Zeedijk, as well as the area around Nieuwendijk between Damrak and Spuistraat.

2 Bicycle Theft

Bicycle theft is rife in Amsterdam. Some are stolen for profit, others on the principle that "someone stole mine, so I'll steal someone else's". Always secure both front wheel and frame to an immovable object with a U-shaped lock.

3 Medical Problems

EU nationals are entitled to receive dental and medical treatment in the Netherlands at a reduced charge. To cover this, British visitors should bring a European Health Insurance Card (EHIC), available from post offices. It is also sensible to take out private travel insurance before you leave, to cover medical emergencies and repatriation *(see p142)*.

4 Dog Mess

It's a strange paradox that the famously house-proud Dutch should put up with fouled streets in their capital city (other towns and cities are much cleaner). A few years ago the problem was dire; it's much better now, but you still need to look where you walk.

5 Losing Possessions

If you lose property at Schiphol Airport, call 0900 0141. For items left on a train, call 0900 321 2100, 9am–5pm Mon–Fri. For trams, buses or the metro, call 0900 8011, 9am–4pm Mon–Fri.

6 Infringing Drug Laws

Amsterdam's enlightened attitude to soft drugs should not be misconstrued. "Coffee shops" are the only places where buying and using small quantities of soft drugs is tolerated. Elsewhere – in the street, or in other bars and cafés – smoking is frowned on.

7 Causing Offence

As the expression "going Dutch" indicates, Amsterdammers will usually share the bill in a restaurant. If you dine at someone's home, bring a small gift such as flowers or chocolates for the host. Try not to annoy cyclists by walking in cycle lanes. Though most Amsterdammers speak excellent English, a few words in Dutch will go down well *(see pp158–9)*. In the Red Light District, don't cause offence by taking photographs of the prostitutes in their windows.

8 Mosquitoes

Summertime heralds the arrival of these irritating insects, attracted to the canal waters. Arm yourself with repellent and a good bite cream.

9 Getting Caught Short

Though there are (albeit very public) men's conveniences on some streets, women are very poorly provided for. Instead, it is acceptable practice to head for the nearest bar or café. You might buy a drink in return, but usually you are not obliged to. Public toilets in stations and museums are staffed by attendants who insist on a tip in a saucer.

10 Tourist Hordes

Amsterdam is busy all year round, but especially from April to September, when you should book up your accommodation well before you plan to visit. Canal cruises and other tours should be booked on arrival. Places like the Rijksmuseum and Anne Frank Huis attract long queues. Order tickets on-line or arrive early in the day, or late, if visiting the Anne Frank Huis and in the case of the Rijksmuseum, use the back, Hobbemastraat entrance until 2010.

Smoking is now banned in all public spaces, hotels, restaurants and cafés.

Left **OBA (Amsterdam Public Library)** Right **Post Office**

TOP 10 Banking and Communications

1 Currency
In January 2002, the Dutch guilder became obsolete and the euro became the official currency of the Netherlands. Euro banknotes have seven denominations: 5, 10, 20, 50, 100, 200 and 500. There are also eight coin denominations: 1 and 2 euros, and 1, 2, 5, 10, 20 and 50 cents. Most shops have now stopped using 1- and 2-cent coins and purchases are rounded up or down. Check exchange rates before you travel.

2 Credit Cards
Major cards including Amex are widely accepted throughout Amsterdam, and you should have no difficulty paying for most things with plastic – but it's always wise to check. Some restaurants do not accept credit cards, and it is common practice to pay small amounts in cash, so you should keep some on you.

3 Cash Dispensers
Amsterdam has no shortage of cash dispensers, many of which will function in several languages.

4 Travellers' Cheques
Travellers' cheques are a safe way of carrying money abroad, and can be exchanged for cash in banks and used to pay hotel bills, as well as being widely accepted in retail outlets. Choose a well-known company such as American Express or Thomas Cook.

5 Changing Money
You can change money in banks, bureaux de change, post offices and American Express offices. To avoid high commission charges, stay clear of independent bureaux de change (like those on Leidsestraat) and choose the official GWK bureaux de change or the post office Postbank. Avoid changing money in hotels.

6 Post Offices
Amsterdam's post offices are recognizable by their TNT logo. Apart from the usual services, they also change currency and travellers' cheques. The main post office on Singel has a poste restante service, parcel service, photocopiers and a philately counter. *Singel 250 • Map M3 • 0900 767 8526 • open 9am–6pm Mon–Fri, 10am–1:30pm Sat*

7 Internet Cafés
You can pick up and send emails, or just surf, for free at the OBA (Amsterdam Public Library) *(see p134)*. There are several other internet cafés in town, and some hotels and bars also have terminals. *Internet City: Nieuwendijk 79. Map N1. Open 9am–1am daily • Freeworld: Nieuwendijk 30. Map N1. Open 9am–1am Sun–Thu, to 3am Fri & Sat.*

8 Telephones
Most public telephones (which are green, with the KPN Telecom logo) require a phonecard – which you can buy at post offices, supermarkets, newsagents and stations – or credit card. The international dialling code for The Netherlands is 00 31. The code for Amsterdam is 020 – you can drop this if you are dialling a local number.

9 Television
Ask a Dutch child where he or she learned to speak such good, idiomatic English, and the answer is likely to be "from the television". British and American imports on Dutch channels are subtitled rather than dubbed, and cable TV brings about 35 stations from around Europe, plus America's CNN. Most of the city's hotels are equipped with cable TV.

10 Radio
For classical music, tune in to Dutch Radio 4 (94.3 MHz); for pop music to Radio 3 (96.8 MHz). There are also several independent music stations, mostly aimed at the young. News is broadcast on Radio 1 (98.9 MHz).

Left **Prescriptions at an *apotheek*** Right **A&E dept, Onze Lieve Vrouwe Gasthuis**

TOP 10 Security and Health

1 Emergency
Dial 112 if you need police, ambulance or fire brigade. English-speaking operators man the 24-hour switchboard, and you can phone free from a call box.

2 Personal Safety
Don't carry your passport, ticket and other valuables around with you. At night, stick to well-lit streets, avoiding dodgy areas like De Pijp, Nieuwendijk and the seediest part of the Red Light District around Zeedijk. Everyone over 14 years must carry a valid means of identification at all times.

3 Theft
Insure your possessions. Should you have anything stolen, report it immediately to the police and ask for a copy of the police report for your insurers. If your passport is stolen, you must also contact your consulate *(see below)*.

4 Police
Police headquarters, the Hoofdbureau van Politie, is in Elandsgracht. There are main police stations in Prinsengracht, Beursstraat, Lijnbaansgracht and Nieuwezijds Voorburgwal. *Prinsengracht 1109. Map E5 • Beursstraat 33. Map P2 • Lijnbaansgracht 219. Map C5 • Nieuwezijds Voorburgwal 104. Map M4 • 0900 8844 (central no.)*

5 Victim Support
Get help from the Amsterdam Tourist Assistance Service (ATAS). Advies-en Steunpunt helps victims of rape and sexual assault. *Amsterdam Tourist Assistance Service: Nieuwezijds Voorburgwal 104–8. 020 625 3246 • Advices-en Steunpunt. 020 611 6022*

6 Hospitals
Of the central hospitals, only Onze Lieve Vrouwe Gasthuis, has an accident and emergency department. *Onze Lieve Vrouwe Gasthuis • Oosterpark 9. emergency: 's-Gravesandeplein 16. Map G6 • 020 599 9111*

7 Pharmacies
For non-prescription drugs or toiletries, go to a chemist *(drogist)*. To have a prescription made up, go to a pharmacy *(apotheek)*. Normal opening times are 8:30am–5:30pm Mon–Fri. A notice will direct you to the nearest pharmacy open outside of these hours.

8 Doctors and Dentists
Your hotel, local pharmacy or tourist office will give you the name and address of an English-speaking doctor or dentist, as will the GP Service Post Foundation Amsterdam (SHDA). EU citizens are entitled to reductions on medical and dental treatment *(see p140)*. *SHDA: 088 003 0600. www.shda.nl*

9 Embassies and Consulates
If you lose your passport or get into trouble with the authorities, you will need to contact your embassy or consulate. Most embassies are in The Hague, but some countries, including the UK and the USA, have consular facilities in Amsterdam. *UK Consulate: Koningslaan 44. 020 676 4343. www.britain.nl • US Consulate: Museumplein 19. 020 575 5309. http://netherlands.usembassy.gov*

10 Sexual Health
The Dutch take sexual health seriously: prostitutes are subjected to rigorous checks. Should you contract a sexually transmitted disease, the GGD provides a Mon–Fri walkin clinic: phone for details. An HIV checkpoint by appointment only, is run by the Servicepunt HIV Vereniging every Friday evening. They also operate an HIV helpline from 2–10pm Thu–Tue. The Schorer Stichting provides information for gays. *GGD: Weesperplein 1. Map F5. 020 555 5822 • Servicepunt HIV Vereniging: Eerste Helmersstraat 17. Map C5. 020 689 2577 • SAD Schorer Stichting: 020 573 9444 • AIDS-STD Helpline: 0900 204 2040*

Left **Inside the UvA Main Library** Right **VU Boekhandel**

TOP 10 Amsterdam for Students

1 UvA Courses

The largest university with buildings in the centre, UvA (Universiteit van Amsterdam) offers English-language International Study Programs in a range of subjects from undergraduate level upwards. For information, contact the Office of Foreign Relations. ✎ *Office of Foreign Relations: Binnengasthuisstraat 9. • Map N5 • 020 525 8080 • www.uva.nl*

2 VU Courses

In a suburb of Amsterdam, VU (Vrije Universiteit) runs English-language courses in economics, law, arts and social sciences for exchange or contract students (whose home university has no official exchange relationship with the VU). ✎ *VU: De Boelelaan 1105, Room OE-49. 020 598 5035 • www.vu.nl*

3 Accommodation

ASVA (UvA's student union) helps students find lodgings. If you are studying at VU, the university has a guest-house in Uilenstede. Alternatively, SRVU, the VU students' union, will help you. ✎ *ASVA: Binnengasthuisstraat 9. Map N5. 020 525 2926 • SRVU: De Boelelaan 1083A. 020 598 9424 • www.srvu.org*

4 Student Cards

Producing your student union or ISIC rail-card in Amsterdam is no guarantee of discounted prices, and only Dutch students are entitled to the *OV Jaarkaart*, which gives them free use of public transport. Anyone under the age of 26 is eligible for a *Cultureel Jongeren Passpoort (see p136)*, which costs €12.50 from Tourist Offices or the AUB *(see p134)*.

5 Unions

Foreign students will find ASVA the most useful of the various Dutch student unions. It offers all kinds of assistance, including an accommodation service. SRVU will also give VU students help and advice *(see above)*. ✎ *ASVA: Binnengasthuisstraat 9 • Map N5 • 020 525 2926*

6 Services for Foreign Students

An independent organization, the FSS (Foreign Student Service) provides advice, support and help for foreign students, as well as arranging social events. Under the auspices of the UvA, the International Student Network (ISN) is a group of students that provides mentors to introduce foreigners and freshmen to university life. ✎ *FSS: Oranje Nassaulaan 5. 020 671 5915. Map A6 • ISN: 020 525 3721. info@isn-amsterdam.nl. www.isn-amsterdam.nl • www.foreignstudents.nl*

7 Amsterdam Summer University

Every year, from the middle of July to the beginning of September, the Amsterdam Summer University offers arts and sciences courses in the Felix Meritis Building. ✎ *Keizersgracht 324 • Map L4 • 020 620 0225 • www.amsu.edu*

8 Bookshops

Most major bookshops stock English textbooks, but the best academic bookshop is VU Boekhandel. ✎ *VU Boekhandel: De Boelelaan 1105 • 020 598 4000*

9 Libraries

To borrow from the UvA Main Library, you need a *Universiteit Bibliotheek* card. Foreign students are eligible if they are studying in the city for at least three months. To borrow from the VU Main Library, you must become a member. ✎ *UvA Main Library: Singel 425. Map M5. 020 525 2301 • VU Main Library: De Boelelaan 1105. 020 598 5200*

10 Visas

All foreign students who plan to stay in the country for longer than three months must register with the *Vreemdelingen Politie* (Aliens Police) within three days of arrival. They must then apply for a MVV (residence permit) and register with the civil registry. ✎ *www.ind.nl*

Left **Crown Plaza Amsterdam American** Right **Grand Hotel Krasnapolsky**

TOP 10 Luxury Hotels

1 Amstel Inter-Continental

Rub shoulders with monarchs and movie stars in Amsterdam's grandest hotel, which just oozes opulence, from the spectacular hall to the pampering bedrooms. Enjoy the state-of-the-art gym, private motor launch and two Michelin-starred restaurant – but don't even think about the bill. ⓝ *Professor Tulpplein 1, 1018 GX • Map F5 • 020 622 6060 • www.ichotelsgroup.com • Dis. access • €€€€€*

2 The Dylan

British designer Anouska Hempel has taken a Catholic almshouse and turned it into a glamorous hotel with an excellent restaurant *(see p103)*. Influenced by Asia, the theme is monochrome, with gorgeous fabrics and furnishings. ⓝ *Keizersgracht 384, 1016 GB • Map L4 • 020 530 2010 • www.dylanamsterdam.com • €€€€€*

3 Grand Amsterdam (Sofitel Demeure)

A sense of history pervades this hotel on the fringes of the Red Light District: the 17th-century building was designed for the Admiralty. It offers five-star comfort and is home to Café Roux *(see p60)*. ⓝ *Oudezijds Voorburgwal 197, 1012 EX • Map N4 • 020 555 3111 • www.thegrand.nl • Dis. access • €€€€€*

4 Pulitzer

Combining 21st-century chic with beams and bare bricks, the Pulitzer is an innovative conversion of 25 canal houses, celebrated for its art exhibitions, courtyard garden and outstanding cellar. ⓝ *Prinsengracht 315–31, 1016 GZ • Map K3 • 020 523 5235 • www.pulitzer.nl • €€€€€*

5 NH Grand Hotel Krasnapolsky

This monumental hotel, with 468 rooms and 36 apartments, has come a long way from its beginnings as a humble coffee shop *(see p35)*. The facilities are phenomenal. Of the four restaurants, the original cast-iron and glass Winter Garden is the most stunning. ⓝ *Dam 9, 1012 JS • Map N3 • 020 554 9111 • www.nh-hotels.com • Dis.access • €€€€€*

6 De l'Europe

Once through the door, you leave the hurly-burly of the Nieuwe Zijde behind and enter a calm oasis redolent of the 19th century. Spacious rooms with empire furnishings are the epitome of plush. ⓝ *Nieuwe Doelenstraat 2–8, 1012 CP • Map N5 • 020 531 1777 • www.leurope.nl • Dis.access • €€€€€*

7 NH Barbizon Palace

Behind a dull façade, a row of 17th-century houses – 19 in all – have been knocked together to create a luxurious hotel. ⓝ *Prins Hendrikkade 59–72, 1012 AD • Map P1 • 020 556 4564 • www.nh-hotels.com • Dis.access • €€€€€*

8 Amsterdam American

This landmark hotel in a splendid Art Nouveau building is for those who want to be close to the action *(see p101)*. ⓝ *Leidsekade 97, 1017 PN • Map C5 • 020 556 3000 • www.amsterdam-american.com • €€€€*

9 The College Hotel

This luxurious "training hotel" for students in the hospitality industry occupies an old school building dating from 1895. The rooms and suites are elegant and include custom-made furniture and WiFi. There is a gourmet restaurant and a cocktail lounge. ⓝ *Roelof Hartstraat 1, 1071 VE • Map C6 • 020 571 1511 • www.collegehotelamsterdam.com • €€€€€*

10 Banks Mansion

This exquisite hotel, formerly a bank, successfully fulfills its concept of being a "home from home". Most notably, many of the facilities – Internet access, the rooms' private bar, morning paper and appetisers from the hotel lounge – are included in the price. ⓝ *Herengracht 519–25, 1017 BV • Map N5 • 020 420 0055 • www.banksmansion.nl • €€€€€*

***Note:** Unless otherwise stated, all hotels accept credit cards and have en-suite bathrooms.*

Canal House salon

Price Categories

For a standard, double room per night (with breakfast if included), taxes and extra charges.

€	under €90
€€	€90–140
€€€	€140–200
€€€€	€200–250
€€€€€	over €250

Top 10 Hotels with Character

1 Canal House

The Golden Age lives on in this tranquil pair of 17th-century canal houses, filled from top to bottom with antiques. Breakfast beneath a chandelier in the ornate salon with a view of the garden. The bedrooms are individually decorated (and priced). The hotel will close for renovation until spring 2010. *Keizersgracht 148, 1015 CX • Map L2 • 020 622 5182 • www.canalhouse.nl • €€€*

2 Ambassade

Overlooking the Herengracht, the Ambassade is truly comfortable and, not surprisingly, often full. Rambling through ten handsome merchant's houses, it blends good antiques with excellent modern service. Popular with writers, the new library has signed copies of their work. *Herengracht 341, 1016 AZ • Map L4 • 020 555 0222 • www.ambassade-hotel.nl • €€€*

3 Seven Bridges

A tired bridge-spotter can count seven from this charming hotel. Immaculately decorated, it has wooden floors, Persian carpets and furniture that would grace any auction-house catalogue. There are no public rooms, so you can have breakfast in bed without a twinge of guilt. *Reguliersgracht 31, 1017 LK • Map E5 • 020 623 1329 • €€ • www.sevenbridgeshotel.nl*

4 De Filosoof

This unique hotel's love affair with philosophy goes beyond its name: philosophers stay and meet here regularly. *Anna van den Vondelstraat 6, 1054 GZ • Map B5 • 020 683 3013 • www.hotelfilosoof.nl • €€*

5 Amsterdam Wiechmann

Made from three well-kept canal houses, the Wiechmann has been polishing its welcome for more than 50 years. Wooden floors, beams and panelling set off antique furniture and Oriental rugs, and the bedrooms, most with canal views, are attractively simple. *Prinsengracht 328–32, 1016 HX • Map K4 • 020 626 3321 • www.hotelwiechmann.nl • €€*

6 Lloyd Hotel

The city's leading art hotel lies in the heart of the gentrified Eastern Docklands. Uniquely, the 117 rooms rank from one- to five-star and have all been individually created by contemporary Dutch designers. *Oostelijke Handelskade 34, 1019 BN • 020 561 3636 • www.lloydhotel.com • €€€–€€€€€*

7 Seven One Seven

This is a luxuriously laid-back hotel in a five-star neighbourhood, where beautiful antiques complement the even more beautiful guests. To simplify your bill, breakfast, tea and evening drinks are included in the cost of the accommodation. *Prinsengracht 717, 1017 JW • Map E5 • 020 427 0717 • www.717hotel.nl • €€€€€*

8 Toro

There is a decidedly English air about this elegant, plant-filled villa south of the Vondelpark. The public rooms are furnished with antiques and oil paintings, and you can take a peaceful tea in the delightful garden. *Koningslaan 64, 1075 AG • Map A6 • 020 673 7223 • www.hoteltoro.nl • €€€*

9 The Toren

Recently renovated, this graceful but comfortable 17th-century canal house has all the modern technology you could wish for, and at modest prices. *Keizersgracht 164, 1015 CZ • Map L2 • 020 622 6352 • www.thetoren.nl • €€€€€*

10 Agora

Overlooking the Singel and conveniently close to the huge floating flower market, this small, intimate hotel also has a peaceful garden. Wooden beams, good furniture, new bathrooms and reasonable rates make this place hard for anyone to resist. *Singel 462, 1017 AW • Map M5 • 020 627 2200 • www.hotelagora.nl • €€*

Recommend your favourite hotel on traveldk.com

Left **Rembrandt** Right **NH Schiller**

Top 10 Family Hotels

1 Owl

Although there are no particular facilities for children (beyond triple rooms and cots for babies), this family-run hotel in the Museum Quarter is noted for its friendliness. A stuffed owl in an alcove provides the name. The hotel has a neat little garden, and fresh flowers in the fairly plain rooms. *Roemer Visscherstraat 1, 1054 EV • Map C5 • 020 618 9484 • www.owl-hotel.nl • €€*

2 Hotel Arena

This hotel enjoys a good location close to the Tropenmuseum *(see p127)* and Artis Zoo *(see p123)*. At weekends the hotel holds club nights for teenagers. Although child-friendly, there are no family rooms and those other than the designer suites may disappoint. *'s Gravesandestraat 51, 1092 AA • Map G5 • 020 850 2400 • www.thehotelarena.com • €€*

3 Singel

Animal-loving children will enjoy staying opposite the Poezenboot *(see p10)*. The family-run hotel has an excellent location on a pretty stretch of the Singel, and small but characterful bedrooms. Under-seven-year olds stay for free, and babysitting can be arranged. *Singel 13, 1012 VC • Map N1 • 020 626 3108 • www.singelhotel.nl • €€€*

4 Amsterdam House

Treat the children to life aboard a houseboat. Amsterdam House has eight of them available for short or long rentals (from €160), as well as apartments and hotel rooms. *'s-Gravelandse Veer 3–4, 1011 KM • Map N5 • 020 626 2577 • www.amsterdamhouse.com • €€*

5 Estheréa

In the same family for three generations, this elegant hotel mixes modern facilities with traditional surroundings and a warm atmosphere. Baby baths and high chairs are available, and babysitting. A new wing with 20 rooms was added in 2005. *Singel 303, 1012 WJ • Map M4 • 020 624 5146 • www.estherea.nl • €€€€*

6 't Jagershuis

This small waterfront inn is a good option for families who prefer to stay outside the city centre. Just 10 km (6 miles) from the city by bus or bicycle, it's in a charming village *(see p128)* and there are family rooms. *Amstelzijde 2–4, 1184 VA Ouderkerk aan de Amstel • 020 496 2020 • www.jagershuis.com • Dis. access • €€€*

7 Aadam Wihelmina

This is an excellent two star hotel in the Museum Quarter, with three- and four-bedded rooms. The yellow breakfast room is particularly jolly. *Koninginneweg 169, 1075 CN • 020 662 5467 • www.hotelwilhelmina.com • €€*

8 Rembrandt

This immaculate, good-value hotel has a wonderful antique breakfast room and spacious contemporary bedrooms that can accommodate up to six people. *Plantage Middenlaan 17, 1018 DA • Map F4 • 020 627 2714 • www.hotelrembrandt.nl • €*

9 NH Schiller

Teenagers might put up with parents in this famous Art Deco hotel overlooking the neon glare of Rembrandtplein, once the meeting-place of artists and poets. There are family rooms, and the kids can escape to the buzzing Schiller Café. *Rembrandtplein 26, 1017 CV • Map N6 • 020 554 0700 • www.nh-hotels.com • Dis. access • €€€€€*

10 Albus Grand

Parents may prefer old-world character, but children usually like their hotels to look spanking new, like this recently opened three-star hotel in the Canal Ring. Some rooms sleep three or four, and there is a brasserie for breakfast and snacks. *Vijzelstraat 49, 1017 HE • Map N6 • 020 530 6200 • www.albusgrandhotel.com • Dis. access • €€€*

***Note:** Unless otherwise stated, all hotels accept credit cards and have en-suite bathrooms.*

Price Categories

For a standard, double room per night (with breakfast if included), taxes and extra charges.

€	under €90
€€	€90–140
€€€	€140–200
€€€€	€200–250
€€€€€	over €250

Grand Hotel Amrâth

TOP 10 Business Hotels

1 Qbic Hotel Amsterdam WTC

Its location within Amsterdam's World Trade Centre makes this pod hotel ideal for business travellers. Its no frills, "cheap chic" concept comes in the form of "Cubi" – a state-of-the-art cube-shaped space with mood lighting and a Hästens bed. *WTC, Strawinskylaan 241, 1077 XX • 043 321 1111 • www.qbichotels.com • €€€€*

2 Radisson SAS

Situated around a dramatic atrium, this well-run hotel takes up most of the street and comprises several old houses, a paper factory and an 18th-century vicarage, part of which has become a lovely candlelit bar. The hotel's health and conference centres are across the road, connected by a tunnel. *Rusland 17, 1012 CK • Map N4 • 020 623 1231 • www.radissonsas.com • Dis. access • €€€€*

3 Victoria Hotel Amsterdam

On the corner of Damrak and opposite Centraal Station, this monumental building has a surprisingly calm and gracious interior. The hotel has a Business Centre, extensive conference facilities and a health and fitness centre. *Damrak 1–5, 012 LG • Map P1 • 020 623 4255 • www.parkplazaamsterdam.com • Dis. access • €€€€€*

4 Renaissance Amsterdam

A wide range of facilities at surprisingly reasonable rates distinguish this central hotel. The business and conference centre occupies a former Lutheran church. The hotel has a health centre, brown café, boat dock, car parking and apartments, in addition to the usual bedrooms and suites. *Kattengat 1, 1012 SZ • Map N1 • 020 621 2223 • www.marriott.com • Dis. access • €€€€€*

5 Crowne Plaza Amsterdam City Centre

A straightforward city-centre business hotel with good business facilities and a leisure centre, and the bonus of Dorrius, a late 19th-century Dutch restaurant *(see p58)*. *Nieuwezijds Voorburgwal 5, 1012 RC • Map N1 • 020 620 0500 • www.amsterdam-citycentre.crowneplaza.com • Dis. access • €€€€€*

6 Okura

Handy for the RAI Congresgebouw, the Okura offers top-of-the-range luxury and facilities to business travellers. It has four restaurants, including the Ciel Bleu perched on its 23rd floor. *Ferdinand Bolstraat 333, 1072 LH • 020 678 7111 • www.okura.nl • Dis. access • €€€€€*

7 Grand Hotel Amrâth

This five-star hotel merges classic Art Nouveau style with modish comforts. Facilities include a board-room with AV equipment and a wellness centre. *Prins Hendrikkade 108, 1011 AK • Map Q2 • 020 552 0000 • www.amrathamsterdam.com • €€€€€*

8 Hotel Omega

With a vibrant colour scheme in red and orange, the Omega has plenty of panache, plus the bonus of a garden, a roof terrace, and particularly accommodating staff. *Jacob Obrechtstraat 33, 1071 KG • Map C6 • 020 664 5182 • www.hotelomega.com • €€*

9 Residence Le Coin

In the University District, this smart new complex of studio bedrooms, each with kitchenette, is patronized mainly by visiting academics. *Nieuwe Doelenstraat 5, 1012 CP • Map N5 • 020 524 6800 • www.lecoin.nl • €€*

10 Atlas

Friendly and efficient, with business-like rooms – though no particular business facilities – the Atlas is in an interesting Art Nouveau house near Vondelpark. Recently renovated. *Van Eeghenstraat 64, 1071 GK • Map C6 • 020 676 6336 • www.hotelatlas.nl • €€*

Left **England** Right **Quentin**

Top 10 Gay Hotels

1 Quentin England
A row of seven unusual houses in this hotel-packed street represent the architectural styles of seven different nations. The England, a cosy, gay-friendly establishment, occupies the English "cottage" amongst them, plus the Netherlands house next door. ✆ *Roemer Visscherstraat 30, 1054 EZ • Map C5 • 020 616 6032 • www.quentinhotels.com • Dis. access • €€*

2 Quentin
A prime example of an Amsterdam hotel that, although not exclusively gay, extends a warm welcome to its many gay guests. Women in particular make this friendly, well-kept little hotel near Leidseplein their base, as do visiting musicians – Paradiso and Melkweg are nearby *(see pp54–5)*. ✆ *Leidsekade 89, 1017 PN • Map J6 • 020 626 2187 • www.quentinhotels.com • €€*

3 Amistad
Exclusively gay, this old hotel has been vamped up by its new, young owners. The rooms are stylish, with red being the predominant colour, and some rooms have shared facilities. Breakfast is served until 1pm. It is close to the clubs and saunas. ✆ *Kerkstraat 42, 1017 GM • Map L6 • 020 624 8074 • www.amistad.nl • €€*

4 Hotel Downtown Amsterdam
In the same gay enclave of Kerkstraat, this friendly hotel has recently been renovated and extended, and a lift installed. There are 24 bright and clean rooms, all with ensuite facilities. ✆ *Kerkstraat 25, 1017 GA • Map L6 • 020 524 6030 • www.hoteldowntown.nl • €€*

5 Golden Bear
First opened in 1948, the Golden Bear has been a popular exclusively gay hotel ever since. With a pretty façade and 11 clean, neat rooms, some with shared facilities, it's situated in Kerkstraat – a street in the Canal Ring where there are several other gay venues. ✆ *Kerkstraat 37, 1017 GB • Map L6 • 020 624 4785 • www.goldenbear.nl • €€*

6 Waterfront
Bedrooms are a cut above at this smart, gay-friendly hotel within easy reach of the artistic treasures of the Museum Quarter and the historic centre. The distinctive reception room has a black-and-white floor and antique furniture. ✆ *Singel 458, 1017 AW • Map M5 • 020 421 6621 • www.hotelwaterfront.nl • €€€*

7 Sander
A gay-friendly hotel situated behind the Concertgebouw in the Museum Quarter. Though plain, most of the 20 rooms are spacious, some with features such as fireplaces and window seats. The breakfast room opens on to a pretty garden. ✆ *Jacob Obrechtstraat 69 • Map C6 • 020 662 7574 • www.hotel-sander.nl • Dis. access • €€*

8 Orfeo
A favourite among Amsterdam's gay hotels, the Orfeo is centrally located near bustling Leidseplein. It has friendly, helpful owners, a convivial bar and free Finnish sauna. ✆ *Leidsekruisstraat 14, 1017 RH • Map D5 • 020 623 1347 • www.hotelorfeo.com • €*

9 Black Tulip
Only in Amsterdam – an exclusive hotel, opened in 1998, for gay men into leather and bondage, with appropriate equipment in each room. It's appropriately located too, near the "leather area" and Centraal Station. ✆ *Geldersekade 16, 1012 BH • Map Q2 • 020 427 0933 • www.blacktulip.nl • €€*

10 Flatmates Amsterdam
Not a hotel but a service offering a variety of accommodation in central Amsterdam: several studios, apartments, a houseboat and an exclusively gay B&B near Amstel River. ✆ *020 620 1545 • www.flatmates.nl • €€*

***Note:** Unless otherwise stated, all hotels accept credit cards and have en-suite bathrooms.*

Amstel Botel

Price Categories

For a standard, double room per night (with breakfast if included), taxes and extra charges.

€	under €90
€€	€90–140
€€€	€140–200
€€€€	€200–250
€€€€€	over €250

TOP 10 Budget Hotels

1 Luckytravellers Fantasia

Close to the Amstel, on a peaceful canal, the Luckytravellers Fantasia Hotel is clean and well organized. The rooms on the top floor have the most character, but all rooms have a shower and a phone. *Nieuwe Keizersgracht 16, 1018 DR • Map Q6 • 020 623 8259 • www.fantasia-hotel.com • €€*

2 De Munck

Originally built for a ship's captain and within hailing distance of the Amstel, an otherwise traditional interior has been given a dose of 1960s retro. Rooms in the De Munck are airy and clean, and there is both a bar and a garden. *Achtergracht 3, 1017 WL • Map E5 • 020 623 6283 • www.hoteldemunck.com • €€*

3 Amstel Botel

The idea of staying on a boat has a certain charm, but the downside of the Amstel Botel is that it is moored outside central Amsterdam and the rooms (or cabins if you prefer) on this floating hotel are small. The upside is getting three-star accommodation at a very reasonable price and good views over the harbour. There is also a ferry that will take you to Centraal Station in 10–15 minutes. *NDSM Pier 3 (Amsterdam-Noord) • 020 626 4247 • www.amstelbotel.com • €€*

4 Van Ostade Bicycle Hotel

Clean, cheap, simple rooms away from the tourist traps, bikes for rent, free maps, and friendly advice on routes and sights attract a young clientele. What might be a lounge elsewhere is "a chill-out zone" here in De Pijp. *Van Ostadestraat 123, 1072 SV • 020 679 3452 • www.bicyclehotel.com • €*

5 Museumzicht

You can peer down into the lovely Rijksmuseum garden from the plain rooms at the back of this modest hotel occupying the top floors of a Victorian house. The Museumzicht's greatest asset is its splendid location. *Jan Luykenstraat 22, 1071 CN • Map C5 • 020 671 2954 • €*

6 Acacia

Steep stairs, simple rooms (some with epic canal views) and a pleasant breakfast room are a quarter of an hour's walk away from the city centre, in Jordaan. The charming owners also offer self-catering studios, and a houseboat on a nearby canal. *Lindengracht 251, 1015 KH • Map C2 • 020 622 1460 • www.hotelacacia.nl • €*

7 Keizersgracht

Great location, rooms for up to four people and budget prices sound like a pipe dream, but this welcoming hotel at the station end of the Keizersgracht has them all – and a bar and restaurant to boot. *Keizersgracht 15–17, 1015 CC • Map M1 • 020 625 1364 • www.hotelkeizersgracht.nl • €€*

8 De Admiraal

At the junction of Herensgracht and Reguliersgracht, and with views over both, this friendly hotel's beamed bedrooms are bigger than most, and it's close enough to the nightlife for breakfast to be optional. *Herengracht 563, 1017 CD • Map N6 • 020 626 2150 • www.admiraalamsterdam.nl • €€*

9 The Winston Hotel

On the doorstep of the Red Light District, this inexpensive art hotel has vibrant rooms, each individually-designed by art students. The hotel attracts a young crowd, in part because of the adjacent club, so expect a little noise. *Warmoesstraat 129, 1012 JA • Map N3 • 020 623 1380 • €–€€*

10 Hegra

Its prime location on the lovely Herengracht, its prices and the warmth of its welcome make up for the (comfortable) rooms being rather on the small side. *Herengracht 269, 1016 BJ • Map L3 • 020 623 7877 • www.hotelhegra.nl • €*

Recommend your favourite hotel on traveldk.com

General Index

C

D

E

F

Acknowledgements

Main Contributors
Fiona Duncan and Leonie Glass are a British travel-writing team of 15 years standing. They are co-authors of three guides in Duncan Petersen's *3-D City Guides* series, including a guide to Amsterdam; *Paris Walks*, in the *On Foot City Guides* series; and several *Charming Small Hotel* guides.

Additional Contributors
Pip Farquharson (Top 10 Bars, Performing Arts Venues and Clubs; all Around Town listings) is a journalist and long-time inhabitant of Amsterdam. She publishes her own alternative listings guide to the city, www.underwateramsterdam.com.

Rodney Bolt (Top 10 Cafés, Bars and Restaurants) also lives in Amsterdam. He is a novelist (History Play), and author of several travel guides.

Produced by DP Services, a division of DUNCAN PETERSEN PUBLISHING LTD

Project Editor Chris Barstow
Designer Janis Utton
Picture Researcher Lily Sellar
Indexer Hilary Bird
Main Photographer Anthony Souter
Additional Photography Max Alexander, Steve Gorton, Rupert Horrox, Kim Sayer, Neil Setchfield, Clive Streeter, Gerard van Vuuren
Illustrator chrisorr.com
Maps Dominic Beddow, Simonetta Giori (Draughtsman Ltd)

FOR DORLING KINDERSLEY
Publisher Douglas Amrine
Senior Art Editor Marisa Renzullo
Senior Cartographic Editor Casper Morris
DTP Jason Little
Production Sarah Dodd
Picture Librarian Charlotte Oster
Fact Checker Gerard van Vuuren
Additional Editorial Assistance
Simon Davis, Carly Madden, Sam Merrell, Marianne Petrou, Sadie Smith

Picture Credits
t-top; tc-top centre; tl-top left; tr-top right; cla-centre left above; ca-centre above; cra-centre right above; cl-centre left; c-centre; cr-centre right; clb-centre left below; cb-centre below; crb-centre right below; bl-bottom left; bc-bottom centre; bcl-bottom centre left; bcr-bottom centre right; br-bottom right; d-detail.

Every effort has been made to trace the copyright holders and we apologize in advance for any unintentional omissions. We would be pleased to insert the appropriate acknowledgements in any subsequent edition of this publication.

Works of art have been reproduced with the permission of the following copyright holders: ©ADAGP, Paris and DACS, London 2002 *Portrait of Bernard's Grandmother*, 1887, by Emile Bernard 18b; ©DACS, 2002, *Children with Dog*, 1950, by Karel Appel 47bl; ©Munch Museum/Munch-Ellingsen Group, BONO, Oslo, DACS, London 2002, *Two Women on the Beach*, 1898, by Edvard Munch 14tl.

The publishers would like to thank the following individuals, companies and picture libraries for permission to reproduce their photographs:
AKG LONDON: 38tr, 49rd, *Dutch Battle Ships*, 1863, by Ludolf Backhuysen 27b; Residenzmuseum, Munich, *Peter the Great*, 1717 by Jean Marc Nattier 10c; Kunsthistorisches Museum, Erich Lessing, *Allegory of Painting*, c1665-66, by Jan Vermeer 46tl. AMSTERDAM ARENA: 71rd, 129tr. AMSTERDAM VILLAGE COMPANY: 54bl. AMSTERDAMS HISTORISCH MUSEUM: 7cla, 24t, 25tc, 25cra, 25bl, 26b, 40b, 107b; *Bird's Eye View of Amsterdam*, 1538, by Cornelis Anthonisz 24c; *The Return to Amsterdam of the Second Expedition to the East Indies*, 1599, by Hendrik Cornelisz Vroom 24b; *The Anatomy Lesson of Dr Jan Deijman*, 1656, by Rembrandt van Rijn 25c; *Dam Square with the New Town Hall under Construction*, 1656, by Johannes Lingelbach 26tl; *Portrait of 17 Guards* by Cornelis Anthonisz 26tr; *Silver Marriage Cup* by Gerrit Valek 27c; *Arrival of Napoleon at Dam Square*, 1811 by Matheus I van Bree 38tl; *Tulp en Spin* by B. Assteijn 83b. ©AFF/AFS AMSTERDAM, THE NETHERLANDS: 7bl, 32tl, 32br, 32-33c, 33cr, 33b, 47br. BIJBELS MUSEUM: Ernest Annyas 99t, 101br; COBRA MUSEUM VOOR MODERNE KUNST, AMSTELVEEN: ©DACS, 2002, *Children with Dog*, 1950, by Karel Appel 47bl. COSTER DIAMONDS: 116b, 117tr. GEMEENTEARCHIEF: Doriann Kransberg 99b; GETTY IMAGES: 47tr. GO

GALLERY: Herman van Heusden 97tl. GRAND HOTEL AMRATH: 147.HET BLAUWE THEEHUIS: 50tl. HOTEL DE L'EUROPE: 52tl. HORTUS BOTANICUS: 67bl. JAN DERWIG ARCHITECTUUR FOTOGRAFIE: 126b. JOODS HISTORISCH MUSEUM: Jeroen Nooter 48tl, 48tr, 48b. JORDAAN FESTIVAL: Jan Willem Groen 70br. KONINKLIJK INSTITUT VOOR DE TROPEN: 127t. KONINKLIJK THEATER CARRÉ: Rob Liot 122tl. MARY EVANS PICTURE LIBRARY: 39br. MUSEUM AMSTELKRING. Gert Jan van Rooij 6b, 20tl, 20cb, 20br, 20-21c, 21cr, 21cb, 21bl, 82c. MUSEUM HET REMBRANDTHUIS: 41t, 76tr. MUSEUM VAN LOON: Maarten Brinkgreve 7cr, 30tl, 30cb, 30cr, 30-31c, 31cr, 31bc; *The Romantic Double Portrait*, 1791, by J.F.A Tischbein 31bl. NEDERLANDS SCHEEPVAARTMUSEUM, AMSTERDAM: 40tr, *Plan of Amsterdam*, 1648, 11b. NEMO SCIENCE AND TECHNOLOGY CENTER: 129bl; NH SCHILLER HOTEL: 113tl; 146tr. OPENBARE BIBLIOTHEEK AMSTERDAM: Annetje van Praag 141tl. PA PHOTOS: 39bl. PATHÉ TUSCHINSKI, AMSTERDAM: 49t, 106cr. PICTURE BOX: 64tl, 64b, 70tl, 70tr; Cuypers, Fotografie Igno 42tl; Amerens Hedwich 23tc, 23c, 40tl; Leeden van der Henk 71tl. PROEFLOKAAL JANVIER: 61tl. RIJKSMUSEUM, AMSTERDAM: 13cr, 13cb, 14tr; *The Kitchen Maid*, 1658, by Johannes Vermeer 6cl, 12b; *The Windmill at Wijk*, 1670, by Jacob van Ruisdael 13tr; *Winter Landscape with Skaters*, 1608, by Hendrick Avercamp 13cra; *Portrait of Woman in Turkish Costume*, 1745, by Jean-Etienne Liotard 13bl; ©Munch Museum/ Munch-Ellingsen Group, BONO, Oslo, DACS, London 2002, *Two Women on the Beach*, 1898, by Edvard Munch 14tl; *Gallant Conversation*, 1654, by Gerard ter Borch II 14tc; *Self Portrait as St Paul*, 1661, by Rembrandt van Rijn 15c; *Company of Frans Banning Cocq and Willem van Ruytenburch* known as *The Night Watch*, 1642, by Rembrandt van Rijn 15b; *Self Portrait at a Young Age*, 1628, by Rembrandt van Rijn 46c. SKINS COSMETICS LOUNGE: 104tr; STADSSCHOUWBURG: 57tl; SUGAR FACTORY: Atilla Tassy 55tr: SUPPERCLUB: Kim van der Leden (www.photo-kim.com) 86tr; DE TAART VAN M'N TANTE: Peter Sabelis 50tr.VAN GOGH MUSEUM, AMSTERDAM (VINCENT VAN GOGH FOUNDATION): Luuk Kramer 16cl; *View of Prins Hendrikkade* by Claude Monet 18tc; Vincent van Gogh Foundation 19cl; *Vase with Sunflowers*, 1889, by Vincent van Gogh 6cb, 16c; *The Potato Eaters*, 1889 by Vincent van Gogh 16cb; *A Pair of Shoes*, 1885, by Vincent van Gogh 17tr; *Self Portrait as an Artist*, 1887, by Vincent van Gogh 17ca; *Wheatfield with Crows*, 1890, by Vincent van Gogh 17b, 46tr; *Exhausted Maenads after the Dance*, 1875, by *L Alma Tadema* 18tl; *Self Portrait with a Portrait of Bernard, 'Les Misérables'*, 1888, by Paul Gauguin 18tr; ©ADAGP, Paris and DACS, London 2002 *Portrait of Bernard's Grandmother*, 1887, by Emile Bernard 18b; *The Bedroom at Arles*, 1888, by Vincent van Gogh 19b. WORLD OF AJAX: 127b; YELLOW BICYCLE: 136tr. XTRACOLD: 52bl.

All other images © Dorling Kindersley. See www.dkimages.com for more information.

Special Editions of DK Travel Guides

DK Travel Guides can be purchased in bulk quantities at discounted prices for use in promotions or as premiums. We are also able to offer special editions and personalized jackets, corporate imprints, and excerpts from all of our books, tailored specifically to meet your own needs.

To find out more, please contact:
(in the United States) **SpecialSales@dk.com**
(in the UK) **Sarah.Burgess@dk.com**
(in Canada) DK Special Sales at **general@tourmaline.ca**
(in Australia) **business.development@pearson.com.au**

Phrase Book

In an Emergency

Help!	**Help!**	Help
Stop!	**Stop!**	Stop
Call a doctor.	**Haal een dokter.**	Haal uhn dok-tur
Call an ambulance.	**Bel een ambulance.**	Bell uhn ahm-bew-luhns-uh
Call the police.	**Roep de politie.**	Roop duh poe-leet-see
Call the fire brigade.	**Roep de brandweer.**	Roop duh brahnt-vheer

Communication Essentials

Yes	**Ja**	Yaa
No	**Nee**	Nay
Please	**Alstublieft**	Ahls-tew-bleeft
Thank you	**Dank u**	Dahnk-ew
Excuse me	**Pardon**	Pahr-don
Hello	**Hallo**	Hallo
Goodbye	**Dag**	Dahgh
Good night	**Goede nacht**	ghoode naht
morning	**Morgen**	Mor-ghuh
afternoon	**Middag**	Mid-dahgh
evening	**Avond**	Ah-vohnd
What?	**Wat?**	Vhat
When?	**Wanneer?**	Vhan-eer
Why?	**Waarom?**	Vhaar-om
Where?	**Waar?**	Vhaar

Useful Phrases

How are you?	**Hoe gaat het ermee?**	Hoo ghaat het er-may
Very well, thank you.	**Heel goed, dank u.**	Hayl ghoot, dahnk ew
How do you do?	**Hoe maakt u het?**	Hoo maakt ew het
That's fine.	**Prima.**	Pree-mah
Where is/are …?	**Waar is/zijn?**	Vhaar iss/zayn
How do I get to …?	**Hoe kom ik naar …?**	Hoo kom ik naar
Do you speak English?	**Spreekt u Engels?**	Spraykt ew eng-uhls
I don't understand.	**Ik snap het niet.**	Ik snahp het neet
I'm sorry.	**Sorry.**	Sorry

Shopping

How much does this cost?	**Hoeveel kost dit?**	Hoo-vayl kost dit?
I would like …	**Ik wil graag …**	Ik vhil ghraakh
Do you have …?	**Heeft u …?**	Hayft ew
Do you take credit cards?	**Neemt u credit cards aan?**	Naymt ew credit cards aan
Do you take traveller's cheques?	**Neemt u reischeques aan?**	Naymt ew raiys-sheks aan
What time do you open/close?	**Hoe laat gaat u open/dicht?**	Hoo laat ghaat ew opuh/dikht
this one	**deze**	day-zuh
that one	**Die**	dee
expensive	**duur**	dewr
cheap	**goedkoop**	ghoot-koap
size	**maat**	maat
white	**wit**	vhit
black	**zwart**	zvhahrt
red	**rood**	roat
yellow	**geel**	ghayl
green	**groen**	ghroon
blue	**blauw**	blah-ew

Types of Shop

antique shop	**antiekwinkel**	ahn-teek-vhin-kul
bakery	**bakker**	bah-ker
bank	**bank**	bahnk
bookshop	**boekwinkel**	book-vhin-kul
butcher	**slager**	slaakh-er
cake shop	**banketbakkerij**	bahnk-et-bahk-er-aiy
cheese shop	**kaaswinkel**	kaas-vhin-kul
chemist	**apotheek**	ah-poe-taiyk
chip shop	**patatzaak**	pah-taht-zaak
delicatessen	**delicatessen**	daylee-kah-tes-suh
department store	**warenhuis**	vhaar-uh-houws
fishmonger	**viswinkel**	viss-vhin-kul
greengrocer	**groenteboer**	ghroon-tuh-boor
hairdresser	**kapper**	kah-per
market	**markt**	mahrkt
newsagent	**krantenwinkel**	krahn-tuh-vhin-kul
post office	**postkantoor**	pohst-kahn-tor
shoe shop	**schoenenwinkel**	sghoo-nuh-vhin-kul
supermarket	**supermarkt**	sew-per-mahrkt
tobacconist	**sigarenwinkel**	see-ghaa-ruh-vhin-kul
travel agent	**reisburo**	raiys-bew-roa

Sightseeing

art gallery	**galerie**	ghaller-ee
bus station	**busstation**	buhs-stah-shown
bus ticket	**ov chipkaart**	o-vay chip-kaahrt
cathedral	**kathedraal**	kah-tuh-draal
church	**kerk**	kehrk
closed on public holidays	**op feestdagen gesloten**	op fayst-daa-ghuh ghuh-slow-tuh
day return	**dagretour**	dahgh-ruh-tour
garden	**tuin**	touwn
library	**bibliotheek**	bee-bee-yo-tayk
museum	**museum**	mew-zay-uhm
railway station	**station**	stah-shown
return ticket	**retourtje**	ruh-tour-tyuh
single journey	**enkeltje**	eng-kuhl-tyuh
tourist information	**VVV**	fay fay fay
town hall	**stadhuis**	staht-houws
train	**trein**	traiyn

Staying in a Hotel

Do you have a vacant room?	**Zijn er nog kamers vrij?**	Zaiyn er nokh kaamers vray
double room	**een twee persoonskamer**	uhn tvhay-per soans-kaa-mer
with double bed	**met een twee persoonsbed**	met uhn tvhay-per-soans beht
twin room	**een kamer met een lits-jumeaux**	uhn kaa-mer met uhn lee-zjoo-moh
single room	**eenpersoons-kamer**	ayn-per-soans-kaa-mer
room with bath shower	**kamer met bad douche**	kaa-met baht doosh
porterr	**kruier**	krouw-yuh
I have a reservation.	**Ik heb gereseveerd.**	Ik hehp ghuh-ray-sehr-veert

Eating Out

Have you got a table?	**Is er een tafel vrij?**	Iss ehr uhn tah-fuhl vraiy
I'd like to reserve a table.	**Ik wil een tafel reserveren.**	Ik vhil uhn tah-fuhl ray-sehr-veer-uh
breakfast	**het ontbijt**	het ont-baiyt
lunch	**de lunch**	duh lernsh
dinner	**het diner**	het dee-nay
The bill, please.	**Mag ik afrekenen.**	Mukh ik ahf-ray-kuh-nuh
waitress	**serveerster**	sehr-veer-ster
waiter	**meneer**	
menu	**de kaart**	duh kaahrt
starter, first course	**het voorgerecht**	het vohr-ghuh-rekht
main course	**het hoofdgerecht**	het hoaft-ghuh-rekht
dessert	**het nagerecht**	het naa-ghuh-rekht
cover charge	**het couvert**	het koo-vehr
wine list	**de wijnkaart**	duh vhaiyn-kaart
glass	**het glas**	het ghlahss
bottle	**de fles**	duh fless
knife	**het mes**	het mess
fork	**de vork**	duh fork
spoon	**de lepel**	duh lay-pul

Menu Decoder

aardappels	aard-uppuhls	potatoes
azijn	aah-zaiyn	vinegar
biefstuk	beef-stuhk	steak
bier, pils	beer, pilss	beer
boter	boater	butter
brood	broat	bread
cake, taart, gebak	'cake', taahrt, ghuh-bahk	cake, pastry
chocola	show-coa-laa	chocolate
citroen	see-troon	lemon
cocktail	cocktail	cocktail
droog	droakh	dry
eend	aynt	duck
ei	aiy	egg
garnalen	ghahr-naah-luh	prawns
gebakken	ghuh-bah-ken	fried
gegrild	ghuh ghrillt	grilled
gekookt	ghuh-koakt	boiled
gepocheerd	ghuh-posh-eert	poached
groenten	ghroon-tuh	vegetables
ham	hahm	ham
haring	haa-ring	herring
hutspot	huht-spot	hot pot
ijs	aiyss	ice, ice cream
jenever	yuh-nay-vhur	gin
kaas	kaas	cheese
kabeljauw	kah-buhl-youw	cod
kip	kip	chicken
koffie	coffee	coffee
kool, rode of witte	coal, roe-duh off vhit-uh	cabbage, red or white
kroket	crow-ket	ragout in bread-crumbs
lamsvlees	lahms-flayss	lamb
mineraalwater	meener-aahl-vhaater	mineral water
mosterd	moss-tehrt	mustard
olie	oh-lee	oil
pannekoek	pah-nuh-kook	pancake
patat frites	pah-taht freet	chips
peper	pay-per	pepper
poffertjes	poffer-tyuhs	tiny buckwheat pancakes
rijst	raiyst	rice
rijsttafel	raiys-tah-ful	Indonesian meal
rode wijn	roe-duh vhaiyn	red wine
rookworst	roak-vhorst	smoked sausage
rundvlees	ruhnt-flayss	beef
saus	souwss	sauce
schaaldieren	skaahl-deeh-ruh	shellfish
scherp	skehrp	hot (spicy)
schol	sghol	plaice
soep	soup	soup
stamppot	stahm-pot	sausage stew
suiker	souw-ker	sugar
thee	tay	tea
tosti	toss-tee	cheese on toast
uien	ouw-yuh	onions
uitsmijter	ouht-smaiy-ter	fried egg on bread with ham
varkensvlees	vahr-kuhns-flayss	pork
vers fruit	fehrss frouwt	fresh fruit
verse jus	vehr-suh zjhew	fresh orange juice
vis	fiss	fish/seafood
vlees	flayss	meat
water	vhaa-ter	water
witte wijn	vhih-tuh vhaiyn	white wine
worst	vhorst	sausage
zout	zouwt	salt

Numbers

1	**een**	ayn
2	**twee**	tvhay
3	**drie**	dree
4	**vier**	feer
5	**vijf**	faiyf
6	**zes**	zess
7	**zeven**	zay-vuh
8	**acht**	ahkht
9	**negen**	nay-guh
10	**tien**	teen
11	**elf**	elf
12	**twaalf**	tvhaalf
13	**dertien**	dehr-teen
14	**veertien**	feer-teen
15	**vijftien**	faiyf-teen
16	**zestien**	zess-teen
17	**zeventien**	zayvuh-teen
18	**achttien**	ahkh-teen
19	**negentien**	nay-ghuh-teen
20	**twintig**	tvhin-tukh
21	**eenentwintig**	aynuh-tvhin-tukh
30	**dertig**	dehr-tukh
40	**veertig**	feer-tukh
50	**vijftig**	faiyf-tukh
60	**zestig**	zess-tukh
70	**zeventig**	zay-vuh-tukh
80	**tachtig**	tahkh-tukh
90	**negentig**	nayguh-tukh
100	**honderd**	hohn durt
1000	**duizend**	douw-zuhnt
1,000,000	**miljoen**	mill-yoon

Time

one minute	**een minuut**	uhn meen-ewt
one hour	**een uur**	uhn ewr
a day	**een dag**	uhn dahgh
Monday	**maandag**	maan-dahgh
Tuesday	**dinsdag**	dins-dahgh
Wednesday	**woensdag**	vhoons-dahgh
Thursday	**donderdag**	donder-dahgh
Friday	**vrijdag**	vraiy-dahgh
Saturday	**zaterdag**	zaater-dahgh
Sunday	**zondag**	zon-dahgh

Selected Street Index